Immigrant Children and Youth

Immigrant Children and Youth

Psychological Challenges

Alberto M. Bursztyn and Carol Korn-Bursztyn,
Editors

PRAEGER™

An Imprint of ABC-CLIO, LLC
Santa Barbara, California • Denver, Colorado

Copyright © 2015 by Alberto M. Bursztyn and Carol Korn-Bursztyn

All rights reserved. No part of this publication may be reproduced, stored in a retrieval system, or transmitted, in any form or by any means, electronic, mechanical, photocopying, recording, or otherwise, except for the inclusion of brief quotations in a review, without prior permission in writing from the publisher.

Library of Congress Cataloging-in-Publication Data

Immigrant children and youth : psychological challenges / Alberto M. Bursztyn and Carol Korn-Bursztyn, editors.
   pages cm
   Includes index.
   ISBN 978-1-4408-0315-4 (alk. paper) – ISBN 978-1-4408-0316-1 (ebook) 1. Immigrant youth–United States–Psychology.   2. Immigrant children–United States–Psychology.   3. United States–Emigration and immigration–Social aspects. 4. United States–Emigration and immigration–Psychological aspects.   5. School psychology. I. Bursztyn, Alberto, 1952–   II. Korn-Bursztyn, Carol, 1953–
   JV6475.I46 2015
   371.7′130869120973–dc23   2015004468

ISBN: 978-1-4408-0315-4
EISBN: 978-1-4408-0316-1

19 18 17 16 15   1 2 3 4 5

This book is also available on the World Wide Web as an eBook.
Visit www.abc-clio.com for details.

Praeger
An Imprint of ABC-CLIO, LLC

ABC-CLIO, LLC
130 Cremona Drive, P.O. Box 1911
Santa Barbara, California 93116-1911

This book is printed on acid-free paper ∞
Manufactured in the United States of America

We dedicate this book to our grandchildren:
Uriel, Julian, and Gordon

and to the memory of our parents:
Celia and Harry Korn
and
Jenny and Valentin Bursztyn

Contents

Preface	ix
Acknowledgments	xv
1. Introduction: Mental Health Risks and Possibilities in Cultural Transition *Alberto M. Bursztyn*	1
2. Acculturation in Immigrant Youths: The Role of Adaptation in Mental Health *Marc Fowler and Alberto M. Bursztyn*	19
3. Identities under Construction: Portraits of Urban Latino Adolescents *Alexandros Orphanides and Alberto M. Bursztyn*	39
4. The Heart Will Know: Loss and Reunification *Anna Malyukova and Carol Korn-Bursztyn*	53
5. Where Is Home? A Narrative of Loss and Resilience *Johnny Thach and Carol Korn-Bursztyn*	61
6. Sadness All About and I'm Wearing Pink Pants: Separation and Reunification *Myrtle Dickson and Carol Korn-Bursztyn*	71
7. On Crafting a Resiliency Narrative *Malya Schulman and Carol Korn-Bursztyn*	81

8. Latino Immigrant Youths and the Transnational Family   91
   Gabriela Santana Betancourt and Carol Korn-Bursztyn

9. Psychological Vulnerability in Second Language Learning   105
   Alexandra Ponce de León-LeBec and Alberto M. Bursztyn

10. Immigrant Youths and the Language of Music   121
    Angelica Ortega and Carol Korn-Bursztyn

11. Sex Trafficking and Migrant Youths   133
    Jacquelin Mueller and Carol Korn-Bursztyn

12. You Learn When You Fall Down: Experience and Adaptation in a Program for Court-Involved Youths   147
    Parvoneh Shirgir

13. Narratives of Immigrant Community College Students   169
    Stacey J. Cooper and Carol Korn-Bursztyn

14. Undocumented Latino Youths Reach for College: Coming of Age in a Time of Uncertainty   185
    Sally Robles

15. Conclusion: Beyond Psychopathology and Toward Resilience   201
    Alberto M. Bursztyn and Carol Korn-Bursztyn

About the Editors and Contributors   209

Index   213

Preface

This preface presents fragments of our own families' migration journeys. These narratives set up a recurring framework of case vignettes that accompany the chapters in this book. They introduce the role that narrative plays as a source of understanding and knowledge about the complicated transitions that migration heralds. They also suggest the ways in which migration provokes resilience and changes the course of people's lives.

ALBERTO

It was the year that Neil Armstrong and Buzz Aldrin would walk on the moon, Woodstock would rally a generation around the motto "make love not war," and half a million protesters would converge on Washington, D.C., seeking to end the war in Vietnam. I landed in New York City. Barely 17, I might as well have landed on the moon. I would later note that the astronauts had rehearsed their mission; I hadn't. In 1969, I arrived with my parents from Mendoza, Argentina, to JFK International Airport where aunts, uncles, cousins, and my paternal grandmother eagerly awaited our arrival. Decades later, I can still recall minute details of the journey. I was aware that I was facing life-changing events and felt a rush of excitement at a new beginning, together with the anxiety of uncertainty. I knew I would never return to live in my hometown; I was leaving behind all that was familiar, but with few regrets. Emigrating to the United States was not my choice—that was my parents' plan—but abandoning my country of birth was something I had already decided on my own. Though apprehensive about the future, I did not mourn severing ties to Argentina.

Migration narratives often have complex, braided motives. In our case, there were reasons that we could easily discuss in the open and other, more compelling reasons, that we could not. By all standards we had been living a comfortable life in Mendoza. My father worked for a local bank whose board of directors was controlled by the local Communist Party. In short order, he rose from bookkeeper to chief executive officer. Breaking class and gender barriers, my mother became a social worker when I was young and worked to improve the health of poor women's and children's health in the local slums. Although a number of family members had already emigrated to the United States or Israel over the years, leaving Argentina was a remote and unlikely prospect for most of my childhood.

The year 1967, though, heralded enormous changes for my family. The 1967 Six-Day War, fought far from home, became a catalyst to the decision to emigrate. Although my father's sympathies for Israel were tolerated largely because of his dedication to the organization and professional competence, post–June 1967, his work environment became increasingly marked by open hostility. Colleagues he had considered personal friends undermined his work, and he resigned the following year. My family began a frightening economic downward spiral.

We talked less and less as my father's growing depression became palpable. My mother, no stranger to depression herself, had a lifetime of experience dealing with hardship. Growing up in poverty, the eldest of three sisters, two of whom had lost their hearing in early childhood, her family identity was that of resilient family caretaker. As my father's emotional state deteriorated, my mother advocated for a new beginning and for migration. They would leave the house they had proudly built, their family and friends, and the country they felt had betrayed them. They hoped, too, that my father's depression would stay behind.

The financial, family, and psychological reasons for migration were all entwined, and I could not point to a central precursor. Family narratives are often revised to serve present needs; later we would tell ourselves that we had no choice and that things turned out all right. We did not dwell on the fact that my mother's family continued to desperately need her; from a distance she could provide financial support but could not lend her reassuring presence. I mostly missed my maternal grandmother, whom I would never see again.

At the time we left Argentina for the United States, my family had already laid down the tracks for recurrent migration journeys. My adolescent immigration story at age 17 was preceded by my father's early emigration from Poland to Argentina when he was eight years old to reunite with his father who had migrated two years earlier. My father, Valentin, was six when his own father, Abraham, left for Argentina. Abraham received his father's blessing for the journey—and his promise to care for Abraham's wife and children until they could join him. He set out for what his wife, Olga, thought was a business trip to Warsaw and journeyed to Mendoza, Argentina, where he joined his two brothers.

Six when his father left and eight when they reunited in Argentina, my father recalled his early childhood years in the small village or *shtetl* in Poland as idyllic. His memories are untouched by the poverty of their surroundings or by the threat of physical violence at the hands of marauding gangs and innocent of the ominous political clouds that threatened their lives. Valentin lived with his parents and baby sister in a room in his paternal grandparents' house, surrounded by loving grandparents, aunts, uncles, and a tribe of boisterous cousins. These memories were a comfort to him throughout his life. After his father's departure, Valentin recalled his sadness and his mother's when night fell. When no one was looking, he would hug his father's heavy overcoat that still hung on the cupboard door.

In 1930, Valentin, his mother, and three-year-old sister left their families and their home to join Abraham in Argentina. The parting was traumatic, and Valentin recalled his small sister Lidia screaming to a young aunt, only three years older than he, as the train pulled away, "Get in, get in!" Little more than a decade later, not a single member of the family they left behind would be alive.

Reunification in Argentina was stormy. Olga did not forgive Abraham for taking her away from her family or for having deceived her. They lived in a rough immigrant neighborhood, but found friendship and emotional support among family and other newly resettled Polish Jews. Although their economic situation was initially better than they had in Poland, the partnership with the brothers soon fell apart, and family relations were tense all around. Reunification with his father was traumatic; Valentin lost his home and extended family in Poland, and later, his father.

In 1937, when Valentin was 15, a brother, Teodoro, was born. Their father, Abraham, contracted rheumatic fever and died a year later, when Valentin was 16. Overnight, he became the primary wage earner for the family, working during the day and attending high school at night. They were poor, maybe hungry, but too proud to seek help from family or community. Abraham died in 1938, unable to anticipate that the upheavals his migration journey provoked also setting in motion the mechanism by which he would rescue his wife and children from the Holocaust that would soon engulf their families in Poland. Valentin rarely spoke about his father.

CAROL

I am the child of refugees who arrived in the United States in early 1950 with my toddler sister, having spent the previous five years wandering about the post–World War II devastated landscape of Eastern Europe. Of my father's extended family in the countryside of southern Poland (now Ukraine), he was the sole survivor. Conscripted into the Red Army at the outbreak of the war, he was granted transfer from Russia to Poland in the war's waning days. There he met my mother and her sister, sole survivors of a large, extended family who had returned to their urban hometown following liberation of the concentration camp in which they were interned, in the hopes of reunification with lost family members.

For my family, the possibility of reunification represented hope—the hope of physical embrace, rather than memory and longing—hope of maintaining a thread to the lost homes and world of Eastern European Jewish life. Their hopes of reuniting with their lost families was dashed, although my father continued throughout his life to hope that a relative or family friend might one day seek him out.

Like my father, we think of reunification as physical refinding of the lost other. But, what if reunification is not an event? What if it is a psychological process that sometimes results in physical encounters but most often resides in the imagination as longed for connections? For my family, finding relatives was a disheartening experience, as they learned upon meeting my father's American aunts, who had migrated decades earlier and had reluctantly sponsored his application for asylum in the United States. The American family, professionally accomplished and thoroughly assimilated, recoiled at their foreign relations. The process of reunification as an imagined homecoming is often fraught with disappointment. The hope of reunification sustains emotional well-being, while the physical act may be profoundly disappointing.

From my father, I learned the art of the heroic narrative. A modestly successful black marketer, he flourished among the far-flung refugee camps my parents inhabited. A raconteur, by nature, his stories—of the Red Army, purloined sausages, and vodka—were embellished with danger and daring, punctuated by the motorcycle with which he returned to camp one day. My mother was the foil to his escapades; it was she who prevailed upon him to sell the motorcycle, and she whose tattoo inked on her left arm provided the context of indescribable horror to his heroic narrative.

For my parents, the narratives they told of their lives emerged in fits and spurts. It was a multilingual affair: Yiddish for reminiscences with fellow survivors (and which I would hang around to accidentally on purpose overhear); English, for rare confidences to the children, and the rare Polish for top-secret-the-children-should-not-know-from-such-things confidences. Yiddish set the emotional tone of the home, well suited for those occasions that called for self-deprecating wit, sarcasm, and especially for raised volume. English was the language of polite discourse, into which my sister and I were ushered.

For my father, his heroic narrative of wit and perseverance became an internalized monologue that helped him to face the fears and enormous challenges that lay ahead. For my mother, her narrative of survival was framed by fierce devotion to family and the capacity to draw on talent and skill—to work as though one's life depended on it. An extraordinary designer and dressmaker, her talents were recognized and exploited by her young, Nazi female captors—to the good fortune of both my mother and aunt—and their many descendants. Fashion saved their lives.

In the chapters that follow, we explore the experience of young immigrants through the lenses of the stories they tell about their own lives and through the stories that others tell about them. We approach narrative not as a means of interrogating or eliding trauma, but as a means of creating resiliency and laying the groundwork for creative approaches to constructing new chapters in the ongoing narratives of our youngest immigrants.

Acknowledgments

While working on this book, we inevitably revisited our own histories of migration and resettlement—the Bursztyns from Argentina, and the Korns from Poland. Migration has deep resonances through the generations; the questions and insights that emerged in teaching and writing about immigrant experience recall our own families' journeys. We acknowledge our own parents' fortitude and resilience as immigrants and as refugees and with gratitude recognize the daring and difficulty of their journeys and the legacy they provided for their descendants.

This project was inspired by our concern for the welfare of immigrant children and youth, a vulnerable population made more so by strident public discourse that too often depicts immigrants contemptuously as a "problem" if not a national threat. Our experience of this population is remarkably different. Having had the privilege of working at the City University of New York and previously with the New York City Public Schools, we both have worked closely with immigrant children and their families and with young immigrants preparing for careers in education and mental health. As a group, these young people represent the future of our city, and we are confident that, as in prior generations, they will contribute to the city's vitality, creativity, and renown.

New York City has historically welcomed immigrants like few other localities in the United States, or the world. Its reputation for nervous energy, relentless entrepreneurship, and merciless competition is balanced by its sanctuary status, relative tolerance of ethnic differences, and civic engagement. These qualities describe the immigrant ethos of this metropolis and represent the vanguard of the demographic shift affecting the entire nation. Diversity is our national strength.

We are most thankful for our contributors, most of whom have been our students at the Graduate Center or at Brooklyn College, for their perseverance, engagement, and thoughtfulness. Their enthusiasm for the book propelled the project forward. Their personal connections to the topic deepened their understanding and strengthened their determination to bring it to print.

Addressing the plight and developmental needs of immigrant children and youth in some of our classes led to deep and fruitful conversations. We recognize that many of our students contributed to this work by offering their own stories and insights, others in more tangible ways by contributing narratives and doing library research. We acknowledge specifically the following former students: Kim Agugliario, Toanna Barker, Lauren Buehler, Kathryn Louise Carpenter, Amanda Dillon, Adrienne DiMatteo, Milushka Elbulok-Charcape, Olivia Gambale, Carly Huelsenbeck, Samantha Hurley, Crystal Lim, Christina Ramos Palau, Maxine Rose, and Jeremiah Sieunarine.

This book could not have been written if not for the time allowed by sabbatical leaves during the spring semesters of 2013 and 2014. We therefore thank our colleagues in the Department of School Psychology, Counseling, and Leadership for approving our request for sabbatical, and Brooklyn College for awarding us the opportunity to focus on scholarship during that time.

At Brooklyn College, we have been assisted in numerous ways by our department's staff, Harriet Bredhoff, Jennifer Milan, and Francine Ward. We are most thankful for their competent and cheerful support.

Our affiliation with the Ph.D. program in Urban Education has been especially helpful in nurturing our research and writing agendas. Teaching at the Graduate Center has brought us into close collaboration with students and colleagues exploring meaningful questions about urban life. We thank Professor Anthony Picciano, executive officer, for making it possible for us to teach regularly in the urban education program, and Christine Saieh, assistant program officer, for her support and friendship.

Finally, we acknowledge with gratitude Debbie Carvalko, senior acquisitions editor for psychology and health at ABC-CLIO/Praeger, who supported our work with patience and confidence.

1

Introduction: Mental Health Risks and Possibilities in Cultural Transition

Alberto M. Bursztyn

Immigration occupies a paradoxical place in U.S. culture. Celebrated in monuments, such as the Statue of Liberty, and in myth, as in the multitude of stories about heroic grandparents arriving with nothing in their pockets, immigrants are rarely embraced in the present. Still, no country in the world has welcomed as many immigrants and refugees as the United States. Since the 1980s, more than a million immigrants, documented and not, have settled on a permanent basis in this country. Welcomed might be an overstatement—most immigrants have not been welcomed; in some quarters, they have been resented and reviled. But immigration is rapidly changing the demographics and character of this nation, and change is no longer something projected into the future—the future is now. Caucasians will soon cease to be the majority of the population in the United States; although the native population has remained stable, immigrants and children of immigrants, the majority of whom are Latinos, account for the net population growth in our nation (Rong & Preissle, 2009; U.S. Census Bureau, 2012).

Writing from Brooklyn, New York, a quintessential port of entry for generations of new Americans, the prospect of a more diverse and multicultural United States may mean that more of the country could become more like Brooklyn—a hopeful prospect. Brooklyn is a place where members of a multitude of ethnic groups that are actively fighting wars in their ancestral lands live with one another as neighbors. Immigration changes everyone. Even among those who intend to cling tightly to their heritage, language, and traditions, the lure of the American way of life—broadly defined by the expectation of fairness, opportunity, and choice—exerts a strong pull toward acculturation and compromise.

Immigration is prominently featured in the news as thousands of unaccompanied minors from Central America have reached the U.S. border after harrowing journeys aboard freight trains. There are arguments in the media about the rights of undocumented "aliens" and the dangers they ostensibly pose. Children of undocumented families brought here at a young age from other lands are beginning to claim the right to citizenship in the country they have always called home. Regardless of legal status, immigrants are often depicted as taking jobs away from "Americans." Immigration, and the political heat it engenders, is as American as Taco Bell.

Beyond the demographic projections and political arguments that define the contemporary discourse on immigrants and refugees, this book will focus attention on the next generation of Americans who will come of age at a time of unprecedented social diversity. New young immigrants' contributions to our society will hinge on their education, sense of belonging, and creativity and mental health (Camarota, 2012). Mindful of the pivotal role this new generation of new Americans will play, this book seeks to address that relative dearth of literature on their emotional well-being, especially as this intersects with acculturation and identity development. Their individual and collective journeys matter in personal, familial, and social spheres. How well they cope with the demands of their new country, how they fare socially and academically, and how they learn to frame the story of their own lives will have repercussions for generations to come.

Historically and at the present, public education has been tasked with addressing the needs of young new arrivals and children of immigrants. Consequently, policymakers have portrayed new immigrant children and youths primarily as students with specific learning needs and expectations (García & Kleifgen, 2010). Unfortunately, defining learning outcomes narrowly, such as measured proficiency in English, has undermined a more holistic view of these children's social, emotional, and developmental needs (Lopez & Bursztyn, 2013).

During the 1970s and 1980s, with increased numbers of Spanish-speaking children attending school, an assertive Latino political agenda, and the Lau decision[1] (Menken & García, 2010) to back it up, the federal government was compelled to promote bilingual education as a right for non-English-speaking children in public schools. In principle, bilingual education looked beyond expedient approaches to teaching English to new immigrant children. It sought to create a transitional space in schools where children could continue using their native language while acquiring English and continue learning content knowledge in their native language. It promised to buffer the experience of dislocations by providing children with teachers who spoke their language, understood their backgrounds, and communicated easily with their families. Explicitly, bilingual education validated the children's prior experiences by promoting not only bilingualism but also biculturalism.

The Ronald Reagan administration sought to curtail the role of the U.S. Department of Education. Concurrently, well-organized and unremitting attacks on bilingualism as un-American eventually succeeded in shifting the focus of bilingual education to English language learning only. Federal support would be limited to transitional bilingual programs that required an expedient exit from bilingual instruction once the students' English language skills were deemed sufficiently developed. These policy changes effectively dismissed the schools' role in addressing bilingual children's cultural background and socioemotional supports for transition.

In the 1990s and early 2000s, there was a parallel movement embodied in the multicultural curriculum, the aim of which was to promote a welcoming school culture for children of all backgrounds (Harris & Goldstein, 2007; Korn & Bursztyn, 2002). Political forces again sidelined this approach by establishing and enforcing unforgiving high-stakes testing policies. Multicultural education was not easily measurable; its aims were to teach children to value their own ethnicities and cultures and expand their capacity to work collaboratively with those from backgrounds different from their own. The emphasis on accepting everyone as a full member of the school community, regardless of race, language, ability level, sexual orientation, and cultural background, drew support from liberal constituents but upset traditionalists and nativists. Multicultural education preserved an approach to pedagogy that addressed the whole child, that is, children's social and emotional development as integrally connected with and necessary for academic success. Multiculturalism in education was further eroded by the national fear of external and internal threats that followed the 9-11 attacks.

Presently, teachers and school administrators are so heavily policed on student performance measures that children's social and emotional developmental needs have been relegated to secondary concerns. Children's emotional states, when considered at all, are considered in relation to test performance, or unavoidably, when they engage in disruptive or violent behaviors. The overwhelming concern with test performance has so disrupted the public school curriculum that young children no longer play or nap in school, while the arts are considered a frivolous luxury. Schools have replaced counselors with literacy coaches and hired behavioral specialists to help control explosive student behavior. Without adequate physical education during the week, increased pressure on mastering a narrow set of skills, and limited opportunities for age-appropriate socialization, behavior specialists have been busy. The prescription of psychotropic medications to school-aged children is at an all-time high. Some schools have responded by instituting programs to help children cope with their stressful lives, rather than consider how school came to be so stressful in the first place.

Despite their burdens, schools continue to serve as the primary acculturating institution for young immigrants. Teachers are the quintessential representatives of American society and wield enormous influence on children's adaptation to the new setting (Suarez-Orozco, Rhodes, & Milburn, 2009). It is in school that immigrant children learn, socialize, and expand their understanding of their new country. In school, they have opportunities to form friendships, practice new skills, including English, and continue their developmental trajectories. But schools have few resources to address children's mental health needs; access to mental health professionals in the public sector is extremely limited and available only in severe cases.

The aim of this book is to contribute to a refocusing of attention on the emotional needs of children, particularly those who are most vulnerable, including recent immigrants and English language learners (ELLs). Their needs must be recognized not only in schools, but also in clinics, hospitals, community-based organizations, and other institutions serving children and families. With greater knowledge and insight, mental health professionals can play a critical role as cultural brokers and advocates for immigrant children, youths, and families (Lopez & Bursztyn, 2013).

The mental health needs of immigrant populations have been recognized by major professional organizations. For example, an American Psychological Association (APA) report states:

> Some recent immigrants face difficulty adjusting to their new home in the United States for a host of reasons, including coping with trauma experienced in their native country, overcoming cultural and language barriers, and encountering discrimination. The effects of immigration on psychological and social well-being are especially profound for certain populations, including children, women, individuals with disabilities, and those with limited financial resources. Despite the critical need for mental health services, immigrants face significant obstacles to receiving quality mental health care. (APA Initiatives, 2014)

Clearly, there are vast gaps between the nature of needs and services available. However, improving services may not be sufficient; mental health professionals must also develop psychologically and culturally informed approaches for working with this vulnerable population.

This chapter will briefly address three common features of the immigrant experience that must be considered in working with immigrant children and youths: (a) trauma and its sequelae, (b) separation and loss, and (c) identity and resilience.

IMMIGRATION AND TRAUMA

Although the experiences of migration, lengthy separations from family, and reunification are so common that we may think of them as normative, these experiences are often psychologically traumatic. There is no painless immigration story—they may become painless in retrospect, in the forgetting or in the retelling; but anyone who has had to abandon everything that was familiar, including people, places, and rituals, for the unknown has likely experienced enormous stress and if not trauma. In traumatic circumstances, individuals feel overwhelmed by stress to a point that they cannot fully integrate their emotional experiences. The need for survival often overrides awareness of stress in the moment; traumatic experiences may be repressed for days, weeks, or even decades. Traumatized individuals may seek to avoid revisiting the experience, thus warding off anxiety, or they may enter potentially self-destructive repetitive patterns to gain a sense of mastery over the initial traumatizing event. Because immigrants tend not to talk about their trauma, mental health professionals may overlook its continuing negative effect on their clients and their relationships.

Children who have experienced the trauma of abandonment by a parent, as occurs when parents migrate ahead of their children, sometimes leaving them vulnerable to maltreatment, abuse, or neglect, will have greater difficulty establishing trusting relationships, following routines, and modulating their emotions. The following case study of Sam illustrates the sequelae of multiple traumatizing events on an immigrant child.[2]

CASE VIGNETTE: SAM

Sam typically sleeps well into the afternoon, but this time he was awake at noon laying sideways on the couch with his feet on the floor, arms at his sides, and no pillow under his head. He stared blankly at a television on the far wall playing some dimly lit daytime drama. He had threatened his social worker the night before and would not speak to other staff at his new group home.

Sam is angry most of the time. He is angry with his family for disowning him, with his school for not doing enough to address his illiteracy, with his girlfriend for leaving him after a fight, and especially with himself for a lifetime of decisions he views as reckless. Along with being angry, Sam is sad, anxious, and looking for support; he seems genuinely regretful after altercations. He is an adolescent suffering from posttraumatic stress disorder (PTSD); his coping skills are limited when he feels stressed and overwhelmed with feelings.

His family lived in a rural area of an African country that was severely affected by famine. Soon after his birth, war broke out and his family was uprooted. Escaping threats and persecution, the family resided in a number of refugee camps until he was three years old. His mother and two older sisters fled to Europe and then found asylum in the United States, but Sam stayed behind with his older brother and father, with the anticipation of a reunion in the future. Shortly thereafter, Sam's father contracted a deadly disease and died; his older brother, then 14, was recruited as a child soldier. He never saw his brother again. Sam remained in the refugee camp for another eight years with no assigned guardian. During this time, Sam was virtually unsupervised. Though enrolled in school, he rarely attended class, opting to play with friends outside or finding ways to make money in the community. He stated that he spent some time (undetermined) with a man who claimed to be a relative in a nearby village. He may have been a victim of emotional, physical, and sexual abuse, but Sam would only say that it got so bad that he tried several times to escape, until he succeeded. Despite gentle probing, he never spoke about that period again.

At the age of 12, Sam's mother sent for him from a large city in the northeast where they had settled. Sam had no memory of them. His long journey was completed among strangers; although frightened, he looked forward to having a family. Upon reaching the United States, Sam was eager to reconnect with his mother and sisters. They had adapted well to their new country. His mother had stable employment, his sisters were diligent students; they were actively engaged in a charitable and religious community organization.

Sam wanted to make them proud, but soon struggled to adjust to the demands of his new life. He rebelled against the rules placed upon him; he felt constrained by disciplinary expectations and felt the urge to flee. He frequently misperceived others as threatening or untrustworthy, often reacting aggressively. His impulsive and threatening behavior created social and legal problems for the family.

In school, his academic deficits and disdain for authority interacted to create behavioral concerns that overshadowed his glaring literacy and academic needs. Though verbally fluent in three languages, Sam was unable to read or write in any of them and was too ashamed to acknowledge he had fallen behind. Truancy became a concern as Sam failed to complete assignments and began avoiding challenging classes altogether. He experienced school staff as oppressive, even frightening; he also saw them as ineffective at helping him catch up with his sisters' accomplishments. Educators did not fully understand the underlying academic and psychological reasons for this behavior and fruitlessly continued to focus on his noncompliant behaviors while overlooking his emotional and academic needs. Complicating matters, he had befriended known gang members.

Sam reported feeling exhausted from lack of sleep. Many nights he would sit awake with racing thoughts or wake up from nightmares only to struggle with falling back to sleep. He felt increasingly like an unwanted outsider in his family. His mother expressed disappointment in his school performance, choice of friends, and oppositional behavior. During a particularly charged argument, Sam hit his mother; subsequently the family called Child Protective Services. Soon after, he was placed in foster care; it had been five months since leaving his native country.

Now 16, he has lived in several group homes over the past four years. He often sleeps through the day, reporting difficulty falling asleep at night and experiencing frequent nightmares. He continues to mistrust others and reacts aggressively to perceived threats in social situations. Sam speaks about his life with bitter regret, blaming himself for his severed family relationships and his failure in learning to read. He insists his current circumstances are due to his failure to capitalize on opportunities and refuses to acknowledge that some setbacks were outside his control. Sam expresses a strong desire for a fresh start, both in school and with his family. However, he has expressed regret before but has been unable to remain compliant for long. Sam may not be able to change his patterns of behavior and angry outbursts until he understands and accepts the role that multiple traumas have played in his life. His disrupted attachment history further complicates his recovery from trauma.

SEPARATION AND LOSS

The following case study of Luba focuses on a well-adjusted young adolescent immigrant girl who has had a strong and loving family bond since birth. At the time of her departure from her native country, she enjoyed school, family, and had an active social life. The immigration experience, suffused with multiple losses, engendered loneliness and sadness. Current developments in her life have heightened the risk for depression.

CASE VIGNETTE: LUBA

Luba is a 13-year-old girl showing signs of depression; she is quiet and withdrawn, rarely participates in class, and generally looks sad and lethargic. She immigrated to the United States from Ukraine less than a year ago with her parents, leaving both sets of grandparents and numerous relatives behind. The family was part of the Russian-speaking minority in their native country. Leaving the populous city of Odessa, her parents hoped to find better work and educational opportunities in the United States. An only child, Luba moved with her family to New York City where members of the extended family (an aunt, uncle, and cousin) had established roots years before. Upon moving to New York, she enrolled at the same junior high that her cousin had attended and was assigned to a seventh-grade class that was created for ELLs.

Speaking in a barely audible voice, Luba describes her life in Odessa as different, though neither better nor worse than life in the United States. She says that although she has left much behind in Odessa, she expects to gain more opportunities in the United States. For example, she explained, "In Ukraine the schools were not as good; only books and chalkboards." Luba references the technology in school as a tangible improvement in her education. Her statement seems rehearsed, as though she were trying to justify her family's decision.

Luba later adds that she misses her friends and the life she left behind. She seems remarkably sad when she speaks about her friends. She explains that she had many friends in the large building complex where she lived. Most of her peers went to the same school and were free to visit one another and to play outside until dark. Now, she is not allowed to go out by herself, and comments, "Where would I go? I don't know anybody!"

The economic status of Luba's family has deteriorated since their migration. She describes her life in Odessa as "comfortable." Her father was a railroad employee with supervisory responsibilities. Her mother worked as a teacher. After the move, Luba's mother was able to find a job as an assistant in a daycare center serving mostly Ukrainian and Russian infants. Her father, however, was out of work for the first five months postmigration. Her father has temporarily moved to Chicago, where a conational found him a job removing asbestos from residential buildings. If the work was good, Luba said, she and her mother would move to Chicago, too. Until that time, the family would live apart. Luba anticipated this separation of the family as being very difficult because her mother has been "very nervous" since they arrived.

Luba described feeling lonely since the family's resettlement, like she had never felt before. Although she studied English in Odessa, she was unable to communicate effectively in English. At school, Luba quickly befriended a Russian-speaking paraprofessional, Olga, a middle-aged woman who acted as an interpreter for Luba. Olga had immigrated from Russia 20 years earlier and sympathetically assisted Luba in understanding the logistics of junior high school—her class schedule, the purpose of a special assembly, and other common school conventions. However, Olga was not assigned to work with Luba, and the two only interacted when Luba sought out Olga's guidance. Typically, this would occur during homeroom each morning.

Luba clearly felt a special connection with Olga, as one of the few people with whom she could speak in Russian. Luba frequently hugged Olga during their homeroom meetings, and Olga began to refer to Luba jokingly as "her daughter." Aside from the maternal relationship that Luba maintained with Olga, she reported having difficulty making friends because her English was not yet fluent. This greatly affected her and was the primary reason she described her first months as overwhelmingly lonely. It took Luba months to connect with her peers. She says, however, that she talks to other kids now, but it is not like they are real friends.

Although Luba's ability to navigate in school situations was improving, at home she felt burdened. Despite her lack of English fluency, Luba frequently acts as an interpreter for her mother, who does not speak English. She said that she translates school notices and everyday conversations, when she herself is able to understand. If Luba is unable to decode an English document or make an important phone call, she turns to her cousin, Sofia, who has already lived in the United States for a few years. Sofia's mother is her father's sister, but they are not close.

Despite feeling lonely, Luba says that things are improving. At first, she explained, she wanted to return to Odessa. Now though, she just hopes that all of her relatives can obtain green cards and move to the United States. It took years for Luba's family to attain visas, and she knows, realistically, that much of her family will not be able to move to the United States, or may not want to. When asked if she would like to go back and visit Odessa, she says that she would, she misses her grandparents and friends, but adds that it would then be even harder to come back to New York. Shortly after our first interview, Luba's grandmother passed away in the Ukraine. What had been posed as a hypothetical question was now a practical one, would Luba and her family return to Odessa? No, she said. They were in the United States now and no matter the circumstances, there was no going back; also, she explained, "We couldn't afford it."

The school counselor was planning to set up a bereavement group and hoped that Luba would agree to take part. Luba's emergent English language skills and feelings of inadequacy in relation to her peers may inhibit her engagement. She is dealing with multiple losses resulting from the family's emigration, her father's departure, and more recently the loss of her grandmother. The loss of her natural network of support, together with the loss of social and academic competence, places Luba at risk of deepening depression. The potential move to Chicago is likely to be experienced as another destabilizing uprooting, further straining family resources and increasing mental health risks.

Loss is part of all immigrants' and refugees' experience, losses of great magnitude, like home and family, but also loss of ability, including linguistic fluency and the intuitive understanding of one's place in social contexts (Arbona, Olvera, Rodriguez, Hagan, Linares, & Wiesner, 2010; Bursztyn, 2006). More subtle but ever-present losses include familiar places, landscapes, and the flora and fauna of the environment of home. In an unfamiliar and strange place, the immigrant must gather and deploy internal resources to adapt. Failing to do so, the pull of depression may be like an undertow sweeping the immigrant to a place of longing and despair. Because children and youths have not typically been part of the plan to move, the new and stressful context can fuel intrafamilial stress.

Young immigrants, particularly teenagers, are still in the midst of forming their own identities. The migration experience, although stressful and potentially traumatizing, also provides opportunities for expanded options in constructing their identities. Adolescents actively search and experiment with different ways of being, often to the consternation of parents. Identity formation is a process that may extend for years (Laser & Nicoleta, 2011). Immigrant youths have the opportunity to explore ways of being in multiple contexts and to observe the relative nature of social norms, an opportunity that is not available to their age peers who have grown up in homogeneous, monolithic social contexts. This perspective provides immigrant youths with multiple lenses through which to consider their experiences and gives immigrant youths the tools for crafting hybrid identities. Immigration can also, therefore, present opportunities for emotional growth and for resilience.

IDENTITY AND RESILIENCE

The short essay below was written by a 16-year-old girl for an English as second language (ESL) class assignment on the subject of life in the United States. In relatively fluent prose, this young author sets out to explore and explain significant differences between Sri Lankan and American relations with their teenage children. She describes how parents restrict dating choices and decide who their daughters will marry and the qualities desirable of a bride. She concludes by expressing her opinion about Sri Lankan and American customs regarding marriage.

Dating and Marriage in Sri Lanka and the United States
Do you think when a teenager has a big problem and she doesn't know what to do, it is o.k. for her to approach her parents to help her out? Do you think that teenagers should confide in parents?

In my opinion I don't think so. I believe that in American culture it is OK for teenagers to talk with their parents. In my culture it is not the right thing to do. In my culture parents are very strict and make all the decisions for you. There is great fear of the mother and her opinions.

The parents decide who the girl should marry. If the girl doesn't want the boy and goes against the parents' wishes, the dowry money and gold will be taken away from her. A girl is not allowed to go out with a boy alone; she must have a girlfriend or a family member with her. If the girl's family accepts the boy, he must have everything she wants. A girl must be pure, clean person without any gossip told about her. In America, everything is so different in choosing a husband. A girl is free to pick her own man, even if she makes a mistake. I think that the American way is better, and maybe one day I will be able to follow it.

A recent arrival from Jaffna, Asanka begins her essay by asking the reader to consider if it is okay for a teen who has a problem to confide and seek advice from her parents. Learning about American culture from sitcoms and movies, the author suggests that a friendly and easy relationship with parents is the American way, but unthinkable in her culture. Focusing on the hierarchical family structure and the relative powerlessness of children, treating a parent as a confidant presents the risk that the parent, particularly the mother, will be critical and disapproving.

Asanka then turns her attention to the matter of arranged marriages, focusing again on the relative powerlessness of the daughter and the restrictions on her marrying choices. She again turns to American culture for contrast. She writes that American women exercise free will; they may even make bad choices without catastrophic consequences. She makes a declarative statement—the American way is better. She concludes by suggesting that "maybe one day" she will follow the American cultural norm.

The essay is brief yet it captures the essence of her dilemma. As a young Sri Lankan woman, she wishes to fulfill the cultural and familial expectation to be a "pure, clean person without any gossip told about her." But living in a culture that promotes a different message—a woman, and not her parents, gets to choose—she implicitly leans toward acculturation.

Considering the power distance between herself and her parents, Asanka cannot yet express her opinion at home; perhaps anticipating a major conflagration at home, she expresses her wish with a degree of self-doubt, "maybe one day." Whether or not she asserts her will, the acculturation process has already distanced this teen from her parents as she actively ponders how to be more like an American woman. She wishes to be free to make the big decisions in her life, free to make mistakes, and, implicitly, able to withstand parental disapproval. Engaging in the act of comparing cultures, the young author is also engaging in redefining her identity. No longer a Sri Lankan girl, she may be in the process of redefining herself as a Sri Lankan American or even an American of Sri Lankan origin.

Along with risks to mental health, immigration presents opportunity for development and growth (Ebin, Sneed, Morisky, Rotheram-Borus, Magnusson, & Malotte, 2001). Young immigrants are worldly; they may capitalize on their intimate knowledge of at least two cultures to form hybrid identities. Asanka, like most young immigrants, explores her own culture simultaneously with learning about American ways. It becomes a dual process, not simply learning about the new society, but also about one's own by contrast. These unavoidable comparisons hold the key to their emerging new hyphenated identities. Acculturation is neither linear nor predictable; having internalized disparate sets of values, norms, and expectations, young immigrants may actively choose to adopt a bicultural identity or may lean in one direction over another. What is predictable is that the immigration experience will present complex possibilities, as well as challenges, for young migrants. As in past generations, their developmental paths, mental health, and aspirations will continue to shape our country's future.

Brief descriptions of the rest of the chapters that appear in this book are found below.

CHAPTER 2: ACCULTURATION IN IMMIGRANT YOUTHS: THE ROLE OF ADAPTATION IN MENTAL HEALTH

This chapter focuses on the immigrant experience of acculturation as an adaptive psychological process. There are two independent features of acculturation: preservation of ethnic cultural heritage and adaptation to the national society. Immigrants of all ages experience the tension between the conflicting cultural systems at the social, familial, and personal levels. For young immigrants, these tensions become a central aspect of their development as they grow up while negotiating different cultures. The chapter contains a substantial review of the extant literature on this topic and explores its implications through a case study.

CHAPTER 3: IDENTITIES UNDER CONSTRUCTION: PORTRAITS OF URBAN LATINO ADOLESCENTS

This chapter, based on an undocumented teacher-research study, looks at the way that bicultural youths in an alternative school negotiate and craft unique identities. The issues and themes emerging in this ethnography point to a complex and dynamic matrix of identity; in a way, their experience refutes discrete paths to identity formation described in the literature. The informants featured in this chapter suggest a much broader, flexible, and often unpredictable path in identity formation. In a truly cosmopolitan setting, distinct ethnic categories may be superseded by hybrid and emerging grouping and referents for identity.

CHAPTER 4: THE HEART WILL KNOW: LOSS AND REUNIFICATION

Drawing on narrative, this chapter focuses on the phenomenon of reunification of a child with a parent whose migration preceded that of the child's, resulting in a lengthy period of separation. It explores the relational tasks of reunification, including reawakening old attachments, building new relationships, and mourning the loss of primary caretakers left behind upon migration. The chapter also considers the impact of the processes of immigration and reunification on the family left behind, with special attention given to grandparents as primary attachment figures. Attachment theory and Winnicott's holding environment provide theoretical frames through which to consider migration, separation and loss, and the capacity for new and renewed family bonds.

CHAPTER 5: WHERE IS HOME? A NARRATIVE OF LOSS AND RESILIENCE

This chapter examines salient elements of unaccompanied migration in childhood and adolescence. These include the meaning of home, the experience of psychological distress during the migration process, and the relation to home postmigration. The authors explore the intersection of documentation status and psychological well-being among immigrant youths. A retrospective case vignette of a young man's migration from the Philippines provides a framework to illustrate some of the characteristics and psychological risks associated with migration journeys of unaccompanied immigrant children. The chapter describes the trauma of family separation and its after effects, as well as the sources of psychic strength and resilience that may augur a hopeful outcome despite the emotional and relational challenges.

CHAPTER 6: SADNESS ALL ABOUT AND I'M WEARING PINK PANTS: SEPARATION AND REUNIFICATION

This chapter presents case studies of two young Caribbean immigrants that point to the complex situations of transnational families, especially regarding separation from mother and reunion. The chapter considers how immigration can provoke possibilities for growth change postmigration. It concludes with a discussion of how multiple attachment relationships with extrafamilial figures, such as teachers, counselors, and mental health providers, can help young immigrants develop confident expectation in their ability to grow. Growth, though, presents a developing capacity to explore new avenues and possibilities that may exist on the postmigration horizon.

CHAPTER 7: ON CRAFTING A RESILIENCY NARRATIVE

This chapter presents a narrative of an unaccompanied child who joins her father whose immigration preceded her immigration by a number of years. It addresses the importance for young immigrants to craft a resiliency narrative. When young immigrants of diverse backgrounds and living situations can draw on their reserves of youthful flexibility and drive, they can frame their own narratives of inner strength and determination that can help them to imagine how they might grow. The authors suggest that migration offers the potential for creative growth. They offer Winnicott's concept of transitional space to explain how the immigrant who inhabits the interstices between past, present, and future is poised to develop creative responses to life's challenges.

CHAPTER 8: LATINO IMMIGRANT YOUTHS AND THE TRANSNATIONAL FAMILY

This chapter addresses Latino adolescent immigrants' experience, focusing on developmental needs, risks for depression, family conflict, and cultural gender expectations. Focusing on three case studies, the authors describe the tension between ambition—for oneself and for one's immediate family—and *familismo*, which assumes a broader definition encompassing the extended family. Latino immigrant youths from transnational families seem poised to promote deep cultural change regarding gender, personal ambition, the meaning and place of family, and language. Change contains loss; the phenomenon of depression in immigrant youths, especially in Latino youths, may signal rapid changes in family structure and cultural assumptions.

CHAPTER 9: PSYCHOLOGICAL VULNERABILITY IN SECOND LANGUAGE LEARNING

This chapter explores the psychological implications of second language acquisition, specifically English in the United States. ELLs engage in the process of acquiring a new language and culture simultaneously and may experience some degree of culture shock and emotional distress that may negatively impact social and academic functioning. The chapter pays particular attention to children in undocumented families and other circumstances, such as racial minority status, that may increase anxiety and feelings of alienation and lead to internalizing symptoms. The literature is reviewed through the experience of a school-aged child.

CHAPTER 10: IMMIGRANT YOUTHS AND THE LANGUAGE OF MUSIC

This chapter describes the important emotional benefits of a music program for immigrant students. Music programs can provide the continuity and stability needed to buffer acculturative stress and create safe spaces where immigrant students can express and work through difficult emotions. The case vignette of a young, transnational student illustrates the way in which music fills the liminal spaces between country of origin and the host country. It demonstrates how music can become integral to the identify formation of emergent bilingual children. The chapter underlines the role that music plays in helping immigrant children develop emotional and academic resilience. It calls for music instruction for students in urban schools, especially immigrant and bilingual students, and calls for music to again become part of schools' multilingual ecology.

CHAPTER 11: SEX TRAFFICKING AND MIGRANT YOUTHS

This chapter addresses the global nature of sex trafficking involving minors and the psychological wounds suffered by the victims. Unaccompanied migrant youths face risk factors for exploitation. Trafficked youths may have been exposed to trauma prior to or during the migration journey. Challenges in providing support for this population include homelessness, language barrier issues, economic needs, drug abuse, the social constraints of family honor, and personal shame. Lesbian, gay, bisexual, and transgender (LGBT) youths face the added trauma of exposure, or fear of exposure, of their sexual orientation. The authors advocate for better ways of identifying victims and for developing treatment options within the school, community-based mental health organizations, as well as residential programs for those who are deeply traumatized.

CHAPTER 12: YOU LEARN WHEN YOU FALL DOWN: EXPERIENCE AND ADAPTATION IN A PROGRAM FOR COURT-INVOLVED YOUTHS

This chapter explores the multiple ways that young immigrants who have experienced difficulties and setbacks in the course of their development and acculturation begin to capitalize on their internal resources to overcome present challenges. The late teens and young adults who provided the background for this chapter attended a court-mandated General Educational Development (GED) program. The author provides insights into their experiences and strivings. She suggests a culturally and developmentally appropriate pedagogical approach to work with urban, socially marginalized youths that has relevance for psychological practice with that population.

CHAPTER 13: NARRATIVES OF IMMIGRANT COMMUNITY COLLEGE STUDENTS

This chapter focuses on freshman community college immigrant students' narratives regarding prior schooling and personal achievements. The emerging themes discussed in this chapter include overcoming difficulties, the importance of relational support, and graduating high school as an achievement. These narratives highlight the role played by peers, friends, and teachers in shaping a supportive school environment. Although the narratives describe past difficulties, they tended to resolve in personal triumphs. The immigration narratives offer a window into new immigrants' sense of personal agency as emotional investment in crafting life stories of perseverance and overcoming of obstacles. In developmentally appropriate ways, they reject a storyline of dependence and neediness borne of dejection. A view of culture, as dynamically transformed by individuals responding to their social circumstances rather than static and based on structural constraints, highlights the critical role of personal and group agency in education and mental health.

CHAPTER 14: UNDOCUMENTED LATINO YOUTHS REACH FOR COLLEGE: COMING OF AGE IN A TIME OF UNCERTAINTY

This chapter explores, through case study and review of the relevant literature, the various psychological, sociocultural, and legal challenges encountered by undocumented Latino college students. It outlines the nature of psychological tensions emerging from cultural expectations for responsibility to family and the achievement orientation associated with college study.

In addition, the chapter presents a preliminary framework for conceptualizing the identity development of undocumented young adults. It proposes an "Undocumented Adult Identity Development Model" that can be used to understand the varied emotional trajectories experienced by undocumented youths and young adults who wrestle with a marginalized immigration status. The chapter concludes with recommendation for counselors working with undocumented youths.

CHAPTER 15: CONCLUSION: BEYOND PSYCHOPATHOLOGY AND TOWARD RESILIENCE

This chapter underlines a major premise of this book: although cultural transitions present psychopathological risks to children and youth that may exacerbate prior stressful life experiences, the process of adaptation may also foster coping capacities and promote psychological growth. Frequently in children's immigrant life-stories, acculturation stress wanes as adaptive mechanisms and new competencies emerge. Rather than focusing on young immigrants' risk for psychopathology and negative outcomes, this book highlights the potential for coping, development, and emotional growth. Insights from the narratives presented may inform the provision of services and supports for this population of young Americans.

NOTES

1. In 1974 the Supreme Court ruled on a civil rights case (*Lau v. Nichols*) asserting that the San Francisco Unified School District had denied equal educational opportunity to Chinese non-English-speaking students by not providing special language instruction. Based on Title VI of the Civil Rights Act of 1964, the court instituted guidelines against discrimination in federal programs, including education.

2. All the names in this book have been changed in order to protect the privacy of individuals. Moreover, other identifying information in the case studies presented has been substantially altered in order to further protect confidentiality of individuals and institutions.

REFERENCES

American Psychological Association. (2014). APA initiatives on immigration and related issues. Retrieved from http://www.apa.org/about/gr/issues/minority/immigration-related-initiatives.aspx.

Arbona, C., Olvera, N., Rodriguez, N., Hagan, J., Linares, A., & Wiesner, M. (2010). Acculturative stress among documented and undocumented Latino immigrants in the United States. *Hispanic Journal of Behavioral Sciences*, 32(3), 362–384.

Bursztyn, A. M. (2006). Psychoeducational assessment of bilingual learners. In A. M. Bursztyn (Ed.), *The Praeger handbook of special education* (pp. 144–146). Westport, CT: Praeger.

Camarota, S. A. (2012). *Immigrants in the United States, 2010: A profile of America's foreign-born population.* Washington, DC: Center for Immigration Studies. Retrieved from http://www.cis.org/print/2012-profile-of-americans-foreign-born-population.

Ebin, V., Sneed, C., Morisky, D., Rotheram-Borus, M., Magnusson, A., & Malotte, C. K. (2001). Acculturation and interrelationships between problem and health-promoting behaviors among Latino adolescents. *Journal of Adolescent Health, 28,* 62–72.

García, O., & Kleifgen, J. (2010). *Educating emergent bilinguals. Policies, programs and practices for English language learners.* New York, NY: Teachers College.

Harris, K. C., & Goldstein, B. S. C. (2007). Implementing culturally sensitive interventions in classroom settings. In G. B. Esquivel, E. C. Lopez, & S. Nahari (Eds.), *Handbook of multicultural school psychology: An interdisciplinary perspective* (pp. 159–178)). Mahwah, NJ: Erlbaum.

Korn, C., & Bursztyn A. M. (Eds.). (2002). *Rethinking multicultural education: Case studies in cultural transition.* New Haven, CT: Bergin and Garvey.

Laser, A. L., & Nicoleta, N. (2011). *Working with adolescents: A guide for practitioners.* New York, NY: Guilford.

Lopez, E., & Bursztyn, A. M. (2013). Future challenges and opportunities: Toward culturally responsive training in school psychology. *Psychology in the Schools, 50*(3), 212–228.

Menken, K., & García, O. (Eds.). (2010). *Negotiating language policies in schools: Educators as policy makers.* New York, NY: Routledge.

Rong, X. L., & Preissle, J. (2009). *Educating immigrant students in the 21st century.* Thousand Oaks, CA: Corwin.

Suárez-Orozco, C., Rhodes, J., & Milburn, M. (2009). Unraveling the immigrant paradox: Academic engagement and disengagement among recently arrived immigrant youth. *Youth & Society, 41*(2), 1–33.

2

Acculturation in Immigrant Youths: The Role of Adaptation in Mental Health

Marc Fowler and Alberto M. Bursztyn

Currently, immigrants comprise one-fourth of the 75 million children in the United States. It is projected that within 50 years, immigrant youths will grow to represent one-third of a population of 100 million children. Dramatic periods of demographic shifts have always taken place in the United States, but the current wave of immigration has created the most racially and ethnically diverse age group in this nation's history (U.S. Census Bureau, 2012). Considering these trends, it is more important than ever to examine the ways that immigrants and their children adjust to life in the United States. Similar patterns of resettlement are observed worldwide, adding relevance and urgency to questions about children's and youths' mental health needs in transnational families.

Similar to other industrialized nations, the history of the United States is greatly influenced by the presence of immigrants and their descendants. For each immigrant group, both similarities and differences define their experience in a new country. Previous examinations of the immigrant experience have primarily focused on the influx of Eastern and Southern European populations during the late 19th and early 20th centuries. More recent explorations of the topic have expanded to include the arrival of immigrants from Latin America, Africa, and Asia from the mid-20th century through the present day (Berry, 1990; Farley & Alba, 2002; Fortuny & Chaudry, 2009; Passel, 2011).

CASE VIGNETTE: ALICIA

Alicia[1] is a 14-year-old shy and petite freshman attending a newly established charter high school in a poor neighborhood in a large urban center. Alicia lives with her mother, father, maternal grandmother, and siblings in a cramped apartment. Her parents are originally from the Dominican Republic. Alicia has five biological siblings and three half-sisters from her father's previous relationship. She is the second oldest in birth order and the oldest girl at home. Her parents were raised in their country of birth, as were her half sisters. Alicia describes her family's perception of her as the "most American" in her family due to her fluent English, light skin color, and long, flowing hair. Alicia mentioned that her family teases her about her light skin color because, according to her, "this means you are more American" than her siblings. She has also mentioned that her cousins sometimes do not invite her to partake in social activities because they are jealous of her "American looks." Alicia states that she is proud of her looks, but upon further examination, her insecurities and ambivalence about looking different from close family members are clearly apparent.

Alicia refers to the Dominican Republic as "home" yet longs for American opportunities "like the women I see on movies and television." Because of her tendency to withdraw from social interaction at home and in her classes, Alicia was referred for counseling at school. During the first meeting with the school psychologist, Alicia's anxieties about growing up in America became immediately clear. She reported that she spends most of her time after school at home taking care of her younger siblings, often watching television in their shared room.

Most notably, Alicia first mentioned she identifies with the Dominican culture and "feels most at home while visiting my father's family in DR." Although she is an American citizen and has been raised in the United States since birth, Alicia said that she struggles to fully identify with American culture because she is so close to her Dominican family. She also noted that her parents expressed disapproval when she tried to incorporate American traditions, such as the Fourth of July and Thanksgiving, into their home life. Alicia mentioned, "We get off from school and teachers ask us how we are celebrating Thanksgiving and I never know what to say. It is more than just celebrating holidays. It is the food, too! I ask my mom every year to make mac and cheese and turkey for Thanksgiving and she never does." This clash in cultural traditions is an obvious source of discomfort for Alicia as she would like to participate in conversations at school and, in her words, "fit in when they ask questions."

Additionally, the family speaks Spanish at home; however, Alicia speaks halting conversational Spanish, but she is most fluent in English. She explained that her English proficiency is helpful when visiting the doctor with her mother and navigating other transactions, but she experiences it as an odd disconnect while at home. Alicia has mentioned several times she feels as though it is "difficult to connect with her Spanish words" in a meaningful way while addressing important topics with her parents. She struggles to find the right words, and, despite her parents' encouragement, she inevitably switches to English. This inability to connect on an emotional level in the same language, as previously mentioned, makes Alicia feel like "a foreigner in her own home," so she prefers spending time alone watching videos or television.

Her uncertainty about where she belongs also interferes with her peer relationships. Alicia has attempted to partake in afterschool activities such as the drama club; she confided that she hopes to be a singer or actress, something she has not shared with her parents. Her family did not consent to her participation in afterschool programs, and they demanded that she return home immediately after school and assist in the care of her younger siblings. Alicia was disappointed that she could not join afterschool activities but accepted her parents' authority. She stated that her father's parenting is "very strict, but in a protective way." When asked to elaborate, she explained that she is not allowed to attend afterschool social activities unless her younger siblings also attend. This includes her friends' birthday parties, going to the movies, or hanging around after school to chat with friends. She is also forbidden to talk to members of the opposite sex or date until after high school. Her parents want her to be a proper young lady, not like "American girls." Because of her limited opportunities to connect with peers outside of school, Alicia said she has no close friends; building peer relationships outside of school has been a challenge. She reported that she is often sad when her classmates talk about their weekends during lunch hour and wishes she could participate in weekend outings. She explained that her parents fear for her safety and feel that "only your family can take care of you." Asked to explain, Alicia said that her parents do not trust outsiders and feel that being Dominican, "they'll try to take advantage of you."

Alicia seeks to please authority figures, especially her parents and teachers. She has expressed several times that her biggest fear is disappointing them. Alicia reliably complies with school rules and expectations set by her mother or father, but she is increasingly conflicted about her need for autonomy and her parents' desires for her future. She stated that is "difficult to get what I want because they never want the same thing for me." For example, Alicia said, "My parents think that I should graduate from high school and then get married and have children and raise a family." Alicia, on the other hand, wants to attend college and study acting. She believes that she can succeed because of "my

American looks, English ability, and I will have a better education than my parents."

The incipient conflict with parents is normative at Alicia's age, but her push for autonomy and personal ambitions are inflected by the acculturation process, affecting the whole family. The personal characteristics that make her feel different from her family are also expressions of her growing internalization of American values and worldviews. Her parents understand her Americanization as a threat and reflexively demand that she be more "Latina" in language use, values, and aspirations. She is conflicted at home and with peers, she struggles to define where she belongs and feels "like a misfit everywhere I go." Although she repeatedly states that she identifies with her Dominican family and culture, she indicates preference for "the American way of life" and hopes to be given the freedom to socialize with her peers outside of school. In counseling, Alicia explores her ties to her family's culture, language, and traditions and her wish to please and make her parents proud, and contrastingly, she envisions herself as a successful, independent, and educated "American woman." She feels guilt and even a sense of betrayal by fantasizing about her future; yet she says "I want something different for myself." The discomfort of living between worlds contributes to her tendency to self-isolate in her room, escaping to a television fantasy.

ACCULTURATION: HISTORICAL PERSPECTIVE

Alicia's personal journey is familiar to millions of immigrants who have experienced the ever-present internal tug between loyalty to a culture of origin and the compelling need to adapt, change, and accept the host culture as one's own. Early research into acculturation assumed that immigrants would inevitably be absorbed into the national culture as part of a unidirectional process. In particular, Gordon's (1964) One-dimensional Assimilation Model stated that immigrants' attitudes move on a continuum, which goes from maintaining their own cultural traits to the adoption of the host society culture. According to this model, to be successful in the new society, immigrants must necessarily become assimilated, meaning that adaptation problems encountered by them in this process would be due to their inability to become assimilated in the host society (Nauck, 2008). The process is now seen as dynamic and bidirectional, which suggests varying degrees of interaction between two independent dimensions: individuals' links to their ethnic culture and to the national society (Chen, Benet-Matinez, & Harris Bond, 2008; Horenczyk, 1996). In Alicia's family, varying degrees of identification with both cultures color everyday interactions and affect relationships. The acculturation is evident in negotiations about food, dress, responsibilities, and freedom.

Acculturation Basics

Various terms, including multiculturalism, globalism, biculturalism, and assimilation, have been used interchangeably with acculturation; however, the latter is preferable because it most aptly describes the process of change that occurs as a result of interaction between cultures. In terms of immigration, this interaction takes place between the immigrant (or ethnic) culture and the host (or national) culture. When two cultures encounter each other, a dynamic interchange takes place that affects a wide range of cultural characteristics such as language, traditions, religion, values, institutions, and economic and political life. Both groups experience, to one degree or another, change during this interaction, but the concerns of immigrant populations are primarily due to the considerable challenge of conforming to an established national culture (Liebkind, 2001).

There are two independent features of acculturation: preservation of ethnic cultural heritage and adaptation to the national society. Accordingly, immigration strategies are understood by evaluating the value of ethnic culture as compared to the value of embracing the host society's culture. This tension between conflicting systems is felt at the social, familial, and personal levels (Navas, Garcia, Sanchez, Rojas, Pumares, & Fernandez, 2005).

Alicia says that she is Dominican and feels most at home in the Dominican Republic; but in fact her spoken Spanish is weak, and her attachment is mostly linked to feelings for her extended family. Her ambitions and fantasies suggest a future break with traditional roles. The anticipation of conflict with her parents leads her to silence, thus increasing the risk of alienation and depression.

Acculturation Attitudes

When immigrants move to a new country, they make choices and employ strategies about how to engage with the new culture. These choices can range from deliberate and conscious, such as efforts to become proficient in the host language while retaining the native language at home, to choices dictated by circumstances that lie outside the awareness but propel the individual toward acculturation. J. W. Berry (2003) identified four categories of acculturation attitudes that describe the range of options for immigrants. *Assimilation* describes individuals who identify more strongly with the national culture than with their ethnic culture. *Integration* applies to individuals who strongly identify with both the national culture and their ethnic culture. *Separation* describes individuals who identify more strongly with their ethnic culture. *Marginalization* applies to individuals who do not identify with either culture. Of course, there are varying degrees of identification within each of these acculturation categories (Korn & Bursztyn, 2002). For example, an individual in the separation category may not only identify with his or her culture of origin but may also completely reject the host culture. Moreover, these are not fixed categories, but rather tendencies that may shift over time and are influenced by circumstances (Rudmin, 2003; Sabatier & Berry, 2008).

Alicia pushes against her parents' exclusive commitment to their ethnic culture, hoping to introduce American holidays, foods, and, more subversively, a more liberal approach to child rearing. Finding little success, she mostly retreats to herself, seeking to balance cultural expectations in her own terms.

While recognizing the importance of strategic attitudes involved in acculturation, differences exist between what immigrants actually do in terms of chosen acculturation strategies (the real plane) and the strategies they prefer (the ideal plane). The relative acculturation expanded model (RAEM) attempts to account for this gap and also highlights the fact that preferred strategies and the actual chosen strategy vary with respect to the sphere of life (e.g., school, family, and religious beliefs) (Sam & Berry, 2010). In the RAEM, the immigrant's ideal and real positions are contrasted with the national culture's ideal (how they would prefer immigrants to acculturate) and real positions (how they perceive immigrants as acculturating in practice). RAEM recognizes that immigrants may simultaneously hold numerous positions, depending on whether the domain is political, work, economic, family, social, or ideological (which includes religious beliefs and customs, principles, or values). These domains are part of a spectrum that moves from public to private. For instance, work is often viewed as a public issue that does not involve deeply held beliefs. On the other hand, religion involves deeply held opinions and is more resistant to adaptation. It follows that individuals in an immigrant group can engage in selective adaptation, choosing one acculturation strategy in one domain while utilizing another strategy in a second domain. The same choices apply to individuals belonging to the national culture, in that they may reject or embrace aspects of the ethnic culture they encounter.

For Alicia's parents, the prospect of her becoming more American than Dominican threatens their idealized set of expectations. Although they have jobs that require them to navigate cultural challenges in American society, they tend to see these as necessary inconveniences that should not translate into their children ceasing to be fully Dominican.

Adaptation

In relation to the acculturation process, adaptation refers to the changes that immigrants experience during their interaction with the national culture. Colleen Ward (2001) identifies two distinct ways of adapting to acculturation. The first, termed *psychological adaptation*, refers to personal well-being and good mental health. The second, *sociocultural adaptation*, refers to the individuals' social competence in managing their daily lives in the intercultural setting. Evidence suggests that both types of adaptation are greatly influenced by acculturation attitude. Generally speaking, an integrated attitude has been shown to result in the most desirable psychological and sociocultural adaptation. However, other factors such as ethnic identity, immigration policies, and discrimination also play a critical role (Nguyen & Benet-Martinez, 2007).

ETHNIC AND BICULTURAL IDENTITY

Theories about acculturation originally focused on group dynamics, which accounted for sociological patterns but shed little light on individual processes. The need to examine individuals within groups was eventually recognized because individuals are affected by their environment in idiosyncratic ways and personal coping mechanisms vary widely (Bursztyn, Afonso, & Black, 2013). Research studies describe vast differences in acculturation among individuals who have the same cultural origin, and even members of the same family. Individual transformation is as inevitable as cultural transformation during acculturation.

Although typical developmental trajectories, which include the evolution of personality and identity, influence acculturation, little is known about the precise nature of the connection. What is known is that both processes are based on change and are particularly relevant in the lives of adolescents. The study of personality has largely focused on characteristics such as attachment style, coping strategies, cultural intelligence, extraversion, motivation, self-esteem, and locus of control. For example, the Five-Factor Model (FFM), a unifying personality framework, defines personality along five domains: neuroticism, extraversion, openness to experience, agreeableness, and conscientiousness. In a study by Roesch and Wee (2006), the FFM was used to examine the impact of personality during acculturation. Viewing coping skills as integral to successful acculturation, the traits of extraversion, openness, and conscientiousness were associated with problem- and emotion-focused coping, whereas neuroticism was associated with psychological distress and lack of impulse control. Although results in this area are far from conclusive, it appears that the characteristics of openness to experience and neuroticism have the most substantial positive and negative effects, respectively, on adaptation during the acculturation process (Oppedal, Roysamb, & Sam, 2004).

In an effort to better understand the impact on personality, Colleen Ward (2001) identified three main areas of life change for an individual during acculturation: affective, behavioral, and cognitive. A focus on the affective is concerned with the emotional well-being of individuals during the acculturation process. One possible affective consequence of acculturation is the onset of stress. Considering that acculturation is a major life event, individuals may experience stress-related difficulties, depending on various factors. In particular, traditionally at-risk populations such as children and adolescents are more susceptible because of their age and lack of social supports. The behavioral perspective considers that some individuals lack the necessary skills to successfully adapt to a new culture. From this viewpoint, verbal and nonverbal language skills are considered essential. Language is necessary to navigate daily activities and engage in interpersonal relations, both of which must occur to gain proficiency in a new culture. The cognitive area deals with an individual's feelings about self, his or her culture, and the new culture. The social identity theory, which examines how and why people identify and behave in groups, provides direction because it suggests that humans, particularly adolescents, require a sense of group identity in order to develop and maintain well-being. During acculturation, individuals compare their identities to their group as well as to the larger society.

In addition to personality, identity development influences adaptation. Similar to acculturation, identity can be viewed along two dimensions. Ethnic and national identity for immigrants—each of which can be strong or weak—may vary independently according to the individual. Ethnic identity is an important aspect of adolescence during which developmental and environmental factors promote change. Ethnic identity refers to subgroups that share common ancestry and elements such as culture, religion, language, and place of origin. Formation of ethnic identity can be thought of in terms of a progression, moving from the unexamined childhood viewpoints, through a period of exploration, to a secure ethnic identity. Progress toward ethnic identity is not certain and relies on socialization experiences with family, community, and the larger society. Ethnic identity is associated with but not equivalent to ethnicity, which is related to a group's shared history. Ethnic identity varies in response to social psychological and contextual factors as individuals examine their group's behaviors and values to determine the extent to which they relate and choose to emulate those characteristics (Oriol, 1989).

Ethnic and national identities and their role in adaptation can be understood as an interaction between the attitudes and characteristics of immigrants and the responses of the receiving society, subject to specific immigrant characteristics and circumstances. Ethnic identity, self-esteem, and group perceptions are closely related. Referring again to the social identity theory, individual self-worth is closely related to the perceived value of the group to which an individual belongs. If a group is viewed favorably as compared to others in a society, the members of that group are more likely to possess positive self-esteem. Individuals belonging to a group with unfavorable social standing may seek to change their social standing in one of two ways. Individuals can attempt to integrate into the larger society, thereby distancing themselves from the negative associations of their ethnic group. Conversely, individuals may reject the larger society and embrace their ethnic group identity. In both cases, self-identity is largely influenced by comparisons to and reactions from group membership.

The impact of negative social standing for ethnic groups does not necessarily result in a diminished self-identity for individuals within that ethnic group. Positive socialization from family and the immediate community can serve to counteract marginalized treatment from the larger society. This socialization encourages a well-developed group and individual ethnic identity. Still, negative social perceptions of the ethnic group increases psychological risk for young people. Traits such as gender, age at the time of migration, and the generation of immigration (first, second, etc.) also serve to mitigate the relationship between identity and adaptation for immigrants (Phinney, Cantu, & Kurtz, 1997).

Attempts by immigrants to meld both aspects of their cultural selves result in the development of a dual culture or bicultural paradigm. Biculturalism involves dynamic identity development that is based in more than one cultural, ethnic, or racial background. Racial and ethnic perspectives can change over the course of an individual's life. This is particularly true of the children of immigrants, whose environment consists of influences from their ethnic culture as well as the larger national culture into which they were born.

In the past, bicultural identity was viewed as a pathway to social estrangement, stress, and depression, the remedy of which was assimilation into the mainstream. More recently, research indicates that bicultural individuals may experience benefits such as higher self-esteem, improved mental health, and increased academic achievement as compared to individuals from a singular cultural background. A preponderance of evidence now supports the advantages of the bidirectional model over the unidirectional model. Recent sociocognitive experiments also demonstrate that bicultural immigrants engage in cultural frame switching depending on the cultural context. It is important to emphasize that bicultural individuals do not experience their two cultures globally and uniformly. Acculturation changes can take place in many different domains of life and may occur independently of changes in other components. Measurement of bicultural identity has developed from single score representations to theories that provide a more well-rounded portrayal. One such model, the bicultural identity integration (BII) model, examines the subjective feelings of individuals with dual culture identities. It uses two factors to determine the level of integration between the culture of origin and the new culture. The first factor, *cultural distance*, represents the degree of dissociation or compartmentalization versus overlap perceived between the two cultural orientations and is associated with a close-minded disposition. The second, *cultural conflict*, which is the degree of tension or clash versus harmony perceived between the two cultures, is associated with a neurotic disposition. These two factors have been shown to be effective measures, as individuals with a high BII rating are more likely to respond to cues in a manner consistent with the new national culture, whereas individuals with a low BII rating are likely to respond to a new national culture's cues in accordance with their ethnic culture. Regardless of the measure used, evidence overwhelmingly supports the idea that bicultural identity contributes to greater well-being and adaptation (Nguyen & Benet-Martinez, 2007).

Biculturalism can be identified with positive feelings such as pride and uniqueness but can also be associated with conflicting expectations, identity confusion, and a sense of isolation. As Mary Waters (1999) indicates in her book about West Indians living in the United States, there may be unforeseen negative consequences during the acculturation process. West Indian immigrants arrive with qualities that distinguish their group from other minority or immigrant groups—many arrive with educational or job qualifications that allow them to immediately join the workforce. Education, particularly in the British West Indies, is an important factor; it can be a predictor of low acculturation stress due, in part, to the fact that European-based education provides immigrants with prior exposure to Western culture. In addition, the absence of experience with entrenched racism in the West Indies helps them to negotiate the complicated nature of race relations in the United States. Over time, however, West Indian immigrants are absorbed into the same racial caste system that African Americans experience from birth. Similar to the offspring of other immigrant groups, West Indian children may have less acculturation support from parents, who often maintain multiple jobs in order to pay for living expenses, save money, or provide support to relatives in their home country. As a result, second- and third-generation immigrant children may become oppositional to the national culture, while relinquishing the group characteristics that initially helped their parents and grandparents succeed.

Studies of bicultural stress in Latino adolescents indicate that they are more likely to experience stress from the pressure of trying to meet the expectations of ethnic and national cultures, intergenerational conflict, and English speaking in a Spanish-speaking home environment (or vice versa).

These stressors contribute to a higher rate of depression in Latino youths as compared to U.S.-born peers. For some adolescents, biculturalism is less a melding of cultures than maintenance of two separate identities. Although maintenance of multiple identities is not necessarily problematic, it may become so if conflict exists between the cultures upon which those identities are based (Romero & Roberts, 2003).

In this chapter's vignette, Alicia's social anxiety is partly rooted in her internal struggle to accommodate two disparate sets of cultural expectations. Dominican culture is collectivistic and hierarchical, while American culture is much more individualistic and egalitarian. Forming a bicultural identity is further complicated by her desire to please her parents and avoid conflict. Alicia envisions a future break from her culture of origin, formulating a different cultural script than the one stated by her parents, namely marrying after high school and raising a family. She plans to attend college and pursue a career as an independent woman. Fearing disapproval and rejection, she is unable to share her internal struggle with family members; consequently, she withdraws, experiencing sadness and a sense of disconnection. This coping strategy, withdrawal and fantasy, is sufficient to maintain family harmony but is affecting Alicia in a negative way. In retreating from age-appropriate social engagement and exploration, she is losing ground developmentally and increasingly at risk for psychopathology.

NATIONAL POLICIES, PARENTING STYLES, AND DISCRIMINATION

National policy has the potential to significantly influence group or individual acculturation attitudes. Immigration policies reflect the extent to which a country supports the process of integration through encouragement of cultural diversity. Phinney, Horenczyk, Liebkind, and Vedder (2001) examined the relation between immigration policies and adoption of immigrant attitudes. The four countries in their study differ significantly in their policies toward immigrants. The United States has officially welcomed immigrants and refugees for many years, but individual states are responsible for providing needed services. Israel's immigrant policy has traditionally focused on assimilation, but this policy is slowly being replaced by an integrationist policy. Although recent legislation in Finland emphasizes integration, its immigrant policy is in practice assimilationist. The Dutch government's immigrant policy, aimed at integration, extends benefits through the provision of school funds and medical and financial support. Findings from the study of adolescents in these four countries showed that only in the United States, specifically within the State of California, did the type of identity adopted by most immigrants parallel the state's official immigrant policy; immigrants adopted proportionally more often an integrated identity than an assimilated, separated, or marginalized attitude. Finnish immigrants had largely marginalized attitudes, immigrants in the Netherlands largely possessed separated attitudes, and immigrants in Israel were divided almost equally between assimilated and integrated attitudes. Although national policies that support immigration provide an incentive for acculturation, evidence for links between policies and ethnic identity is weak. It appears that other factors weigh more significantly on acculturation attitudes.

Discrimination is a significant risk factor in mental health development of immigrant adolescents. Research indicates that a relatively small percentage of immigrants demonstrate related problem behaviors; however, those who do are at higher risk for significant maladaptation. Family life, where children initially gain self-esteem and learn about social interactions, is a vitally important protective factor. In fact, families function as a microcosm of the larger society in the respect that family members utilize individual acculturation strategies that in turn interact with other relatives to influence the overall family adaptation.

Parents who have moved to a new country in pursuit of a higher standard of living must balance the maintenance of cultural continuity with the need to conform to the demands of their new environment. Despite differences between immigrant and national parenting styles, immigrant parents attempt to maintain cultural points of reference for their children while encouraging new competencies that will be useful in the larger culture. Parenting style refers to the child-rearing attitudes and behaviors that contribute to a family's emotional climate—three parenting styles relevant to acculturation have been identified. Parents using the *authoritative* style establish rules and boundaries for children's behavior but balance enforcement with communication, caring, and support. The *authoritarian* style emphasizes rules and compliant behavior without consideration of the child's feelings. Parental use of the *permissive* style involves a nurturing attitude with an absence of demands and discipline for the child. Parental style, which is linked to adolescent self-esteem and academic performance, varies according to culture and context. Parental style that emphasizes empathy, epitomized in the authoritative approach, is most effective for the transmission of ethnic pride, familial values, and psychological well-being.

Adolescent attitudes about family climate are based on views of cultural harmony with parents and self-disclosure. Cultural harmony refers to the adolescent's view of how congruent his or her values and orientations are compared to their parents. Some degree of disagreement between parent and child is a typical aspect of adolescent development—parents attempt to maintain control as children struggle for independence. However, it is important to determine whether the adolescent attributes conflict to normal disagreements or deeper cultural separations. Self-disclosure concerns the willingness of children to express their feelings to their parents. In the absence of such willingness, it is difficult for parents to gain insight into their child's emotional state. Although most children talk about school, they are less forthcoming with important information about their friends and social life.

Colette Sabatier and John W. Berry (2008) studied the interaction of acculturation, parenting style, and discrimination on immigrant youths in France and Canada. Evidence supports the idea that both ethic and national identification resulted in positive adaptation. The array of positive outcomes, depending on the context, supports the theory of domain-specific acculturation. For instance, French paternal support of ethnic and national identities aids in the reduction of deviant behavior, whereas the embrace of ethnic and national identities by Canadian youths contributes to increased self-esteem. The results also indicate that integrated acculturation promotes positive adolescent adaptation.

Important differences in adaptation and family climate exist between the two countries. Adolescents in France experience a lower level of psychological and sociocultural adaptation and more distant family climate. The differences appear to be consistent with national characteristics in that French society advocates a less involved parenting style. Although French adolescents report experiencing more discrimination, they tend toward higher levels of national acculturation than their parents. French immigrant parents endorse national orientations less than Canadian immigrant parents, while the reverse is true for adolescents. Consequently, French adolescents are more oriented toward the country of settlement than their parents, while Canadian parents and adolescent endorse relatively similar views (Sabatier & Berry, 2008).

Acculturation Trends

For immigrant youths confronted with the challenge of balancing ethnic and national cultures, what does successful acculturation look like? Successful acculturation is based on the immigrant's acculturation attitude as well as his or her level of adaptation to the national culture. Recent research indicates that involvement with both ethnic and national cultures contributes most to immigrant well-being (Phinney & Devich-Navarro, 1997; Portes & Rumbaut 2001; Rumbaut, 1994; Ward, 1996). The path to successful adaptation, however, is more complicated. Depending on the context, psychological adaptation is associated with an orientation toward ethnic culture, while identification with national culture is associated with better sociocultural adaptation.

One transnational study examined acculturation and adaptation in a sample of over 5,000 immigrant adolescents in 13 different countries. The study found that in terms of acculturation, the largest number of youths (36.4%) was classified in the integration category, meaning that they sought to acculturate by being involved with both their ethnic culture and the national culture. The second largest group (22.5%) was in the separated category. They sought to acculturate by being primarily identified with their own ethnic group, seeking limited involvement with the national culture. In contrast, the assimilated category was the smallest group (18.7%) among the participants, indicating that tendencies to reject ethnic culture were rather limited among these youths. Even more surprising was the rather large size of the marginalized category (22.4%), representing the third largest group, which was almost equal to the separated category. These young people lack a clear identity and appear to be confused; they thus represent a group in which, according to previous research, personal and social problems are likely to appear (Sabatier & Berry, 2008).

Results from the study also illustrate the importance of individual and environmental factors. The length of residence in the new country proved to be a strong indicator of acculturation attitude—the more time spent exposed to the national culture, the more likely the adolescent held an integrated attitude. The place of residence was also an important factor. Adolescents who lived in an ethnically mixed neighborhood were more likely to exhibit an integrated attitude, while those in ethnically segregated areas expressed separatist attitudes. Psychological and sociocultural adaptation fluctuated, depending on gender. Girls expressed higher levels of psychological distress, as indicated by depression and anxiety, compared to boys, who demonstrated higher levels of sociocultural distress, as indicated by behavioral and personality disorders. The link between perceived discrimination and acculturation attitude, as suggested in the theory of reciprocity, was also supported by the study (Sabatier & Berry, 2008).

Reciprocity, which posits that likes or dislikes are reciprocated accordingly, was demonstrated by the fact that when there is little perception of discrimination, young immigrants are most likely to embrace an integrated attitude; however, when there is more perceived discrimination, they are likely to exhibit separated or marginalized attitudes. This suggests that when immigrant adolescents experience discrimination, they are likely to reject close involvement with the national society and are more oriented toward their ethnic culture or ambivalent about their involvement with both. An integrated acculturation attitude is associated with psychological and sociocultural adaptation; conversely, a marginalized attitude reduces the likelihood of any adaptation. Ethnic acculturation was shown to promote psychological adaptation but produced both positive and negative outcomes concerning sociological adaptation. The assimilated acculturation attitude indicated modestly poorer psychological and sociological adaptation, but these results were inconsistent, depending on the type of analysis used to evaluate the data. Despite the inconsistency, the results suggest that strong ethnic and national identities are crucial to an appropriate level of adaptation (Sabatier & Berry, 2008).

Relative preference for acculturation attitudes seems to vary with respect to the ethnic group and the national society, as well as contextual factors. In another study that involved 7,000 immigrant youths in 13 different countries, researchers found that among all the immigrants combined, integration was the preferred strategy. However, separation appeared to be the most preferred strategy (40.3%) for Turkish immigrants. In contrast, those in the Vietnamese sample seemed to prefer assimilation (25.6%) nearly as much as integration (33.1%); their preferences were directly related to the nature of the national culture (Berry, Phinney, Sam, & Vedder, 2006).

School adjustment is generally regarded as the primary sociocultural and developmental task for adolescents (Hirschman, 2001). Within many immigrant communities, the importance attributed to school adjustment is particularly high; newcomers tend to see schools as avenues to participation and mobility in the new national culture. This positive attitude toward achievement contributes to a phenomenon known as the *immigration paradox*, which is defined as immigrant youths adapting as well as or better than national youths. This paradox has also been observed in children of immigrants as compared to the children of American-born second and third-plus generations. Focus on family, community, and educational achievement in immigrant communities is viewed as a distinguishing characteristic that may account for disparity in achievement (Gibson, 1991).

The educational attainment of immigrant youths is an area of increasing study. The Children of Immigrants Longitudinal Study found that 1.5-generation (those who arrive before age 13) and second-generation children tend to do better than their native-born schoolmates in grades, rates of school retention, and behavioral aspects such as homework (Portes & Rumbaut 2001). Similarly, the New York Second Generation Study found that second-generation West Indians do better than native-born blacks in the city, and Dominicans, Colombians, Ecuadorans, and Peruvians do better than Puerto Ricans (Kasinitz, Mollenkopf, & Waters, 2004). Chinese perform better in high school graduation rates and college attendance than all the other groups, including native whites of native parentage.

On the other hand, ethnic identity is not always associated with academic achievement. School performance may only be enhanced if a particular ethnic identity includes achievement as an aspect of that culture. For example, although second-generation Mexican Americans compare favorably with the very low education levels of their parents, there is some evidence of third-generation decline among the grandchildren of Mexican immigrants. The inconsistencies between ethnic identity and national identity may be related to the fact that the process of adaptation to a new society involves complex communication transactions in which immigrants attempt to make sense of what they expect and what is expected from them by the national society. Research suggests that an integrated acculturation attitude is conducive to better school performance, but, in some environments, depending on the country, region, and school, embracing a national identity may encourage higher achievement. In any case, it does not appear that one form of acculturation is conclusively superior to others in terms of school adjustment (Marks, Patton, & Garcia Coll, 2011).

CONCLUSION

As major demographic shifts continue to take place in the United States and around the world, it is increasingly important to understand the factors that contribute to the acculturation of immigrant youths (Flannery, Reise, & Yu, 2001). When immigrants and their children move to a new country, their acculturation attitude determines the degree to which they will embrace the national culture or retain their ethnic culture (Roesch & Wee, 2006). As immigrant youths adapt, their personal well-being and social competence are affected by various factors such as personality, identity, national immigration policies, parenting style, and discrimination (Kasinitz, Mollenkopf, & Waters, 2004). Research suggests that characteristics such as an integrated acculturation attitude, openness to experience, and balance between ethnic and national identities, as well as extenuating factors such as authoritative parenting style, integrationist immigration policies, and minimal experience with discrimination, contribute to positive mental health in immigrant youths (Benet-Martinez, Lee, & Leu, 2006).

In the chapter's vignette, counseling Alicia in the school setting offered her an opportunity to reflect on and share her struggles; in counseling she explored sources of stress, anxiety, and discomfort. Although her withdrawal from social engagement in school may have deeper roots than her acculturation experience, her feelings of alienation at home contributed to her overall sense of isolation and heightened her level of anxiety. Negotiating with her parents to expand her autonomy may alleviate some of her sadness and isolation. More importantly, the family needs to become more aware and empathic as Alicia enters a developmental phase that pivots on developing a healthy sense of personal and group identity.

NOTE

1. All the names in this chapter have been changed in order to protect the privacy of individuals.

REFERENCES

Benet-Martinez, V., Lee, F., & Leu, J. (2006). Biculturalism and cognitive complexity: Expertise in cultural representations. *Journal of Cross-Cultural Psychology, 37*, 386–407.

Berry, J. W. (1990). Psychology of acculturation. In N. R. Goldberger & J. B. Veroff (Eds.), *The culture and psychology reader* (pp. 457–488). New York, NY: New York University Press. (Reprinted from Nebraska symposium on motivation: Cross-cultural perspectives, by J. J. Berman [Ed.], 1989, Lincoln: University of Nebraska Press.)

Berry, J. W. (2003). Conceptual approaches to acculturation. In K. Chun, P. Balls-Organista, & G. Marin (Eds.), *Acculturation: Advances in theory, measurement and applied research* (pp. 17–37). Washington, DC: APA Press.

Berry, J., Phinney, J. S., Sam, D., & Vedder, P. (2006). Immigrant youth: Acculturation, identity and adaptation. *Applied Psychology: An International Review, 55*(3), 303–332.

Bursztyn, A. M., Afonso, A. G., & Black, K. (2013). Through a cultural lens: Psychopathology within and across borders. In T. Plante (Ed.), *Abnormal psychology through the ages*. Westport, CT: Praeger.

Chen, S. X., Benet-Martinez, V., & Harris Bond, M. (2008). Bicultural identity, bilingualism, and psychological adjustment in multicultural societies: Immigration-based and globalization-based acculturation. *Journal of Personality, 76*(4), 803–837.

Flannery, W. P., Reise, S. P., & Yu, J. (2001). An empirical comparison of acculturation models. *Personality and Social Psychology Bulletin, 27*, 1035–1045.

Fortuny, K., & Chaudry, A. (2009). *Children of immigrants: Immigration trends*. Washington, DC: Urban Institute.

Gibson, M. (1991). Minorities and schooling: Some implications. In M. A. Gibson & J. U. Ogbu (Eds.), *Minority status and schooling: A comparative study of immigrant and involuntary minorities* (pp. 357–381). New York, NY: Garland.

Gordon, M. (1964). *Assimilation in American life*. New York, NY: Oxford.

Hirschman C. (2001). The educational enrollment of immigrant youth: A test of the segmented assimilation hypothesis. *Demography, 38*, 317–337.

Horenczyk, G. (1996). Migrant identities in conflict: Acculturation attitudes and perceived acculturation ideologies. In G. Breakwell & E. Lyons (Eds.), *Changing European identities* (pp. 241–250). Oxford, U.K.: Butterworth-Heinemann.

Kasinitz, P., Mollenkopf, J. H., & Waters, M. C. (Eds.). (2004). *Becoming New Yorkers: Ethnographies of the new second generation*. New York, NY: Sage.

Korn, C., & Bursztyn A. M. (Eds.). (2002). *Rethinking multicultural education: Case studies in cultural transition*. New Haven, CT: Bergin and Garvey.

Liebkind, K. (2001). Acculturation. In R. Brown & S. Gaertner (Eds.), *Blackwell handbook of social psychology: Intergroup processes* (pp. 386–406). Oxford, U.K.: Blackwell.

Livingston G., & Kahn J. R. (2002). An American dream unfulfilled: The limited mobility of Mexican Americans. *Social Science Quarterly, 83*, 1003–1012.

Marks, A., Patton, F., & Garcia Coll, C. (2011). Being bicultural: A mixed-methods study of adolescents' implicitly and explicitly measured multiethnic identities. *Developmental Psychology, 47*, 1, 270–288.

Nauck, B. (2008). Acculturation. In F. J. Van de Vijver, D. A. van Hemert, & Y. H. Poortinga (Eds.), *Multilevel analysis of individuals and cultures* (pp. 379–410). Mahwah, NJ: Erlbaum.

Navas, M., Garcia, M. C., Sanchez, J., Rojas, A. J., Pumares, P., & Fernandez, J. S. (2005). Relative acculturation extended model: New contributions with regard to the study of acculturation. *International Journal of Intercultural Relations, 29*, 21–37.

Nguyen, A., & Benet-Martinez, V. (2007). Biculturalism unpacked: Components, measurement, individual differences, and outcomes. *Social and Personality Psychology Compass, 1*(1), 101–114.

Oppedal, B., Roysamb, E., & Sam, D. L. (2004). The effect of acculturation and social support on change in mental health among young immigrants. *International Journal of Behavioral Development, 28*, 481–494.

Oriol, M. (1989). Modeles ideologiques et modeles culturels dans la reproduction des identities collectives en situation d'emigration [Ideological and cultural models for the reproduction of a sense of collective identity in the emigration situation]. *Revue Internationale d'Action Communautaire, 21*, 117–123.

Passel, J. S. (2011). Demography of immigrant youth: Past, present, and future. *Future of Children, 21*(1), 19–41.

Phinney, J. S., Cantu, C. L., & Kurtz, D. A. (1997). Ethnic and American identity as predictors of self-esteem among African American, Latino, and white adolescents. *Journal of Youth and Adolescence, 26*, 165–185.

Phinney, J. S., & Devich-Navarro, M. (1997). Variations in bicultural identification among African American and Mexican American adolescents. *Journal of Research on Adolescence, 7*(1), 3–32.

Phinney, J. S., Horenczyk, G., Liebkind, K., & Vedder, P. (2001). Ethnic identity, immigration, and well-being: An interactional perspective. *Journal of Social Issues, 57*(3), 493–510.

Portes A., & Rumbaut R. (2001). *Legacies: The story of the immigrant second generation*. Berkeley: University of California Press.

Roesch, S. C., & Wee, C. (2006). Relations between the Big Five personality traits and dispositional coping in Korean Americans: Acculturation as a moderating factor. *International Journal of Psychology, 41*(2), 85–96.

Romero, A. J., & Roberts, R. E. (2003). Stress within a bicultural context for adolescents of Mexican descent. *Cultural Diversity and Ethnic Minority Psychology, 9*(2), 171–184.

Rudmin, F. W. (2003). Critical history of the acculturation psychology of assimilation, separation, integration, and marginalization. *Review of General Psychology, 7*, 3–37.

Rumbaut, R. G. (1994). The crucible within: Ethnic identity, self-esteem, and segmented assimilation among children of immigrants. *International Migration Review*, 28(4), 748–781.

Sabatier, C., & Berry, J. W. (2008). The role of family acculturation, parental style, and perceived discrimination in the adaptation of second-generation immigrant youth in France and Canada. *European Journal of Developmental Psychology*, 5(2), 159–185.

Sam, D. L., & Berry, J. W. (2010). Acculturation: When individuals and groups of different cultural backgrounds meet. *Perspectives on Psychological Science*, 5(4), 472–481.

U.S. Census Bureau. (2012). The foreign-born population in the United States: 2010. Retrieved from http://www.census.gov/population/foreign/.

Ward, C. (1996). Acculturation. In D. Landis & R. Bhagat (Eds.), *Handbook of intercultural training* (2nd ed.; pp. 124–147). Thousand Oaks, CA: Sage.

Ward, C. (2001). The A, B, Cs of acculturation. In D. Matsumoto (Ed.), *The handbook of culture and psychology* (pp. 411–445). Oxford, U.K.: Oxford University Press.

Waters, M. C. (1999). *Black identities: West Indian immigrant dreams and American realities*. Cambridge, MA: Harvard University Press.

3

Identities under Construction: Portraits of Urban Latino Adolescents

Alexandros Orphanides and Alberto M. Bursztyn

With Latinos representing the fastest growing segment of the U.S. population, there is an abundance of scrutiny about where these young people are headed (Hemphill & Vanneman, 2011). There are many ideas as to what constitutes a Latina/o person and the psychological and societal factors that impact his or her life choices and school performance. In his anthology of Spanish–English poetry, Gustavo Pérez Firmat (1995, p. 1) asks the reader "how to explain to you that I don't belong to English though I belong nowhere else." This sense of alienation, of belonging to an ambiguous third kind of culture, is not uncommon to the child immigrant in the context of his or her new home. Their experiences are fraught with difficulties of a different and compounding nature.

Traditionally, Latino immigrants in the United States have faced racial, cultural, economic, and linguistic challenges. Yet immigration as a process is extended through acculturation, and we find that fluid, hybridized cultural identities exist for adolescent Latinos. In the large metropolitan areas, Latino students are not linguistically or culturally engaged by an educational system that replicates the dominant culture and its rigid understanding of subcultures, yet this population is an ever-growing section of the national student body. Additionally, they may live in communities where they "are likely to experience a high number of life event stressors and daily hassles" (Suarez-Morales & Lopez, 2009, p. 335). Further complicating any analysis of these young people is the attempt at defining such a group; the term Latino is broadly used to categorize a conglomeration of people with some ancestral ties to approximately 20 different countries with wildly different norms, cultures, and historical contexts located in North America, Central America, South America, and the Caribbean. We find that the use of such reductionist terminology further obfuscates the theoretical understanding among researchers, educators, and mental health professionals. Culturally responsive therapeutic and educational practices must acknowledge that new cultural identities are constantly forming that do not fit neatly within our outdated modes of cultural identification.

This chapter is based on an ethnography conducted over a period of an academic year at an urban alternative high school. The school primarily served poor ethnic minority youths who had previously abandoned their studies or had been expelled or transferred from another site. About 30% were foreign born and more than 12% qualified for English language support services. Student participants were interviewed individually and in groups. They were also observed in classrooms and in interactions with peers, teachers, and other school personnel. The thematic direction of inquiries focused on the overarching theme of identity that these young people struggle to locate within themselves in relation to their communities, families, the school system, and society at large.

PARTICIPANTS

The participants in the study were all teenagers attending an alternative school, and they shared certain commonalities, among them difficulty adjusting to a standard academic program. Through their eyes, memories, and insights, we gain access to their social and personal realities. In this chapter, we chose to narrow our focus to four participants in order to highlight individual challenges and trajectories instead of drawing broad generalizations without an underlying narrative. Although these four young adults are somewhat representative of the population served by the focus school and others like it, we do not generalize from their experience, but rather seek to portray their individuality in the context of social and academic demands common to their peer group.

CASE VIGNETTES: ADDISON, SASHA, FERNANDO, AND LETTY

Addison[1] is a young man originally from the Dominican Republic. Approaching the age of 20, he immigrated to the United States before starting primary school, but returned to the island for a year in the second grade. He transferred to his current high school last year and was subsequently a long-term absence. The causes of his truancy were two separate incidences of family illness, one in the Midwest and the other in the Dominican Republic. He is the firstborn in his family and the only male; this distinction carries along with it much responsibility and pressure. He often cares for his mother and younger female sibling.

Socioeconomically, Addison's family struggles—his mother works exhaustive hours and is often sick.

In the social environment of the school, he is identified by most as Latino—his appearance indicates a likely mix of European and Afro-Caribbean ancestry. He is tall and dark skinned with short curly hair; he maintains a manicured and well-groomed appearance. He likes to wear flashy, form-fitting graphic T-shirts and slim-yet-slouchy designer jeans resembling the style of *bachateros* and *reggaetoneros* like Prince Royce, Don Omar, and Plan B. At school, he has a small group of friends, all of whom are Latino. Within this group and in classrooms, he displays a relaxed attitude and a sense of humor. The group includes a female of Ecuadorean descent and two males, one of Colombian Dominican descent and the other of Mexican ancestry. Their conversations are bilingual—in both English and Spanish. Addison participates primarily in Spanish and exhibits some degree of difficulty expressing himself effectively in English.

Sasha is a 17-year-old mainland-born Puerto Rican female. She transferred to her current high school at the start of the academic year. She is boisterous and extraverted—a social leader in the classroom. It is common to find her laughing in the hallway, working after school with a teacher, or volunteering her opinion. She has an older sister and aspires to join the navy. This year she has been accepted at a private college in Florida but is uncertain as to whether she will attend.

Petite and dark skinned, Sasha is often confused for Dominican, a point she is quick to correct. When describing herself, she uses terms such as Hispanic, American, and often references her *blackness*. She communicates primarily in English and has rudimentary knowledge of Spanish. Her style vacillates between hip-hop and hipster-chic; she wears Jordans (sneakers), jeans, and urban hip-hop brands, as well as anachronistic thrift store fashions. She lives in a community best described as a working-poor Puerto Rican enclave that borders the frontier of hipster gentrification. Her community is struggling to hold on to apartments that are being transferred to young, affluent whites.

Fernando is an 18-year-old student who transferred to this school after having been stabbed and involved in gang-related activity in his previous school. The gang he was a member of comprised Dominican Americans involved in petty crime, drug trafficking, and territorial squabbles with other Dominican and Latino American gangs. He is of mixed parentage; his mother is from the coastal city of Barranquilla in Colombia, and his father is from the Dominican Republic. Fernando was born in the United States. He is the youngest child and has two older sisters. His father works in property management and provides a lower-middle-class life for the family. At school, he is friendly with most students and socializes with a group of other Latino students. Their social interactions are bilingual, in both English and Spanish.

Tall and light skinned with brown eyes and brown hair, his ethnic identity is ambiguous to others due to the lighter tone of his skin and lack of any noticeable markers of Spanish in his English. Fernando is clear that he identifies as Dominican. He wears high-end baggy jeans, new Jordans, designer sweat shirts, and fitted baseball caps in pristine condition. In the popular culture, his attire parallels rappers like Drake and Wiz Khalifa. He carries himself with confidence through the hallways and engages with students of various racial and cultural groups comfortably.

Letty, who is 18 years old, was born in Puerto Rico but raised in New York since the age of two. She does speak Spanish as a second language and has strong conversational skills in the language. She is new to the school environment and is still finding her place in the school's social dynamic. She is the youngest of two, having an older sister who is married and out of the house; Letty now lives with only her mother in a neighborhood that is experiencing gentrification. She is friendly with her peers and instructors. She is light skinned with brown hair and brown eyes. Her fashion sense is heavily influenced by the East Village bohemian style, with large nonprescription glasses and various hipster fashions. She works in the food and hospitality industry, keeping late nights and struggling to make it to school on time.

FAMILIES

Studies indicate that there are dynamic changes occurring within many Latino families. Splintering of the traditional family structure challenges Dominican families as a transnational body (Dicker, 2006). "Puerto Rican mothers indicate a variety of acculturated views that range from highly traditional to mainstream American" (Hammer, Rodriguez, Lawrence, & Miccio, 2007, p. 218). Neither of these groups is homogenous. They all have a variety of complicated and idiosyncratic details that populate this bouquet. We find Dominican families often deal with relocation, which jeopardizes the educational stability of their children. In addition to this, there may be a tenuous immigration status. In the case of the child, birth order is a factor. The strain of the immigrant experience can be heavy in the Dominican community, where the responsibilities usually associated with adults are often entrusted to children. These factors are often overlooked in psychological and educational studies.

Within the Puerto Rican diaspora, there is the relationship to the heritage language as well as the generations since migration from the Spanish-dominant island to the mainland. One of the complications of the Puerto Rican population is that as an older immigrant population, they hold a long-established niche and subculture population in New York, evidenced by the identity of the *Nuyorican*.

In both groups, as in all families, there is the diversity of the very notion of family. In some of the studies, the family is a traditional two-parent system. Other studies highlight the single mother, and still others reference nontraditional families in the immigrant experience characterized by patterns of separation and reunification. Any study attempting to be comprehensive will at the very least be conscious of these differences.

A study that focuses on Puerto Ricans and Dominicans in New York has the challenge of accommodating a third group, namely the hybridized Latino identity that exists in urban centers. These groups have their own idiosyncrasies and distinctions that challenge many traditional concepts of ethnic group or nationality. Their inclusion is, however, fundamentally important to a fuller understanding of either group in the United States.

The study from which we extracted these data sought to arrive at a more nuanced understanding of how linguistic and cultural differences affect young Latinos' education and mental health. We also considered how new insights might improve psychological services in and out of school.

IDENTITY AND RACE

In the song "Race Card" by rapper Ice Cube, we are warned "please don't believe the hype, not everything in this world is black and white" (Jackson, 2006). There is a general obsession in the cultural ethos of the United States with identity. Perhaps this fascination with skin color, economic status, and sexual orientation is the manifestation of historical developments surrounding the foundation of the country, its immigrant past, settlement history, and struggle to accommodate people from the world over beneath one banner. The thrust of this way of thinking in the context of a heterogeneous environment may even be a societal neurosis. Whether in the name of institutional discrimination or social justice, this taxonomical approach to understanding society is insufficient because identity is not a monolithic entity nor is it rooted entirely in one category, be it race, skin color, musical preference, career specialization, or sexual orientation. What makes identity is the soup of circumstance, historical phenomena, personal experience, and an innumerable number of other factors, but fundamentally identity. To the immigrant or child of immigrants, the expectation of providing a definitive response to questions of identity can be confusing, stressful, and exasperating.

Social identity theory posits that identity is "that part of an individual's self-concept which derives from his/her knowledge of his/her membership of a social group (or groups) together with the value and emotional significance attached to that membership" (Tajfel, 1978, p. 63). All the youngsters involved in this study answered questions regarding their identities in a thoughtful manner; some struggled a bit or were slightly unsure, but generally discussed identity with a reasonableness and familiarity of someone who has answered the question many times before.

IDENTITY, EXPECTATIONS, STRESS, AND FATALISM

These young people may be somewhat different from their demographic group in that they are all sticking with the pursuit of their high school diploma, despite academic struggles, high stress environments, and community expectations formed around high dropout rates. One may inquire as to whether their sense of identity is a factor contributing to their hopeful and aspirational behavior in the face of difficult odds. It is important to note that these participants are all students at an alternative school. They have arrived at this school after struggling at their previous school. Practically all students at these schools are behind in graduation requirements; and more often than not they have had negative experiences in the school system. Their resilience was evident, so was their realistic view of their lives and challenges.

ADDISON

Addison, the participant who spent considerable time in the Dominican Republic, identifies as Dominican point-blank: "I'm Dominican, my whole family is Dominican—but we live here." When asked about living in Brooklyn, Addison expounded "I been living in Brooklyn for more time than I was living in the Dominican Republic but I feel proud that I am Dominican." In social situations, Addison would best be described as boisterous, as long as the others are members of the same in-group, Hispanics or Latinos. I vividly remember seeing Addison interact with store owners in the local Dominican-owned and operated bodega, where he stood tall and spoke to them in Spanish with a volume and verbosity that exuded confidence. His body language betrayed his confidence and sense of masculinity. This is markedly different from his dealings with black or white peers or adults—Addison shrinks, his speech becomes uncertain, his posture slouches, and his confidence appears to erode. When speaking with other Latino teens in English, he shows very little hesitance and his confidence returns. It is in academic settings and when dealing with people he presumably identifies as different that we observe insecurity. He struggles to explain his sense of inadequacy with regard to academic matters; his shrinking during interactions with non-Latinos also indicates that his identification as Dominican is as much an identification as a non-American.

Addison is the only male in his household. He lives with three women—his mother, sister, and grandmother—and shows a great deal of respect and reverence for his mother. Still, he finds a specific meaning in the role of man of the house. He frames his responsibilities as male responsibilities: "My sister needs me to take her to school; with my mom working, I have to be the man who takes care of things." His distinction is that with the absence of his mother, he must ascend to the role of man of the house, even if the responsibilities of tending to children are traditionally, in the Dominican Republic, a female concern. One senses traces of pride in describing his duties as those of "the man who takes care of things." The identity of man, which he associates with accountability and duty, must be complicated and a source of stress when he encounters struggles and challenges in his school life.

Addison explains that he has a lot of respect for his mother, and, as he recollects, listened earnestly to her instructions as a child. The dynamic of the single mother household undermined many of the traditional family roles, and the responsibility of caring for both a younger sister and an ailing grandmother has shifted his role in the house as well. "My mom is my hero," he says, "she works a lot . . . she is a home attendant . . . so she has to work all the time. . . . I take care of my sister . . . and my *abuela* is sick." While he feels that he is an adult and responsible for himself, he is clear that his mother has played an important role in his development. "She taught me everything, she told me what to do when I was little and how to behave—what not to do." Discipline was doled out in the traditional manner as a young child: "If I did something wrong she would tell me . . . if I didn't listen she'd hit me, but nothing hard, like a little slap if I deserved it." He notes that his mother does not discipline his sister in this manner. This may be a result of acculturating to American norms or developing an awareness of American laws or it may be reflective of gender differences.

His mother does not deal with schools because "she doesn't speak English so good and she's always busy with work. . . . I can take care of those things." This creates an interesting situation where Addison must be responsible for garnering information on his sister's academic progress, but this begs the question: Who was responsible for *his* academic development? Addison explains, "My mother doesn't like coming to school because of her English, but she always told me to do good in school, it is important for her that I finish high school." Herein lays a stressful contradiction. Addison identifies as an adult and a male, and he associates these two roles with the ability to successfully complete duties and responsibilities. Yet he is not successful in school or academic pursuits.

Additionally, confronted with the strong possibility of aging out of the school system, Addison expressed trepidation: "I'm not so sure I'm going to finish," he explained, "it's tough because I have so many other things happening, and sometimes you try and you just can't [succeed at school], and I try, but I don't think I'm going to finish." Despite this, he continues to attend, to struggle, and fail. Bearing in mind his family's economic challenges, Addison could easily abandon school for paid employment. If his words and physical responses are not aspirational, at the very least his activity is in that he continues to attend. We see him inhabit the space of adult and child—the adult in the world of his family, personal responsibilities, and Spanish speakers, and the insecure child in the school setting or world of "other" people.

SASHA

When asked about her background, Sasha adamantly says "I'm American." When asked further about her Puerto Rican ancestry, she continues, "I guess, a little bit, but I'm American. I don't even speak Spanish good." Sasha identified as two things, American and Puerto Rican, with the former playing the dominant role. She equates her lack of Spanish language abilities with not Puerto Rican. Another identity central to her concept of self is geographically bound; she has lived in New York since moving from Connecticut as a young child. Sasha explains that Connecticut, where she was born, is "really wack, there is nothing to do there, it is not like Brooklyn." She is proud of her neighborhood and particularly proud of the city she lives in. The neighborhood is primarily Latino, and her lack of Spanish language fluency magnifies her sense of being American. The music she listens to is primarily in English as she prefers hip-hop and rhythm and blues, two genres generally associated with black culture.

Yet she noticeably reaffirms her Puerto Rican or Latina sense of identity a number of times. In one instance she is being teased by some black students for eating *mangu*, a Dominican dish made primarily of garlic and mashed plantains, in the classroom. They comment on its strong odor and pulpy appearance, likening it to vomit and excrement. Visibly upset, Sasha vigorously curses them, calls them racists for insulting "Spanish food," and finishes the verbal melee by loudly declaring "I'm blacker than you anyway!" Here she inhabits two identities she did not openly declare when asked the initial question; she sees herself as Latina and yet embraces a sense of blackness. This is worth noting because historically, Latino groups with African ancestry have had a tenuous understanding of American terminology like black or African American and have resisted being grouped within such classifications.

Her sense of being Latina may actually be broader than specifically Puerto Rican, as evinced by another tense interaction she had with some black students who were making remarks to a student of Mexican descent about whether he ate tacos daily and his legal status. Sasha, who does not regularly interact with the boy, loudly told the other students, all of whom were physically larger than she, to "shut the f**k up" and told them to stop making fun of "us Spanish people." She finished off this salvo by asking them how they would like it if they were referred to by racial epithets and stereotypes, which she briefly summarized. The students generally laughed and called Sasha "crazy" but subsequently stopped teasing the young man. Herein lays her sense of Latina identity—perhaps organic, but also a product of American ideas surrounding identity and the imposition of a group that elsewhere in the world would most likely not exist.

Sasha lives with her mother and sister. "I don't talk to my dad," she says, "he said something mad f***ed up to me." She was uncomfortable discussing her father, but explained that "I do what I want really; I don't do nothing bad, my sister—she crazy." In referring to her sister as crazy, Sasha is making a point about her sister's social life, full of parties and substance use, not her mental health. Yet Sasha herself is often absent for long periods of time, a behavior that by her own admission is irresponsible. Doing what one wants is often associated with a sense of adulthood by adolescents. A striking moment occurred when Sasha expressed that her father had half-jokingly denied her: "One time, I went to see my dad and he was like, 'maybe I'm not your father'—that was mad f***ed up—but whatever, I don't talk to him, it's not like I need him." Sasha betrays a sense of not needing anyone, she is fiercely independent, and while she socializes with many other teenagers, she does not seem to be a member of a particular clique. Her fierce independence may indicate another of the roles she occupies, that of an independent woman.

In the Puerto Rican community, there are other stories like hers—children raised in single-parent households where ingenuity and resourcefulness take the place of the traditional family dynamic, where both parents and young people must cope with nontraditional situations and the experience of membership in a minority group. As a single parent, her mother works long hours to provide for the family, and Sasha is often home alone. She frequently looks for employment, transiently working at various retailers, fast-food chains, and local businesses. Sasha generally displays strong confidence in most interactions and settings.

When asked about school, Sasha asserts that she intends to graduate and aspires to attend college or join the armed forces. There is what may appear to be an incongruity in her behavior; her days playing hooky and long-term truancy hamper her chances at graduating. Some may see an incompatibility in her sense of identity; in mainstream parlance Latino is not black, and

Americans like Sasha carry hyphenated identities, and yet she less than comfortably slips into these identities at different times and under different circumstances. These struggles are real; on the surface the decision to wear Jordans and large doorknocker hoop earrings on one day and a bourgeois bohemian skirt and boots the next day may seem like just a fashion choice, but to an adolescent, these choices represent more. They embody the definition and redefinition of her fluid identity.

FERNANDO

Fernando is of Dominican and Colombian descent and was born in the United States. Fernando, who lived in a bilingual household and in the United States his entire life, describes himself as mostly Dominican, in spite of geography: "I was born in Brooklyn and I only lived here, nowhere else." He offers his musical choices as validation of that identity: "I'm mostly Dominican, people don't think I am but then they hear me speak Spanish. . . . I listen mostly to *bachata*, *reggaeton*, and hip-hop." *Bachata* is a musical genre of the Dominican Republic; *reggaeton* is a recent Spanish-language genre with roots in various Caribbean musical art forms and hip-hop; and hip-hop is a music form born in black communities in the inner cities of the United States.

He lives at home with his mother, father, and two older sisters. His father is from the Dominican Republic and his mother from Colombia. Fernando's mother is the authority who deals with the children and with the school. Fernando explains that "my mom, she raised me mostly, my dad too, but mostly my mom." Discipline was swift: "If I did something wrong—I would get hit—but not anymore." He is quick to explain that his mother never abused him: "She would hit me for something wrong if I wasn't listening to her, but never a lot, just a little bit." Now that he is older, he explains that "they [his parents] don't hit me or punish me—they really can't—they just make sure I come to school." The information on school is usually transmitted through grades: "If she [his mother] sees I'm failing," he says, "she knows I'm either not going to school or doing bad; she only speaks Spanish and it's tough for her to talk to people." Here we have a young man, who, despite living in an organized two-parent household that holds education in high regard, at one point joined a gang.

In his previous school, Fernando joined a gang of other Dominican American youths. The gang incorporated Dominican American slang and inner-city hip-hop style. These traits indicate a great degree of acculturation into a subculture outside the bounds of mainstream Dominican and U.S. culture. Fernando never expressed a sense of alienation from his family, just the opposite, but the gang membership does denote a contradiction between the culture of his family and that of the gang. It is possible that each provides a different sense of belonging—his family life connects him to traditional Dominican culture and his gang affiliations offer a sense of belonging to a larger group of youths with similar musical, fashion, and social interests. Fernando identifies strongly as Dominican but speaks primarily in English and listens to a great deal of English language music. Additionally, his fashion choices of baggy jeans and Jordans betray an appreciation for hip-hop clothing styles.

He left the gang and transferred schools after a violent incident left him critically injured and hospitalized. At his new school, Fernando expresses determination to graduate. He generally does well on assignments and participates actively in class. Fernando echoed the idea that education was important but might not always be accessible. "I want to get my high school diploma, I'm going to get it, but sometimes school just feels so long—and you ask why you have to learn some things and not others, sometimes it's cool—a lot of the friends I used to have though, they didn't finish school and some of them was smart—but school just doesn't work for some people." His insights here offer a glimpse into his and others' ambivalence surrounding educational goals.

His social life is full of friends, family members, and parties, which he is probably too young for, at nightclubs that play mostly *reggaeton* and *bachata*. Here his musical affiliation forms part of his social identity. His attire, resembling that of a polished hip-hop artist, is not out of place among other members of his musical community. His identities, like theirs, are simultaneously dependent and independent of one another.

LETTY

Letty, born in Puerto Rico, says "I feel that I'm Puerto Rican and American, but I was born in Puerto Rico—I go back all the time." The irony, of course, is that Puerto Rican legal status includes American citizenship, and yet culturally Puerto Rico is very much a separate nation. As a child, her family relocated to Brooklyn, and she has lived most of her life on the mainland, but still feels her identity is tied to the island of Puerto Rico: "I eat mostly Spanish food, my mom plays all the Spanish music, all the old stuff . . . [referring to the salsa music from the 1970s], so that's mostly Puerto Rican to me." Letty consciously identifies as a person between two identities, offering linguistic, geographic, culinary, and musical rationales for her bicultural identity.

At the age of 18 and still living at home in a Puerto Rican neighborhood undergoing gentrification, Letty explains that her mother has ceded authority: "I can take care of myself now . . . she want to know that I am passing my classes," but her role is more as a concerned observer. Letty explains that "my mother and I get along . . . she has given up on trying to wake me up for school. . . . I sleep so much, that's why I'm always late; she used to try to wake me up, but she gave up." Her mother's parenting style was always progressive, as Letty describes, a mother who "never used to punish me like that [corporal], she would tell me, or I wouldn't be allowed to do something when I was a kid." She explains, "If it has to do with my school I can take care of it." Age is a variable factor here, because this dynamic was not always the case: "She used to talk to my teachers when I was doing bad before, but when I came to this school, and since I'm older, she doesn't anymore." This degree of autonomy for a young person with a history of academic struggles related to poor attendance and very active nightlife suggests parental helplessness and possibly depression.

She is clear that her goal is to graduate high school. She continues to struggle academically because of attendance-related issues. In the classroom, she is full of enthusiasm and often aims to impress, but struggles to perform well due to her frequent absences. When pressed about her attendance, she expresses the idea that she lives in the moment, pursues her desires, and enjoys an adult level of autonomy. When the conflict between her goals and lifestyle is pointed out, she becomes uncharacteristically arrogant and dismissive.

Another source of stress in Letty's life is her father's incarceration for drug-related charges. She visits him from time to time and is always somber when mentioning the subject. She comes from a community where incarcerations are a common family experience. Everyone knows or knows of someone who is serving time, often for drug-related offenses. Letty generally expresses the sentiment that she lives in the moment and comes and goes as she pleases. The conflict between her goals of graduating, her active social life, and lackadaisical approach to school attendance—as well as her sense of autonomy—may correspond to her view of and relation to institutions like prisons and schools that limit choice, independence, and life outcomes.

CONCLUSION

These portraits of Latino adolescents suggest that identity development is dynamic, complex, and nonlinear; identities are fluid, asserted, and contested within various contexts and over time. Diverse identity markers are deployed by young people to broadcasts identities; language, clothing, music, and affiliations support different identities in differing contexts as they actively explore where they feel at home or, aspirationally, how they wish to see themselves.

For the educational practitioner, adolescent counselor, or mental health professional working with minority and immigrant teenagers, it soon becomes clear that acculturation is an ever-present tension between native culture(s) and the dominant American society (Lopez & Bursztyn, 2013). In educational settings, the emphasis on multiculturalism and culturally responsive inclusive practice should be encouraged, but in a way that allows students to explore different identities rather than assignment by the institution (Korn & Bursztyn, 2002). The concepts raised in this chapter point to a complex matrix of identity, so basing these discussions and ideas on static understandings of identity limits the discussion, narrows our understanding, and forecloses communication with young people. From a counseling standpoint, with much of the multicultural literature centering on discrete paths to identity formation, the voices of the participants in this study suggest a much broader, flexible, and often unpredictable path. In a truly cosmopolitan setting, distinct ethnic categories may be superseded by hybrid and emerging grouping and referents for identity.

When considering the identities of immigrant children and youths, mental health professionals may reflect on the words of philosopher Kwame Anthony Appiah in his work *The Ethics of Identity*:

> Each of these categories [ethnic, racial, gender groupings] has served as an instrument of subordination, as a constraint upon autonomy, as, indeed, a proxy for misfortune. Some identities, we can show, were *created* as part of a classificatory system for oppression. And in the context of antidiscrimination law, say, these identities are treated as a sort of handicap, to be disregarded or remedied. Yet the reversible-raincoat nature of these terms is demonstrated by the fact that categories designed for subordination can also be used to mobilize and empower people as members of a self-affirmative identity. (2007, p. 111)

These identities, Appiah contends, are essential to the process of "creating a self—shaping one's identity—one determines the parameters of one's life and thus defines one's ambitions" (Appiah, 2007, p. 170). The words of the four participants demonstrate that conventional ethnic grouping of adolescents and general understandings of identity are not ontologically sound. To be truly responsive is to take the journey of discovery and establish a culture where multiple identities are welcome.

Additionally, if social, educational, and mental health outcomes are to change, finding new ways to engage immigrant students is pressing. Engaging students on their terms means developing an understanding of how new cultural identities form, what their psychological implications are, and what their significance is with relation to the dominant culture. Students like Fernando, who form recurring associations with informal organizations like street gangs, find within the structure and cultural norms of the gang a sense of identity that matches and validates their personal sense of self and feel closer than familial ties and school social groupings might. An appropriate mental health approach requires considerable rethinking and theorizing about adolescent identity and identity exploration. Hybrid identities among immigrants and children of immigrants are normative; therefore, psychological stress surrounding self-definitions are inherently part of their personal struggles.

NOTE

1. All the names in this chapter have been changed in order to protect the privacy of students.

REFERENCES

Appiah, K. A. (2007). *The ethics of identity*. Princeton, NJ: Princeton University Press.

Dicker, S. (2006). Dominican Americans in Washington Heights, New York: Language and culture in a transnational community. *International Journal of Bilingual Education and Bilingualism*, 6, 713–729.

Hammer, C. S., Rodriguez, B. L., Lawrence, F. R., & Miccio, A. W. (2007). Puerto Rican mothers' beliefs and home literacy practices. *Language, Speech, and Hearing Services in Schools*, 38(3), 216–224.

Hemphill, F. C., & Vanneman, A. (2011). U.S. Department of Education, National Center for Education Statistics. Achievement gaps: How Hispanic and white students in public schools perform in mathematics and reading on the national assessment of educational progress. Retrieved from http://nces.ed.gov/nationsreportcard/pdf/studies/2011459.pdf.

Jackson, O. (aka Ice Cube). (2006). "Race Card." *Laugh now cry later*. Retrieved from https://prezi.com/dncprd8dqdpb/oshea-jackson-aka-ice-cube/.

Korn, C., & Bursztyn A. M. (Eds.). (2002). *Rethinking multicultural education: Case studies in cultural transition*. New Haven, CT: Bergin and Garvey.

Lopez, E., & Bursztyn, A. M. (2013). Future challenges and opportunities: Toward culturally responsive training in school psychology. *Psychology in the Schools*, 50(3), 212–228.

Pérez Firmat, G. (1995). *Bilingual blues*. Temple, AZ: Bilingual Press.

Suarez-Morales, L., & Lopez, B. (2009). The impact of acculturative stress and daily hassles on pre-adolescent psychological adjustment: Examining anxiety symptoms. *Journal of Primary Prevention*, 30(3), 335–349.

Tajfel, H. (Ed.). (1978). *Differentiation between social groups: Studies in the social psychology of intergroup relations*. London: Academic Press.

4

The Heart Will Know: Loss and Reunification

Anna Malyukova and Carol Korn-Bursztyn

Immigration is a complex process that entails opportunity and hope, but it also entails loss and longing. It has profound effects on the family—including both the family members who migrate and those who are left behind. The discourse on immigration is often at the macro level, dominated by discussion of borders, education, work, and economy. At the micro level, we need to consider what immigration does to a family on an individual level. We need to consider the consequences of the process of immigration, which often involves separation, loss, and reunification for children and their families.

When we talk about immigrant families, we often assume that families migrate as a unit, with parents creating a buffer between the strangeness of the new country and their children. The reality of immigration, however, is often quite different. A parent or parents may migrate ahead of the children; children are subsequently reared by family or community members. When parents migrate first, seeking to gain an economic foothold in the new country before bringing their children, the role of primary caregiver often shifts to the grandparents. The role of the new primary caregiver is underrecognized as critical to the well-being of the children left behind, essential to the ability of the parent to initiate the immigration process and to facilitate reunification between parent and child.

The child who embarks on the process of immigration may experience multiple losses: first separation from the parent(s) who leaves first, then from the substitute primary caregivers—often the grandparent(s). Reunification presents particular challenges. Like immigration, reunification is a process rather than a discrete event that concludes with physical reunification.

The psychological tasks of reunification are many. This chapter will explore the relational tasks of reunification, include reawakening old attachments, building new relationships, and mourning the loss of primary attachment figures (Suárez-Orozco, Bang, & Kim, 2011; Suárez-Orozco, Suárez-Orozco, & Todorova, 2008). We will also consider the impact of the processes of immigration and reunification on the family left behind.

The narrative that follows illustrates the complex processes of separation and reunification and the critical roles of the family members. Special attention is provided to the role of the grandparents who stepped in as primary caregivers.

CASE VIGNETTE: MATTHEW

The Heart Will Know

"What if I don't recognize my mom?" said five-year-old Matthew[1] to his grandma in a quiet voice that gave away his worry. He was sitting on her lap on the way to the airport to meet his mother and her new husband, who were coming to Russia from the United States to bring him to their new home. Grandma was worried too. It had been three and a half years since she last saw her daughter and her daughter had last seen her son. The inevitable reunion was finally here, the waiting was over, and a new chapter would soon begin. Matthew voiced the worries of the whole family: What will it be like to be reunited?

"Of course you are going to recognize her," reassured Grandma. Her confident voice surprised her. "Do you remember the story I told you? Your life began inside your mommy's stomach, and you could hear mommy's heartbeat when you were in her belly. And she could feel your every move," Grandma murmured, petting his head as if telling him a bedtime story for the hundredth time. "When Mommy sees you and hugs you, your hearts will recognize each other, even if your eyes will not at first. And after that you will feel like you were never apart," continued Grandma softly, her voice catching. She could already anticipate how the old ties would be renewed, while she would be left with memories of the time when the boy with the curly hair looked up at her as if she were his mother.

"I am still going to sleep with you, Grandma. And you can hold my hand tonight, okay?" said Matthew decisively. "Of course. But if you want to sleep with Mommy that will be fine too," replied Grandma not quite knowing what she would prefer herself: for Matthew to be content with his mother or for him to hold her own hand. Without little Matthew, her bed would feel strangely empty. She looked up at Grandpa who nodded in her direction, and turned to the window, keeping his own emotions in check. In a few hours, they would be at the airport waiting for their daughter Anna and her husband, Rashid.

Arrivals Hall

Finally, customs were cleared, luggage collected, and Anna and Rashid walked around the corner to the arrivals area. Grandma and little Matthew were standing up front; Grandma saw them first and nudged Matthew to run toward his mother. Anna ran toward him, hugging and swooping him up before she greeted her own mother, who hugged them both. Voices filled the room with laughter and tears. Grandpa, in tears, hugged his daughter and kissed her on the cheek. Anna's brother, Victor, was there with his son, and he too hugged her tight. Still in Anna's arms, Matthew held tight and trembled in her embrace. Anna's cousin, who had seen her off three and half years earlier, was there, too. Grandma's sister came too, holding a bouquet of spring flowers—surprising for February. The family took turns hugging Rashid, who was meeting his wife's family for the first time. Pictures were taken and jokes exchanged. Matthew still clung to his mother's neck; Anna was determined to never let go of him again.

The Visit

The house buzzed with conversation, laughter, and energy. Matthew and his cousins played with the presents his mother and new father brought. From time to time, older family members stooped to hug and kiss him. Anna was never too far away; at dinner he sat on her lap, even though he was a big boy.

When night came, Matthew's earlier worries evaporated and he headed off to sleep with his mother and his new father. He held his mother's hand all night long. Grandma and Grandpa, overcome by feelings of happiness for their grandson and daughter, forgot for an evening their own foreboding about the inevitable parting.

The next two weeks were a blur of activity: visits with family members and friends and trips to the American embassy to prepare Matthew's travel documents. There was little room for quiet moments of reflection and little inclination to face the impending losses that the next phase of the immigration process would entail. Anna's family was getting to know Rashid, and he was getting to know them—and their expectations for him.

Anna was learning everything about her son firsthand. Her parents kept her up to date about her son while she was gone; at first with letters and videotapes, and later with phone calls. Anna called them as much as she could, even though Matthew had a hard time connecting with her by phone—he seemed not to remember who she was and would not talk for more than a few minutes.

Matthew's documents were finally ready and it was time to say goodbye. The two weeks at home had flown by, but not before Grandpa showed Rashid photos from his childhood and army days, weddings, and grandchildren. He played chess with Matthew and Rashid, helping them to establish an initial connection with each other. Grandma cooked and talked with her daughter about Matthew, instructing both Anna and Rashid to be patient and loving with their son and cautioning them to keep what she referred to as their "strict rules" at bay until he was ready. Rashid got to know and love Anna's family and felt the weight of responsibility of fatherhood. Anna happily looked ahead, dreaming about her new life in the United States, with Matthew finally being a part of it.

Departure

At the airport, Matthew held tight to Grandma's hand. Grandpa periodically stepped out to smoke. The mood was quiet and somber. Everyone who was there to greet Anna and Rashid two weeks ago was there again to see them off. Grandpa's brother joined them in the airport as well, as if knowing that his brother needed extra support. Little was said; tears were on the verge of falling. When it was finally time to leave, Anna held Matthew in her arms; he looked back at his grandparents, fear written across his face. Once they were out of sight, Grandpa wiped his tears and said, "Let's go," to his wife, who was not holding back any more and was weeping uncontrollably.

DISCUSSION OF CASE VIGNETTE

In this vignette, we see how stressful and complex the migration process is for each individual family member and for the family as a whole. The main focus of attention here is the child, Matthew. Separated from his mother since age two; now, three and a half years later, reunited with her and her new husband, and leaving for a new land, leaving behind all that is familiar and loved. Matthew's worry that he would not recognize his mother reflects his feeling that she is now a stranger to him. His grandmother clearly served as a surrogate mother, helping him to overcome the confusion and fear his mother's leave-taking undoubtedly provoked. The attachment relationship that he had with his grandmother prior to his mother's departure smoothed the path to the grandmother's assuming a primary attachment role.

The story that the grandmother told Matthew about his relationship with his mother "Your hearts will recognize each another . . . and after that you will feel like you were never apart" was repeated many times over the years. It demonstrated the grandmother's support of her daughter, while providing a comforting metaphor for Matthew's relationship with his mother. It also acknowledges the protective power of multiple attachments in children's lives—Matthew could experience both his grandmother and his mother as secure attachment figures. The grandmother's support of her daughter reveals the depth of the attachment relationship between herself and her daughter, extended now to encompass the child. Although Matthew recalled little of his mother in her absence, he had the benefit of a warm and loving relationship with her for the first two years of his life.

A word about the grandfather's role is in order, too. The grandfather was clearly deeply attached to Matthew; this was evidenced in a manner different from that of the grandmother, but one more likely culturally consistent with traditional gendered role relationships. The grandfather played a protective role in meeting his new son-in-law, communicating to him the seriousness with which he expected him to assume his responsibilities as father to Matthew and spending time with him talking and reviewing family photos. In a manner parallel to his wife's suggesting that Matthew might want to spend the night with his mother, the grandfather orchestrated chess games between Matthew and his new father, with the aim of facilitating their developing relationship. The grandfather seems to have in a very deliberate way, tried to transfer his paternal role vis-à-vis his grandson to his new son-in-law.

Little is known about Matthew's emotional understanding of his mother's leaving when he was two. What seems clear is that the multiple attachment relationships that he had with his mother and with his maternal grandparents buffered him through what was likely a traumatic separation. They formed "a cooperative triangle of caregivers" that clearly benefited both Matthew and his mother (Suarez-Orozco et al., 2008, p. 68). We also know little about the emotional toll of separation on the mother and the related difficulty of securing documentation for herself and for her son.

The role of the maternal grandparents in providing a holding environment (Winnicott, 1964, 1971b) for the mother, and for her child who remained with the grandparents, is significant. The safe, secure, and loving environment that the grandparents created and maintained throughout the years of separation likely provided an optimal emotional environment for the stressors of reunification that lay ahead for the young family. Their continued presence in the family's life in the United States through exchange of gifts, frequent phone and, later, Skype contact helped the grandparents to maintain their traditional role of providing a holding environment for their adult children, providing a touchstone of emotional connection and security during a time of great transition and development of the new family.

GIFTS

In the narrative above we see a reference to gift giving. Sending gifts was a way for Matthew's mother to maintain contact—and to introduce her husband to him. Gift giving is significant to maintenance of the emotional relationship between absent parents and their children (especially young children) and functions in a manner consistent with what Donald Winnicott (1971) referred to as a transitional object. The transitional object is imbued with emotional meaning and functions symbolically as a representation of the loved person.

Typically, transitional objects are soft items children themselves choose that help them tolerate developmentally expectable separations from parents, such as occur during sleep or naptime or upon brief separations such as entry into child care. The transitional object represents the physical presence of the parent when the parent is not there to protect and buffer the child from harm. The child, who has little control over the events leading to separation—as in bedtime—can now exert control over the transitional object. The transitional object is suffused with ambivalent feelings—the target of adoration and cuddling; it can also at times be misused, neglected, and damaged.

Migration of a parent, however, while not uncommon, represents a traumatic separation rather than a developmentally expected separation as typically occurs when children learn to sleep in their own beds or when they begin child care or school. For children who have been traumatically separated from their parents, a gift's physicality is comforting; one can hold the gift when one can no longer hold the absent parent. Its presence reminds the child of the love and attention the parent has bestowed on the child from afar. Gift giving provides a salve for children, especially young children, who have been separated from their parents (Suárez-Orozco et al., 2011). Consistent with the psychological function of transitional objects, older children often reject the substitution of an object as representation for the missing person, as it is the relationship they crave, rather than the simple comforts of physical presence.

GRANDPARENTS

Matthew's grandparents put on a brave face for the sake of their grandchild, hiding their own grief and fear. While Matthew's parents were happily anticipating their new lives together, Matthew's grandparents were facing another separation and loss at a time in their lives when they were increasingly vulnerable as a function of advancing age. Children lose their closest attachment figure twice: once when their parent leaves, and again when they must leave their beloved caretakers in order to rejoin the parent (Suárez-Orozco et al., 2011). Matthew, who already had a secure attachment to his maternal grandparents when his mother left, deepened his attachment to his grandparents in her absence. While Matthew's mother and grandparents reminded him—and themselves—that he would eventually be reunited with his mother, their everyday lives continued and their relationships became increasingly close.

For the grandparents, family reunification meant sundering their own family's lives once again, resulting in feelings of grief and loss. Both parents and grandparents were cognizant of how difficult it would be for Matthew to lose his connection to the people he experienced as his parents for most of his life. Historically, grandparents have provided additional support for the family in times of need. Parental migration is a pronounced time of need; grandparents' role in providing care for children who are left behind and for the parent(s) who have migrated is underexplored.

Attachment theory ascribes an important role of caregivers in the establishment of an internal working model of relationships (Bowlby, 1989). "Children who are exposed to sensitive and responsive caregiving are more likely to develop a set of beliefs about relationships that are highly adaptive and flexible and that promote optimal developmental outcomes" (Lussier, Deater-Deckard, Dunn, & Davies, 2002, p. 364). The role of grandparents as surrogate parents to grandchildren whose parents have emigrated is complex. It is clearly critical in the process of maintaining children's emotional and physical well-being. An additional factor here is the financial responsibility that grandparents often assume for the grandchildren in their care.

The narrative in this chapter hints at the complexity of the migration process and the critical role of the grandparents in their daughter and, later, their grandchild's migration story. The holding environment that they created played a role in helping their daughter's family to establish themselves in the new country. They supported their grandchild, while separated from their own daughter, and served as primary caregivers for three and a half years. Critically, they maintained their daughter's presence in Matthew's life as his "real" mother, who would soon return to reclaim him. At the same time, they knew their role was temporary and that a successful outcome to their daughter's migration process would mean reexperiencing the loss of their daughter, but this time also losing their grandchild.

POSTSCRIPT

Despite the complexity of the migration process for the family described in this narrative, all of the family members described have weathered the process with great resilience. A teenager now, Matthew still considers his grandparents to be his main caregivers and travels to Russia as often as possible to see them. His emigration to the United States was emotionally difficult for his grandparents, who experienced deep grief. With the passage of time, they have recast their experience of raising their grandchild as a rare opportunity to feel young again and to experience parenthood one more time. Anna has taken a lot of time reflecting on her family's migration process. And I know all of this because this is my story.

NOTE

1. All the names in this chapter have been changed in order to protect the privacy of students.

REFERENCES

Bowlby, J. (1989). *Secure and insecure attachment.* New York: Basic Books.

Lussier, G., Deater-Deckard, K., Dunn, J., & Davies, L. (2002). Support across two generations: Children's closeness to grandparents following parental divorce and remarriage. *Journal of Family Psychology, 16*(3), 363–376.

Suárez-Orozco, C., Bang, H. J., & Kim, H.Y. (2011). I felt like my heart was staying behind: Psychological implications of family separations & reunifications for immigrant youth. *Journal of Adolescent Research, 26,* 222–257.

Suárez-Orozco, C., Suárez-Orozco, M. M., & Todorova, I. (2008). *Learning a new land: Immigrant students in American society.* Cambridge, MA: Harvard University Press.

Winnicott, D. W. (1971a). *Playing and reality.* London: Routledge.

Winnicott, D. W. (1971b). *Therapeutic consultation in child psychiatry.* London: Hogarth Press.

Winnicott, D. W. (1964/1992). *The child, the family, and the outside world.* London: Perseus.

5

Where Is Home? A Narrative of Loss and Resilience

Johnny Thach and Carol Korn-Bursztyn

How does migration impact the lives of immigrant children and youths separated from their parents in the course of the migration process? Through personal narratives and interdisciplinary perspectives from academic research and studies, the aim of this chapter is to help us understand migration in childhood and adolescence as an emotionally transformative experience accompanied by significant trauma and distress.

This chapter examines salient elements of migration in childhood and adolescence. These include the meaning of home, the experience of psychological distress during the migration process, and relationship to home postmigration. It concludes with the intersection of documentation status and psychological well-being among immigrant youths. A case vignette, of Loretta, a retrospective account of a young woman's migration from the Philippines to the United States as an unaccompanied child, runs throughout the chapter, providing an instance of particular lived experience that illustrates some of the characteristics associated with migration journeys of unaccompanied immigrant children. Loretta's[1] story, it should be noted, is a story of separation from family, but it is also a story of an unaccompanied child who is delivered safely into the home of caring family members.

THE MEANING OF HOME

> Home is where you are safe.
> Home is where you are understood.
>
> (Lee, 2002, p. 4)

As an educator at the Museum of Chinese in America in New York City, one of the central questions the first author raises is "Where is home for you?"

This question asks visitors to engage in a moment of reflection about their place in the world. In *Where Is Home? Chinese in the Americas*, author Cynthia Lee (2002) describes home as an intimate space that contains feelings of familiarity, comfort, and, importantly, of being understood. The meaning of home invariably changes with migration, particularly for children who bear the emotional brunt of the migration process. Often, this includes separation from one or both parents. While some children are left behind in the native country and their parent or parents migrate first, seeking a foothold abroad, children are increasingly those who embark on the migration process first, preceding their parents. The first-person case study of Loretta that follows describes the migration process of a young, undocumented immigrant from the Philippines, marked by a profound sense of loss of home.

CASE VIGNETTE: LORETTA

> It's been over a decade since I last saw my parents. I was 11 years old when I came to the United States from the Philippines. My parents wanted a better life for me—they believed that there were more opportunities in the United States—you know, the American dream. They arranged for me to live with my aunt in Arizona. I remember boarding the plane and thinking of it as a short trip. I never knew that I would never see my parents again. I never even said "goodbye."

An undocumented immigrant, Loretta has been unable to travel to the Philippines to see her parents. In the first couple of years postmigration, she believed that she would not be separated from her parents for a long period of time.

> But, when I found out the truth—that I was undocumented, I started to concentrate on my life here. I miss the Philippines, but it is too different to go back. I have a life here: a boyfriend, family, and friends. I cannot imagine myself living in the Philippines. I cannot even go back to visit since without a passport, there is no guarantee that I would be able to come back [to the United States].

The months and even years of postmigration may be particularly difficult for children and youths. Poulsen, Karuppaswamy, and Natrajan (2005, p. 413) conducted a study that found that the immigrants they questioned shared ambivalence about creating a new physical and psychological home in their new country and questioned whether they could ever return to the culture they left behind, concluding that the process of immigration was a lifelong process.

Home is a dynamic construct—at once physical and material, it also registers psychologically for its connections to the family of origin and to the original site of one's personal origins. People find and create new homes with new people throughout their lives. And yet, when people are asked to consider the meaning of home, their reflections often turn to their childhood homes and to the primary figures who created the experience of home. It may well be that all the spaces of home that we create in adulthood oscillate between re-creating the lost home of childhood and the creative impulse toward new iterations. Nowhere is this process more profound than when we consider the unique situations—material and psychological—of immigrants who arrived in childhood or adolescence.

PSYCHOLOGICAL DISTRESS AND TRAUMA

Childhood immigration is often accompanied by intense feelings of distress and reactions to trauma. One of five children who are of school age in the United States is an immigrant or a child of an immigrant (Urban Institute, 2006). Family separation during migration has a negative impact on the children's academic functioning. Children who were separated from their parents during or after migration are more likely to fall behind in school and to drop out of high school. Youths who were separated from their mothers had poorer outcomes than youths who lived with their undocumented parents or who were separated at an early age but reunited with their parents as teenagers (Gindling & Poggio, 2010).

The migration process may be sudden or protracted; in most cases it involves enormous psychological stress and the potential for trauma. Four migration stages that have the most significant potential for traumatogenic experiences that may lead to serious psychological repercussions: (1) premigration trauma; (2) traumatic events experienced during transit to the new country; (3) continuing traumatogenic experiences during the process of asylum-seeking and resettlement; and (4) substandard living conditions in the host country due to unemployment, inadequate supports, and minority persecution (Foster, 2001). Grinberg and Grinberg (1989) argue that the migration process continues to a lengthy period of time, potentially inducing psychological collapse and psychic wounds. The childhood experience of migration trauma is characterized by helplessness, especially with regard to children who are mostly excluded from the decision-making process that results in their migration.

Immigrant children and youths who are separated from one or both parents are even more likely to develop symptoms of anxiety and depression in the initial years of postmigration (Suárez-Orozco, Bang, & Kim, 2011). Furthermore, feelings of depression, confusion, loneliness, anxiety, and bewilderment affect a child's psychological and social processes when adapting to a new environment in the country of immigration. Separation from family, a regular feature of migration in its various iterations, profoundly impacts immigrant children and their parents (Jensen, 2007; Lacroix & Sabbah, 2011; Smith, LaLonde, & Johnson, 2004).

Bar-Yosef (2001) also argues that immigrant children and youths often do not understand the reason for migration as a consequence of their inability to use adult reasoning. Perhaps motivated by a desire to avoid painful topics—and perhaps their own ambivalence about the migration decision—parents and other family member often avoid talk about the migration process, offering the children little consolation. Loretta describes her attempts to console herself in the postmigration period.

> Growing up in Arizona was different. The weather was dry and I missed not being near water. It was definitely a change. I did not do so well in school. Sometimes it was very difficult to understand when people spoke. People also saw that I was different; I guess it was the cultural cues that made me stand out. It was also a challenge to catch up on other subjects. I never asked for help. It was important for me to be strong and not let others know that I was struggling. I was definitely the quiet and shy person in the class.
>
> My grades were higher in high school and I started to make a lot of friends and fit in. I also started running and joined the track team. It felt like freedom and made me feel happy.

Loretta omits the painful period of middle school, but returns to this later.

> In middle school all of the emotions boiled up all inside and I struggled with depression. I was lonely. I was confused and did not understand why my parents had abandoned me. I did not choose this life; I cried for days. But no one knew. I never showed these emotions to others. I actually used writing as a coping strategy back then. I just started writing one day. I wrote letters to my mother, complaining over and over. This made me realize my parents' sacrifices. I was not ready to give up.

Loretta recounts how her schoolwork deteriorated. Unable to sleep at night, she dozes off in class, is inattentive, and skips class, resulting in after-school detention. The school's approach is largely punitive. No one seems to recognize her distress or to question her downward academic trajectory. She begins to write, expressing and working through conflicted feelings about her parents' decision to send her away and about her own life choices. Loretta's narrative is tightly constructed; she is proud of her ability to wrestle with feelings of abandonment and rejection and especially proud that she did so without help.

Loretta's experience raises a concern of mental health providers that, on their own, adolescents will often shield their troubles from helpful adults. The push for autonomy is typically experienced by teens as the need to solve problems independently. Loretta's restricted social ties meant that she could not turn to friends. For adolescents, seeking help from peers does not seem to threaten their autonomy, perhaps as a result of the reciprocal nature of self-disclosure and help among young peers. She confronts and confides in her mother, writing letters she does not mail. The writing itself seemed to have recalled the mother's soothing presence for Loretta, who was comforted by this imaginary connection.

Loretta's capacity to draw on a psychologically internalized or introjected representation of mother has a calming effect, which enables her to draw on her emotional reserves to cope with the pain of separation and the challenges of being a new arrival. Another way to consider the soothing effects of addressing her mother in writing is that calling up her image also called up representations of the attachment relationship between the two. Through a child's eye, Loretta recalls the idyllic life in the Philippines from which she was abruptly sent forth.

An alternative version of her migration story—one that was not available to her as a child—becomes available as she matures and begins to decenter, rendering her better able to take the perspectives of others (Piaget, 1929/2007). This alternative version, existing in an almost alternative psychological universe, is suddenly available to her one night as she calls up the deep attachment to her mother from the perspectives of a maturing youth. This new way of thinking, a qualitatively different cognitive style, which Piaget termed "formal operations," affords her the ability to reflect on abstractions, including the complicated motivations of her parents (Piaget, 1937/1954, 1936/1963).

In the alternative universe that is now available to her, Loretta is deeply loved by her parents and family in the Philippines. Her parents struggle with their desire for their daughter to have a better life and decide that she will join her trustworthy, loving aunt in the United States. Pained at the impending separation from their daughter, her parents avoid talking about the journey, reluctant to have her read sorrow in their faces. Their matter-of-fact air disarms their young daughter, and maybe themselves too, and leaves hope for a swift family reunification.

The following sections will return to Loretta's story from time to time to illustrate various psychological phenomena associated with the experience of separation and migration in childhood and adolescence.

TIES TO HOME POSTMIGRATION

Loretta grew increasingly distant from her parents and seldom spoke to them. Smith et al. (2004) suggest that migration, accompanied by separation from one or both parents, may significantly impact the parent–child relationship; longer separations make reunion less likely. Reunification of an entire family can take many years, especially when complicated by legal and economic burdens (Suárez-Orozco, Suárez-Orozco, & Todorova, 2008).

> As time went on, the letters stopped, and we started to grow more distant and apart. I guess there are also mixed feelings. It has been many years, and I have grown up. Sometimes I'm not too sure if my parents would be able to recognize me, if I would be able to recognize them. Sometimes we talk on the phone, but our conversations are short. How could they understand how I feel? They feel like strangers. I try not to think about it.

Reflecting on her postmigration experience, Loretta recalled her envy of peers who lived with their parents. "The sad part is, I was jealous of the other kids. They had parents and I didn't. I missed the love and affection that only comes from parents."

Loretta observes that caring teachers became parental figures for her. The close, loving ties with parents that she recalled from home undoubtedly formed the basis of her ability to emotionally connect with helpful adults in her new environment. Children who grow up being loved are typically better able to connect with other helpful adults, such as teachers. We might even speculate that any feelings of anger toward the parents who sent her away betray a deep attachment to her parents and perhaps a longing for the happy, secure home of childhood so abruptly lost.

Loretta's observation about the role of caring teachers underlines the important role they can play in safeguarding the emotional well-being of unaccompanied immigrant youths. She recalls her early postmigration school experience in the United States:

> I was lucky to have a teacher in fifth grade that made me feel special. I stayed with her during lunch breaks and helped her organize the classroom. I didn't fit in with the other children at lunch—she understood this. Some of my teachers became parental figures to

me. They listened and helped me through a lot of my problems. I don't know where I would be without their support.

Undocumented immigrants face exceptional challenges. They have higher levels of acculturative and other stressors related to their legal status in the country and chronically fear deportation (Jensen, 2007). Additionally, fewer job options and academic opportunities are available. Negative portrayals by the media are an additional source of strain. As a result, undocumented immigrants are often socially isolated. Like Loretta, undocumented children and youths often do not learn about their status until they are teenagers.

Loretta first learned she was undocumented in late adolescence, when she was unable to obtain a driver's license. She was shocked and dismayed to learn what this meant for her future plans. For this first time since her arrival in the United States she felt even more isolated and different—now she had a secret. She began to suffer from recurring nightmares in which immigration officers would suddenly show up at her home and take her away. Meanwhile, her friends went on to college, while Loretta reluctantly readjusted her goals.

Undocumented immigrant children and youths are at a distinct disadvantage as compared with their documented peers. Undocumented children and youths tend not have medical coverage, have poor living conditions, and if they are united with their parents, regularly face the threat of losing them to deportation. Many undocumented high school students are shocked to discover that they cannot secure a driver's license, social security card, or apply for financial aid to four-year colleges or universities. Suárez-Orozco and Suárez-Orozco (2001) found that these youths feel a terrible sense of injustice when they discover the limitations imposed by their documentation status and typically experience feelings of anger, hopelessness, and depression.

After high school, because of her undocumented immigrant status, Loretta could not afford to go to college without financial aid, and her grades were not high enough to qualify for scholarships. She struggled with finding purpose in going to college and was uncertain what her future possibilities would be as a result of her undocumented status. After a few semesters, she left school. She lived in fear that she would be deported and that her parents would find out she was no longer attending college. She began a small business that brought in income for the family, which she believed demonstrated she could be self-reliant and help support the family.

Last year, Loretta applied for Deferred Action for Childhood Arrivals (DACA) with the help of a pro bono lawyer. Although DACA does not provide amnesty or a pathway to citizenship, undocumented immigrants are allowed to request consideration for deferred action for a period of two years or more to stay in the United States and work. Loretta began to work in the hospitality industry and now speaks about making positive strides toward her professional dreams.

CONCLUSION: FINDING HOME AGAIN

Loretta's experience of separation from family and migration is a story of losing home and finding the capacity to create a new home. It is framed by the poverty of the Philippines and parents who hope to provide their child with opportunities they can ill afford in their home country. Like all children who are sent forth by parents with hopes for a more secure future, Loretta feels alone and lost, maybe abandoned and rejected. At 11 years old, she was on the cusp of being able to understand cognitively the complex reasons for her parents' decision; emotionally she cannot yet comprehend the difficult choices her parents faced. Despite the traumas of separation and migration, Loretta presents as a well-related youth, easily responding to friendly overtures by teachers, and over time, making friends and developing a healthy social life.

Loretta's narrative is a story of resilience. When we last encountered her, she was a young adult, hopeful and excited about her future. Family is on her mind; it is important to Loretta that she demonstrates to her parents—and to herself—that she is growing into a responsible adult, self-directed and concerned about supporting her family. Loretta has a seriousness of purpose borne of confronting great, potentially overwhelming challenges.

Although these are her own personal achievements, the role of others in buffering her through the difficult migration process—her American family, helpful teachers, counselors, and friends—may be considered as playing strong supporting roles in Loretta's performance. It is worth noting that the strong feelings of connection with her family of origin that resulted in her despair in the immediate postmigration period suggest deep bonds of love. Loretta's is a hopeful narrative. Home is important to her, and it is likely that she will go on to establish a home that captures the warmth and love of her childhood home. It is even possible that adulthood will bring the growing emotional capacity to understand her parents' dilemmas and decisions.

NOTE

1. All the names in this chapter have been changed in order to protect the privacy of individuals. Moreover, other identifying information in the case studies presented has been substantially altered in order to further protect confidentiality of individuals and institutions.

REFERENCES

Bar-Yosef, R. W. (2001). Children of two cultures: Immigrant children from Ethiopia in Israel. *Journal of Comparative Family Studies, 32*(2), 231–246.

Foster, R. P. (2001). When immigration is trauma: Guidelines for the individual and family clinician. *American Journal of Orthopsychiatry, 71*(2), 153–170.

Gindling, T. H., & Poggio, S. Z. (2010). The effect of family separation and reunification on the educational success of immigrant children in the United States. The Institute for the Study of Labor (IZA). Retrieved from http://ftp.iza.org/dp4887.pdf.

Grinberg, L., & Grinberg, R. (1989). *Psychoanalytic perspectives on migration and exile.* New Haven, CT: Yale University Press.

Jensen, B. (2007). Understanding immigration and psychological development. *Journal of Immigrant & Refugee Studies, 5*(4), 27–48.

Lacroix, M., & Sabbah, C. (2011). Posttraumatic psychological distress and resettlement: The need for a different practice in assisting refugee families. *Journal of Family Social Work, 14*(1), 43–53.

Lee, C. (2002). *Where is home? Chinese in the Americas.* New York, NY: Museum of Chinese in America.

Piaget, J. (1929/2007). *The child's conception of the world.* Lanham, MD: Rowman & Littlefield.

Piaget, J. (1936/1963). *The origins of intelligence in children.* New York: Norton.

Piaget, J. (1937/1954). *The construction of reality in the child.* New York: Basic Books.

Poulsen, S., Karuppaswamy, N., & Natrajan, R. (2005). Immigration as a dynamic experience: Personal narratives and clinical implications for family therapists. *Contemporary Family Therapy, 27*(3), 403–414.

Smith, A., LaLonde, R., & Johnson, S. (2004). Serial migration and its implications for the parent-child relationship: A retrospective analysis of the experiences of the children of Caribbean immigrants. *Cultural Diversity and Ethnic Minority Psychology, 10*(2), 107–122.

Suárez-Orozco, C., & Suárez-Orozco, M. (2001). *Children of immigration.* Cambridge: Harvard University Press.

Suárez-Orozco, C., Bang, H., & Kim, H. (2011). I felt like my heart was staying behind: Psychological implications of family separations & reunifications for immigrant youth. *Journal of Adolescent Research, 26,* 222–232.

Suárez-Orozco, C., Suárez-Orozco, M., & Todorova, I. (2008). *Learning a new land: Immigrant students in American society.* Cambridge: Belknap Press of Harvard University Press.

Urban Institute. (2006). Children of immigrants: Facts and figures. Retrieved from http://www.urban.org/UploadedPDF/900955_children_of_immigrants.pdf.

6

Sadness All About and I'm Wearing Pink Pants: Separation and Reunification

Myrtle Dickson and Carol Korn-Bursztyn

Immigration in adolescence provokes trauma of dislocation and loss, but also offers possibilities of expanding boundaries of personal identity. Adolescence is a time of psychological change; migration can provide access to new social landscapes and to new understandings of how one's life might be lived. This chapter presents two adolescent migration vignettes; one marked by poverty, the other by privilege. The youths in both vignettes experience abrupt loss of mothers, whose migration preceded theirs, and strained ties upon reunion. Both become quiet and withdrawn, and both do well in school. The role of school in the educational trajectories of both are explored for the critical emotional support and academic scaffolding schools can provide.

CASE VIGNETTE: ANTON, OR SADNESS ALL ABOUT

A decade or so ago, he appeared at the door of my crowded junior high school English classroom one morning. (The vignettes presented are told from the perspective of the first author.) My first impression was that he was misplaced and that he should be in one of the elementary schools; but he was accompanied by the seventh-grade guidance counselor. Alas, he must be in the right place! His name was Anton;[1] slight, with a shock of jet black hair. Huge eyes looked up at me unsmiling. Instead, he seemed frightened and sad. As was our custom, the class welcomed this new student, and the student monitor for that week provided Anton with a copy of Jack London's 1903 book, *Call of the Wild*— in retrospect an odd choice for a new arrival from the Caribbean. Despite efforts over the coming weeks to engage Anton in class activities, he remained quiet and aloof, his large eyes sad.

Anton was from the English-speaking island nation of Jamaica, but his speech was mostly unintelligible to me. Hailing from the Caribbean myself and priding myself in having developed a keen ear for accents and speech patterns, I found Anton almost impossible to understand. He possessed only rudimentary penmanship skills and knew next to nothing about writing. In hindsight, the guidance counselor who assigned Anton to my class, and to a specific group of seventh-grade teacher colleagues, must have done so deliberately. Soon, we teachers were discussing him regularly. We concurred that Anton was intelligent but lacked academic preparation. His math teacher observed that he could quickly grasp new concepts, but his reading and writing skills were woefully inadequate. We asked the usual types of questions that teachers ask in these circumstances: What do we do with this child? How can he ever catch up? Does he require special education placement? How do we teach him along with the rest of our students? What resources are needed or even available?

Our team of women teachers decided that we would meet Anton where he was academically and move him forward from there. We included his mother, who worked nearby, in formal and informal conversations. Ms. Smith was a quiet, soft-spoken woman who spoke Jamaican Creole. Since I was the closest ethnically and culturally to Anton's mother, having emigrated from the Caribbean myself, I was designated to accompany the social worker to meet with her. Ms. Smith was remarkably forthcoming and trusting. She told us that Anton was sometimes sad, would stay alone for long periods, and would respond to her with one-word answers.

On those rare occasions when he would open up to her, he would tell her that he missed his grandmother and was worried about her and how she was getting along without him. "Sadness was all about" her home, she said. However, Ms. Smith also reported that Anton liked his school and teachers and wanted to achieve. She confessed that she felt awkward talking to us, did not know what to say or ask, and did not know how to help her son academically. Nevertheless, she attended school events whenever she could and appeared genuinely grateful for our efforts.

Soon Anton began to become more comfortable with us; blank stares were replaced by smiles, and he became a very amenable student. We created an afterschool homework center that he faithfully attended. Over time, he continued to make progress and became more outgoing and talkative. He made progress in math, but language-related subjects continued to be challenging. We learned that Anton's mother left Jamaica for New York when he was five, leaving him in the care of her mother in rural Jamaica. His elderly grandmother needed him to be her eyes and ears and to assist with household chores. Anton's attendance at school was erratic at best. He would later tell us that many days were spent playing with goats in the mountains.

Although Anton was an immigrant from an English-speaking country, he spoke Creole and had minimal command of standard English. As an immigrant from an English-speaking country, Anton did not qualify for programs for English language learners (ELLs); we informally arranged for daily English as a second language and reading support. He progressed to eighth grade, and by the end of ninth grade, we hoped that he was ready to leave us and to successfully continue his academic career. We hoped that he had learned in middle school that we cared, and that he was worth the effort. Although we feared that he might not find the same care and support as he moved into tenth grade and beyond, we felt that he had achieved a degree of industry, perseverance, and resilience that could propel him forward. Today, Anton is a successful businessman; he continues to be in touch, from time to time, with his middle school teachers.

CONTEXT: IMMIGRANT YOUTHS FROM THE ENGLISH-SPEAKING CARIBBEAN

A major challenge that schools face is addressing the needs of immigrant students and preparing them for higher education. Over the past decade, the population of ELL students in the State of New York has increased by 20%, according to statistics from the State Education Department (SED). More than 230,000 ELLs make up 8.9% of the total public student population. In the face of the recent and continuing influx of children and families crossing this nation's borders, it is expected that these figures will spiral upward. These students speak 200 languages, with nearly 45% of ELL's born outside of the United States.

The SED reports that the high school graduation rate of ELLs is 31.4%, compared with an overall rate of 74.9% for all students statewide. In an effort to address the needs of immigrant students, the board of regents recently publicized their beefed-up requirements for school districts in which they require school districts to implement actions that better serve this population of students and parents and better protect the retention of specific instructional staff in the event of the need to trim back teaching positions (NYSSBA, 2014).

Anton's story illuminates several key obstacles to college and career readiness for immigrant youths. There is a tendency to view immigrant students as only those students who speak languages other than English. As a result, those students who emigrate from English-speaking countries are often overlooked. Despite the fact that Anton spoke Jamaican Creole—a language with its own syntax, grammar, and lexicon—and was wholly unfamiliar with standard English, he was ineligible for designation as a second-language learner, as the official language of his home country is English. As a result, Anton had limited access to mandated interventions and supports available to immigrant students who speak languages other than English.

Acquiring the language of the host country presents monumental challenges to all immigrants. For immigrant youths arriving with inadequate academic preparation, including academic language skills, linguistic challenges can often seem insurmountable to both children and their teachers. The emotional upheavals that immigrant youths carry within them are less obvious and frequently overlooked by school personnel, even by well-intentioned, generous, and caring staff such as Anton had the good fortune to encounter in his first school experience in New York.

Another great challenge that immigrant students face that is underrecognized by schools is the likelihood that newcomers have personal histories of multiple occasions of traumatic separation and loss. Anton left a grandmother who had raised him since he was five and who depended on him. His relationship with her was reciprocal—she cared for him, becoming his primary parent over the course of the next seven years, and he provided her with necessary support and assistance as she aged. We know little about how his leaving impacted his grandmother's life or what the nature of the contact with her was subsequently. Smith, LaLonde, and Johnson (2004) refer to this common pattern of serial migration in their description of single parents migrating first, with their children following at a later date. A newcomer to New York and to the first author's middle school, Anton was undoubtedly dealing with the loss of his grandmother, his primary attachment figure. Suárez-Orozco and Bang (2010) tell of the pain of children having to break attachments first from the parent who has migrated and then from the caretakers with whom they have become attached.

We know little about Anton's reaction to the initial separation from his mother or how he was prepared for leaving his grandmother and his native home. We also know little about the process of reunification with her after a separation that spanned early childhood to adolescence. We do know that postmigration, his mother maintained a quiet presence in his life and was deeply grateful for the care and concern of his teachers. In retrospect, the phenomena of separation and loss and the shoals of migration and reunification went under the radar with Anton's worried teachers and school counselor. Although they met frequently to discuss his academic progress, the major stressors of migration, separation, and loss were not on their horizon. This is understandable, as the psychological consequences of immigration in childhood and adolescence are underrecognized in precisely those settings where young people are found—schools, recreational facilities, and community-based organizations. In schools, the narrowing of focus to exclusive concern with academic performance works to the detriment of immigrant youths.

In Anton's case, the teachers in his school intuitively created a warm, holding environment (Winnicott, 1965), which undoubtedly helped him transition to his startlingly new life. The genuine welcome he experienced from staff generalized to a warm reception from the other students and was sustained by continued interest and concern on the part of the dedicated group of teachers. The warm and welcoming school environment that was created by staff and students likely served a linking function between Anton's lost Jamaican home with grandmother and his new home with his mother.

Anton's story is an exceptional story of gratitude and striving, with little evidence of youthful rebellion. Glad to be in school, excited by what he was learning, and especially pleased to be making his teachers so happy with his achievement, Anton uncritically accepted their direction, hopes, and aspirations, making these his own. His group of female teachers embraced their maternal transferences (Freud, 1922/1990), eagerly taking this frightened, slight child—who appeared younger than his given age—under their collective wing. In this story of exceptionality—most immigrant adolescents who arrive in the United States with minimal educational background do not replicate this story—Anton becomes their successful son, who grows under their tutelage, heeds their advice, and returns their love with achievement. He goes on to a successful high school and college career, and today, is a successful businessman, occasionally flying high over the hills where he once played with goats.

The vignette that follows offers a contrast to Anton's humble upbringing in rural Jamaica. Like Anton, Devon has also experienced separation, loss, and, much later, reunion with a barely known mother. Unlike Anton, Devon is the child of a well-to-do Trinidadian transnational family, with an extended network in Trinidad and in the United States. Devon's story presents a counter-narrative to Anton's with regard to their families' economic, educational, and social standing, but also with regard to how each young person goes about constructing his new postmigration identity.

CASE VIGNETTE: DEVON, OR I'M WEARING PINK PANTS

Devon was 13 years old when he was permanently reunited with his mother in New York. When he was four, his mother left him with her parents and older sisters in the island nation of Trinidad and Tobago. A bright boy, he was doted upon by his grandparents and aunties and attended an elite, private school for boys, where he excelled. By all accounts he was an outgoing, friendly, and sociable child, with a sunny disposition. Devon took private piano lessons and was encouraged to show off his musical ability on the old piano that stood polished and dusted in the family's living room. Slender, he learned to swim and was an active and valuable member of his school's soccer team. By all measures, he was a happy, well-adjusted youngster.

During this period of separation, Devon's mother visited Trinidad once or twice a year. In turn, Devon and his grandparents would spend a few weeks every year in New York with his mother. Eleven years into this arrangement, Devon's mother's living situation was finally more secure, and she sent for her then 15-year-old son. He arrived and was soon settled into his new home and a public high school. Devon became quiet and stayed mostly to himself. He maintained an emotional distance from his mother; he was compliant, but distant and reserved at home and at school.

As he grew into late adolescence, Devon continued to heed his mother's household rules, was respectful, and did well at school. However, like many of his contemporaries, he began to push back against his mother's traditional assumptions of how he should dress. When Devon emerged from his bedroom one Saturday morning wearing tight pink pants, his mother was horrified and ordered him to change his clothes. Devon refused and continued to wear his pink pants—yet remained respectful and tidy at home and conscientious at school. His mother fretted about his friends, too.

For Devon, the tribulations of emigration may well have been balanced by the newfound opportunity to craft his own identity in the United States. From a traditional cultural perspective, Devon's pink pants represented a rebellious act, flying in the face of traditional, gendered social and cultural expectations. At least this seems to be how his mother interpreted his fashion statement. To her, Devon's insistence on pink pants was a challenge—and an affront—to her expectations of gender conformity, with pink an entirely unsuitable color choice for a teenage boy. Gendered expectations, including fixed gender roles, are consistent with traditional cultural views of what constitutes maleness and femaleness. Immigration, though, bestows upon immigrants the opportunity to recast their identities and to rewrite their own narratives.

Earlier generations of immigrants cast off adherence to religious rituals and practices upon disembarking at Ellis Island; some threw personal items that marked their premigration identities overboard. For young, contemporary immigrants, the ability to liberate oneself from culturally defined gendered expectations may represent a new frontier of personal freedom and choice. The ability to make autonomous choices is an American tradition. In the Western tradition, adolescence is a time of crafting one's personal identity (Erikson, 1950/1993), whereas in more traditional societies (even as traditional societies undergo rapid change), this is a period in which the young are expected to settle into the lives their elders scripted for them.

It is entirely possible that pink pants represent an autonomous choice associated with crafting of personal identity, rather than provocative behavior whose sole aim was to upset a mother with whom Anton was polite, but distant. Both Anton's story and Devon's story are similar in their emotional reactions of distance from mothers following reunification after long periods of separation. Both mothers were dismayed and pained by the distance that sprang up between themselves and their sons during their lengthy periods of separation.

Both Anton and Devon describe strong feelings of attachment to their grandparents in their respective home countries. Despite his youth (four when his mother left), Anton was his grandmother's eyes and ears—as well as her legs. In the mornings, he would run the goats up the hill for them to graze, and in the evening, return them for tethering, milking, and for whatever other chores needed to be done. Devon was also deeply attached to his grandparents and aunts and thrived under their care. In contrast to Anton's upbringing, Devon's was an environment of affluence and privilege. He was introduced to music and to a range of extracurricular activities, encouraged to excel in whatever he undertook, and was praised for his efforts. Devon grew up secure in the knowledge that he was loved and doted on by his grandparents and aunts.

Whether in circumstances of privilege or poverty, abrupt detachment from those one has come to love best—and who return that love faithfully—yields similar emotional reactions. Both Anton and Devon became quiet and withdrawn, unable to draw close to the mothers they rejoined. Both did well in school; Anton's success hinged largely on the warm embrace of the school staff, while Devon's achievement appears largely the result of his strong academic training in the exclusive private school he attended in Trinidad and his own drive to achieve.

DISCUSSION: A RELATIONAL APPROACH TO WORKING WITH IMMIGRANT YOUTHS

The case vignettes of Anton and Devon illustrate another phenomenon that significantly affects young immigrants. Youthful immigrants, who come from impoverished circumstances in their countries of origin, typically settle in neighborhoods with underserved schools. These students are often placed in troubled school districts that serve poorer families and have fewer resources. The school district in which Anton was placed, for example, was a Title 1 school district with a 50% free and reduced lunch designation. Underresourced schools have fewer resources to expend on addressing the additional needs of poor, immigrant youths. Wen-Jui Han (2008) writes that children of immigrants typically attend schools with multiple risk factors, putting them at a disadvantage for school achievement. Anton's success in this school environment is decidedly exceptional.

In contrast, Devon attended school in a better-resourced, middle-class neighborhood. Yet for Devon, the public school he attended in New York was a far cry from the exclusive all-boys private school he attended in Trinidad. Anton, who was largely unschooled in rural Jamaica, was gathered in by the maternal group of teachers and staff at his middle school, who took their en loco parentis role with great determination. His experience demonstrates the powerful role that teachers and other school staff can take, even in underresourced schools. The teachers' maternal transference, a key factor in Anton's academic success, is a common phenomenon with young, dependent children in early childhood settings but is less common with physically more mature and challenging middle and high school students.

Unlike Anton, Devon went from the smaller, more intimate private school setting, where his achievement was closely monitored and encouraged, to a larger, more impersonal setting, where he became one of many. Although Anton lost the closeness of home when he left Jamaica, he found a proxy in his new school in New York. Devon, however, lost his home when he left Trinidad but did not find a proxy for home in his new school. Despite his more secure economic circumstances, Devon may well have been on shakier ground.

Anton's story and Devon's story point to the complex situations of transnational families, especially regarding separation from mother and reunion. The two protagonists of these stories present exceptional stories: Anton's for his surprising academic success in the face of poverty and inadequate academic preparation, and Devon's for the privilege he came from in his country of origin. Both Devon and Anton present widely disparate demographics, yet their emotional reactions to emigration and reunion with mother were similar. We cannot help but wish that Devon too had the benefit of a school that could have provided a warm, holding environment postmigration (Korn, 1997). It was truly Anton's good fortune to chance upon a school that would offer him so much emotionally and that would open his mind to new possibilities. It is too risky, however, to leave the fate of immigrant youths to chance.

The relational angle to adolescent emotional well-being warrants further exploration. Positive transferential relationships that recall the best of nurturing parental figures are protective of young people. In a manner that parallels early child development, the older child and adolescent can form attachment relationships with other helpful, caring figures who can promote their own development. Anton clearly created reciprocal attachment relationships with the teachers in his middle school. Secure feelings of attachment are reflected in exploration and learning in young children; children who exhibit behavior consistent with secure attachment engage in the kinds of exploratory behavior implicated in cognitive growth (Ainsworth, Blehar Waters, & Wall, 1978; Bowlby, 1969/1982; Bretherton & Mulholland, 1999).

Patterns of multiple attachments are characteristic of traditional societies. Both Anton and Devon are products of traditional societies with deep cultural traditions of extended families that provide childcare, including for extended periods, for young relations. Children who grow in extended family networks, where multiple caregivers are deeply invested in caring for them, form multiple attachments at an early age. Young immigrants who hail from cultures with traditions of multiple attachments and caregiving arrangements may be especially open to building relationships with other, helpful adults. Reciprocity is key here; the teachers' collective interest in, and concern about, Anton suggests that they developed relationships with him characterized by protective maternal transferences (Freud, 1922/1990) that promote feelings of care, concern, and connectedness.

Multiple attachment relationships, including attachment relationships with extrafamilial figures, including teachers, counselors, and other mental health providers, can help young immigrants develop confident expectation in their ability to grow. Growth, though, presents the developing capacity to explore new avenues and possibilities that may exist on the postmigration horizon. Immigration provokes possibilities for change and for new directions that one might not—or could not—have envisioned in the country of origin.

Devon's audacious pink pants may signal a way in which migration affords young immigrants the opportunity to push against the boundaries of their identities, crafting a new sense of self in their adopted home countries. It may signal, too, despite the distance that often springs up between parent and child following lengthy separations, resonances of strong, positive multiple attachments, first with the parent who left and later with loving caregivers (in these two case vignettes, their grandparents). It is likely that the residue of strong, emotionally laden, positive attachment relationships emerges in autonomous, self-directed behavior, sometimes expressed in academic achievement and other times by pink pants.

NOTE

1. All names are pseudonyms.

REFERENCES

Ainsworth, M. S., Blehar, M. C., Waters, E., & Wall, S. (1978). *Patterns of attachment: A psychological study of the strange situation.* Oxford, Engl.: Erlbaum.

Bowlby, J. (1969/1982). *Attachment and loss:* Vol. 1. *Attachment* (2nd ed.). New York: Basic Books.

Bretherton, I., & Mulholland, C. (1999). Internal working models in attachment relationships: A construct revisited. In J. Cassidy & P. Shaver (Eds.), *Handbook of attachment* (pp. 89–111). New York, NY: Guilford.

Erikson, E. (1950/1993). *Childhood and society.* New York, NY: Norton.

Freud, S. (1922/1990). *New introductory lectures on psycho-analysis.* New York, NY: Norton.

Han, W. J. (2008). The academic trajectories of children of immigrants and their school environments. *Developmental Psychology, 44,* 1572–1590.

Korn, C. (1997). "I used to be very smart": Children talk about immigration. *Education and Culture, 14*(2), 17–24.

London, J. (1903/2003). *Call of the wild.* New York, NY: Barnes & Noble.

New York State School Boards Association. (2014). *Serving English language learners.* A special report by NYSSBA's Department of Legal & Policy Services.

Smith, A., LaLonde, R. N., & Johnson, S. (2004). Serial migration and its implications for the parent-child relationship: A retrospective analysis of the experiences of the children of Caribbean immigrants. *Cultural Diversity an Ethnic Minority Psychology, 10,* 107–122.

State Education Department; the University of the State of New York. (2014). Memorandum to: Deans and Directors of Institutions Offering Teacher Preparation Programs in New York State. Albany, NY.

Suarez-Orozco, C., & Bang, H. J. (2010). Contributions to variations in academic trajectories amongst recent immigrant youth. *International Journal of Behavioral Development, 34,* 500–510.

Winnicott, D. (1965). *The maturational processes and the facilitating environment: Studies in the theory of emotional development.* Oxford, Engl.: International Universities Press.

7

On Crafting a Resiliency Narrative

Malya Schulman and Carol Korn-Bursztyn

This chapter presents the story of Michael (which is a pseudonym), a young immigrant from Ukraine, who began his own migration journey at age 11 when he left Ukraine for Vancouver to join his father, whose own migration journey had begun five years earlier. Between the lines of this terse narrative is a story of epic dimensions, repeated in greatly differing versions by children from around the globe in often startlingly different circumstances, but who all hold in common the emotional experience of being left behind by a parent who migrates.

This story is a tale of vulnerability and loss but also of great resourcefulness, autonomy, and mastery. It is retrospective and significant for how the storyteller positions his young self as the hero of his own narrative. His story is one of exceptional resourcefulness in difficult circumstances. Although we cannot be assured of the accuracy of all elements of the storyteller's account, the narrative of inner strength, independence, and resiliency emerges as an important feature of this retrospective account. The critical reader will note an emphasis on details connoting resilience, self-sufficiency, and purpose with minimal attention to the inevitable feelings that accompany loss and the major life changes that migration typically entails.

The narrative is followed by a discussion that amplifies the skeletal structure of Michael's story, connecting elements of his story to features significant to many young immigrant narratives. The role of academic ability, understated in the story our narrator tells, presents an important pathway to thinking about the role of educators and mental health professionals in helping young immigrants to craft life stories of resilience and hope.

CASE VIGNETTE: MICHAEL

The Journey

Michael was born in a small city in Ukraine. When he was seven, his father emigrated to Vancouver. Following his emigration, Michael's mother worked long hours, and Michael began to spend more time away from home in various afterschool programs.

From age seven to 11, when Michael joined his father, he spoke with his father once every few months. At age nine, he visited his father in Vancouver, and upon his return to Ukraine, proposed to his mother that he join his father, and she agreed. Two years later, 11-year-old Michael joined his father in Vancouver. Upon arrival, Michael recalled his sense of pride and self-satisfaction in orchestrating his migration despite his youth.

Reunification

Reunification with his father, Michael observes, was surprisingly untouched by the geographic distance that preceded their reunification. He felt close to his father, able to draw on the strong bonds that were formed in his early childhood years, prior to his father's migration. There were compelling new needs to attend to: mastering a new language and adjusting to a new school environment.

Michael says that he began school in Vancouver in mid-year, where he was placed in a mandatory English as a second language class. He was determined to learn English over the summer; a steady menu of English-language television helped. In the fall, he was mainstreamed, and by the end of the semester, he earned honor roll.

The story that Michael tells then skips ahead to the end of high school, when he studies abroad for three years. In the interim, we learn that his father has remarried, and that both he and his new wife encourage Michael to return home to prepare for a professional career. He agrees, returns home, and begins graduate school. Reflecting on his three years living abroad, far from family, Michael connects this period to his own personal growth and to his decision to enter a profession that involves caring for people in which he would be able to support himself well.

Unlike most immigrant youths who are not party to the decision to migrate, Michael's decision was self-motivated and voluntary, casting the migration experience in a very different light (Grinberg & Grinberg, 1989). His father's migration appears to have set a migratory path in motion, triggering

Michael's own migration journey. In his absence, Michael seems to have idealized his father and recalls him as a model of unconditional love. Idealization of the absent father is a common phenomenon, described by children left in the care of their mothers following the fathers' emigration. In her moving memoir *The Distance between Us*, Reyna Grande (2012) speaks to her fantasied father, with whom she develops an imagined relationship. Unlike her true-to-life mother, who she recognizes as troubled and flawed, Grande's imaginary father escapes relatively unscathed, even as their actual reunion is deeply disappointing. Her book is dedicated to him.

Michael's successful trajectory in his new home, like Grande's story, begs the question, What accounts for a young immigrant's success? What can we learn from narratives of young people who successfully negotiate the intimidating obstacles that immigration in youth presents and go on to carve out productive and creative lives? In the sections that follow, we will examine Michael's story for the characteristics that emerge with the hope that this can provide guidance for those who work with young immigrants.

We begin with consideration of the place of academic ability as a potentially protective factor. We examine other community venues, including religious institutions, as potential sites of warmth and emotional support and consider how qualities of inner strength and emotional resilience can be nurtured. Finally, we consider the role of narrative and the importance of how young immigrants can craft narratives of strength, resilience, and creativity.

ACADEMIC ABILITY

One might expect that Michael's entry into his new school would be trying, as "the analysis of parental separations [has] revealed complicated relationships between various dimensions of the separation experience and resulting academic trajectories" (Suárez-Orozco, Bang, & Onaga, 2010, p. 506). However, despite the challenges in his home life, migration history, in combination with his entering early adolescence, he maintained strong academic performance, avoiding the downward educational spiral that is not unusual in early adolescent immigrants.

Though immigrant children are likely to attend underperforming schools that can put them at risk of school failure (Han, 2008), Michael was placed in a school that presented few risk factors; his ability was recognized and he thrived in the new environment. Exemplary academic performance in immigration children is atypical but not unusual. Suárez-Orozco et al. (2010, p. 500) observe that "despite the cumulative stresses of migration, not all immigrant youth fall prey to school failure and disengagement . . . [students] demonstrate varying levels of achievement during the course of their education. It is likely that newcomer students' academic adjustments over time are sensitive to a range of family, school and individual factors." From an early age, Michael identified with his father's intellectual bent. He recalls: "My father was an academic, whom I spend my first few years of life watching write his dissertation. He is a complex and deep thinker."

Michael's identification with his father and ease of reunification are likely implicated in his motivation and academic success. Jensen (2007) explains that the young immigrants' experience of loss can be mitigated by the positive feelings that result from reunion with lost loved ones. Premigration characteristics may be salient here. Grinberg and Grinberg (1989) offered that emigration requires a strong ego and an ability to face risks. Michael's inner strength, greatly assisted here by his strong cognitive ability and by the felt security of his early years in the parental home prior to his father's emigration, may be at play in his rapid adjustment to his new home. Michael, though, also points to the cultural roots of his determination and perseverance. He explains:

> Like many Jews in the former Soviet Union, my family had defined themselves as survivors. We had to differentiate ourselves from the culture that often placed Jewish quotas in educational and professional spheres. Jews had to find creative outlets in a society that would discourage individualism in the true sense of developing oneself as a unique individual, setting oneself from the masses.
>
> As an immigrant, in order to survive, one has to figure out what your strengths are and how you can make yourself employable or create ways to support oneself. I learned not to be frivolous with money, things and people. Once you have watched your parents struggle and succeed in creating a good life from scratch, you come to appreciate other people's struggles, diversity, and depth of character. It made me appreciate how people from completely different backgrounds can pursue self-oriented goals for themselves, while managing to co-exist with those around them.

It is possible that the process of migration itself has the potential to encourage new growth. "Migration is one of life's emergencies that exposes the individual who experiences it to a state of disorganization and requires a subsequent reorganization that is not always achieved. . . . If, however, he has sufficient capacity for working through [the conditions of his migration], not only will he overcome the crisis but there will be a quality of rebirth to his recovery and a development of his creative potential" (Grinberg & Grinberg, 1989, p. 15).

However, we need to ask under what conditions can migration open possibilities for creative growth, rather than stagnation? This is especially salient when considering the young immigrant, whose personality is not yet fully formed and who is developmentally in a state of rapid growth. It is useful to consider the ideas of Donald Winnicott (1965a, 1965b, 1986), a pediatrician who turned to psychoanalytic practice as a result of his work with young patients and their parents. His concept of the holding environment is especially relevant for young immigrants whose development task upon arrival in their new home is to craft a new narrative of themselves that includes the vicissitudes of their migration history.

SEARCH FOR HOME: THE HOLDING ENVIRONMENT

Taking a developmental approach, Winnicott references the idea of home as an optimal site that functions as a holding environment for the child. It is conceptualized as the seat of burgeoning independence from which the young child progressively moves from a state of absolute dependence to relative dependence and eventually toward a state of independence (Winnicott, 1965a, p. 45). This progression, he explains, "is a matter of the inheritance of a maturational process, and of the accumulation of living experiences; this development does not occur, however, except in a facilitating environment" (1965a, p. 27).

Winnicott's early thinking about the holding environment and its importance to furthering the child's autonomous growth has relevance to both the fields of education and mental health (Korn-Bursztyn, 2012). It has added significance to children whose life stories include loss—including the loss of home—dislocation, and migration. In typical development, which assumes stability of home and environment over the course of childhood and adolescence, in order for the growing child to make strides toward autonomy, the child must feel the secure base of a safe home to which it is possible to return (Korn-Bursztyn, 1998). The facilitating environment is that which projects confidence in the child's ability to grow and to move beyond the confines of home. Further, it is the loved objects within the environment that make it possible for the child to both move into the world and to return home.

Taken metaphorically, the holding environment is that which offers the safety and security of unconditional acceptance and regard and that projects confidence in the ability of the growing individual to sally forth independently. The holding environment is an essentially bittersweet concept that is firmly rooted in contemporary Western notions of autonomous development, as well as in the more classic tropes of heroic journeys and epic tales. Home as holding environment is the site that creates the conditions for growth, synonymous here with departure.

In immigration, the immigrant leaves the environment that has provided, for better or worse, the functions of a holding environment. Under the best of circumstances, that environment has provided immigrants with an inner sense of resourcefulness and with a now imaginary space peopled by those whose love was once felt daily. Optimally, over the course of childhood and into adulthood, the holding environment becomes internalized—an imaginary, portable home. When young people immigrate, their relationship to the holding environments of their youth—if they are lucky enough to have had homes, communities, even schools that have served as holding environments—is abruptly changed. Their tasks are now complex: they must seek new spaces that can serve as holding environments, and they must make sense of the spaces in between their lives pre- and postmigration.

MIGRATION, TRANSITIONAL SPACES, AND CREATIVITY

Migration offers the potential for creative growth. The act of migrating propels migrants into new spaces: launched from the known environment to a new, strange place. The migrant resides in the interstices between the familiar past, the unfamiliar present, and the unknown future. Winnicott's (1971) concept of transitional space—the potential space between the individual and his environment—is the potential space of creativity, of playfulness, cultural productivity, and of the development of creative responses to life's challenges. The psychological task of immigration is to make meaning of the immigrant's complex pre- and postmigration narratives and to construct a personal story that is not only coherent, but that also provides a framework for moving into the future (Korn, 1997).

For Michael, his chosen career in the medical field may have served as a touchstone to the familiarity of home and family and served to strengthen his emotional connection to her father. He observed that his paternal grandmother was a physician. If Michael's choice of career represents a nod to the original holding environment of home, which emotionally he connects to identification with father, then his choice of workplace (i.e., hospital) may represent a transitional space in which he transforms traumatic experiences into creative and generative responses, aimed toward healing and soothing.

Michael's professional life is spent in an environment that is itself intrinsically a transitional space: patients are checked in and checked out—either through discharge or death. The transitional space of work and hospital may well serve as a creative outlet in which Michael works in the in-between spaces of trauma (illness and hospitalization) and its aftermath.

Michael's turn to religion postmigration provides another insight into the role of organized religion in the lives of immigrants. The experience of migration is unsettling and anxiety inducing in any event. For unaccompanied children and for children who are reuniting with parents from whom they have been separated, the act of voluntary migration represents a huge leap of faith—faith in the constancy of the waiting parent's love and trust in the parent's desire to again offer a secure holding environment in which the child can relax into parental care.

In his book *Home Is Where We Start From*, Winnicott (1986) comments on how we come to possess an innate trust of our surroundings, a confidence, he writes, that has roots in the earliest interactions between mother/parent and infant. He locates belief in the earliest relationship of trust between child and parent.

> We are believing people. Here we are in this large hall and no one has been worried about the ceiling falling down. We have a belief in the architect. We are believing people because we are started off well by somebody. We received a silent communication over a period of time that we were loved in the sense that we could rely on the environmental provision and so get on with our growth and development. (p. 147)

For Michael, whose early life was marked by the loss of his father through migration and the consequent loss of the secure home of early childhood, organized religion may have provided a reassuring postmigration holding environment. Religious institutions often serve as sources of assistance and support of immigrants and their families and provide "spaces in which they could hold on to their ethnic identity" (Menjivar, 2010, p. 10). In *Finding Space: Winnicott, God and Psychic Reality*, the Christian theologian Ann Belford Ulanov (2001) discusses the relationship between the concepts of transitional space and religion. Ulanov posits that the transitional space between the infant and its mother is a template for the relationship between the individual and a higher power. Michael's turn to religious belief and to the structures of organized religion may well have provided him with a holding environment that met his needs for community, connection to cultural identity, and to a longed-for sense of trust and belief.

DISCUSSION: FOSTERING RESILIENCE

Follow-up conversations between Michael and the first author revealed a more nuanced account of the period following his father's departure. He recalls the warmth and support of a maternal aunt, whom he visited frequently.

> My weekends were spent at my aunt's house—my mother's sister who never married and who treated me as if I were her own child.

> She was warm, caring, and stern when needed, but fun most of the time. She was the type of person one can talk to about anything; she was deeply superstitious, a great storyteller. My aunt was very spiritual in a pragmatic kind of way.

In describing the positive outcomes to his migration story, Michael emphasizes his "natural curiosity" and "motivation" in combination with what he refers to as his "resources." These include family, including the maternal aunt in Ukraine, his religious community, and other mentors with whom he forged a relationship along the way. Michael's acknowledgment of the role of curiosity suggests early formation of habits of intellectual interest and a love of learning. This intrinsic attitude toward learning, fostered by family, clearly contributed to Michael's resilience by promoting a disposition to the outside world as an interesting, stimulating place from which one can learn and in which one can test oneself. Strong cognitive ability is a recognized factor in resiliency; curiosity about the world and a desire to learn and make a mark in the world are underrecognized characteristics that Michael's narrative presents. Although curiosity is implicated in cognitive ability, it is a typical feature of early childhood. The capacity to sustain a curious approach to the world postearly childhood may well be dependent on the intellectual tenor of children's surroundings.

His age may have also played a part. Children are known to exhibit surprising resilience in the face of painful separations from family members and to draw upon reserves of strength and a capacity for flexibility and rapid adjustment to changed circumstances (Michael, 2009; Suárez-Orozco, Suárez-Orozco, & Todorova, 2008). The experience of immigration is at best stressful and, in its most complex variants, traumatic. Jensen (2007) presents Urie Bronfenbrenner's ecological model as creating a continuum of resistance, explaining that Bronfenbrenner's conception of mediating processes explains how ecological circumstances interact so that an immigrant's experience could range from vulnerable to resistant.

Fergus and Zimmerman (2005) also view resilience, specifically in adolescence, as a dynamic process that incorporates both risk and protective factors for adolescent development. As in Michael's narrative, they too underline how assets and resources promote positive outcomes and reduce the risk of negative outcomes. Like Michael, they equate assets with internal characteristics, such as competence, coping skills, and self-efficacy, and resources with factors external to the individual, such as support, adult mentoring, and community organizations. However, the interaction between internal and external characteristics, as Michael's story reminds us, points to the mutual influence of inner qualities derived from deep attachments to family, home, and cultural traditions and trustworthy figures from the past and in the present.

The importance to young immigrants of crafting a resiliency narrative cannot be underestimated. All immigration stories hold inner experiences of fear and dread, loss, and longing; for some these take the form of nightmares realized, while for others, buffered by family and community, these complex feelings can be stowed away to be retrieved in the retelling of a migration epic. Michael's arrival in Vancouver as a documented immigrant, reuniting with his father, and entering an organized household and school situation place his immigration story in a far more secure context than that of many young, impoverished, and unaccompanied migrants today. And yet, when young immigrants of diverse backgrounds and living situations can draw on their reserves of youthful flexibility and drive, they can frame their own narratives of inner strength and determination, which can help them to imagine how they might grow.

REFERENCES

Fergus, S., & Zimmerman, M. A. (2005). Adolescent resilience: A framework for understanding healthy development in the face of risk. *Annual Review of Public Health, 26,* 399–419.

Grande, R. (2012). *The distance between us.* New York, NY: Atria Books.

Grinberg, L., & Grinberg, R. (1989). Chapter 2, Migration as trauma and crisis (pp. 10–15); Chapter 3, The emigrants (pp. 16–24); Chapter 12, Age and migration (pp. 113–128). In *Psychoanalytic perspectives on migration and exile.* New Haven, CT: Yale University Press.

Han, W. (2008). The academic trajectories of children of immigrants and their school environments. *Developmental Psychology, 44,* 1572–1590.

Jensen, B. T. (2007). Understanding immigration and psychological development: A multilevel ecological approach. *Journal of Immigrant & Refugee Studies, 5,* 27–48.

Korn, C. (1997). "I used to be very smart": Children talk about immigration. *Education and Culture, 14*(2), 17–24.

Korn-Bursztyn, C. (1998). How young children make sense of their life stories. *Early Childhood Education Journal, 25*(4), 223–228.

Korn-Bursztyn, C. (2012). Cultivating imagination and creative thinking. In C. Korn-Bursztyn (Ed.), *Young children and the arts: Nurturing imagination and creativity* (pp. 51–67). Charlotte, NC: Information Age Publishing.

Menjivar, C. (2010). Immigrants, immigration, and sociology: Reflecting on the state of the discipline. *Sociological Inquiry, 80,* 3–27.

Michael, S. (2009). Continuities and discontinuities: Patterns of migration, adolescent immigrant girls and their family relationships. *Qualitative Social Work, 8,* 229–247.

Suárez-Orozco, C., Bang, H. J., & Onaga, M. (2010). Contributions to variations in academic trajectories amongst recent immigrant youth. *International Journal of Behavioral Development, 34,* 500–510.

Suárez-Orozco, C., Suárez-Orozco, M. M., & Todorova, I. (2008). Network of relationships. In *Learning a new land: Immigrant students in American society* (pp. 55–87). Cambridge, MA: Harvard University Press.

Ulanov, A. B. (2001). *Finding space: Winnicott, God and psychic reality.* Louisville, KY: Westminster John Knox Press.

Winnicott, D. W. (1965a). *The family and individual development.* London: Tavistok.

Winnicott, D. W. (1965b). The maturational processes and the facilitating environment: Studies in the theory of emotional development. *International Psycho-Analytical Library, 64,* 1–276.

Winnicott, D. W. (1971). *Therapeutic consultation in child psychiatry.* London: Hogarth Press

Winnicott, D. W. (1986). *Home is where we start from.* London and New York: Norton.

8

Latino Immigrant Youths and the Transnational Family

Gabriela Santana Betancourt and Carol Korn-Bursztyn

Research examining the role of immigration in outcomes of depression among first- and second-generation Latino youths is rather limited. Studies have found that Latino adolescents in the United States have a higher prevalence of depression compared with their white and African American peers, and that Latina teens may be at even higher risk than Latino adolescent males. However, several studies have also shown that first-generation Latino immigrant youths may be at lower risk for depression than second-generation Latino teens, despite low socioeconomic and "minority" status, creating an "immigrant paradox." This phenomenon has been attributed to various factors (such as resilience, family characteristics, level of acculturation, and the "healthy migrant" effect) that may act as protectors against deleterious mental health outcomes. This chapter explores the relation between immigration, family dynamics, and the outcome of depression among Latino youths.

My (the first author's) interest in the topic of depression among Latino immigrant youths stems from my professional experiences working as a health educator and counselor for immigrant youths for a community-based clinic in a large urban high school. The youths I worked with were from a variety of countries, but as a native Spanish speaker, I worked most closely with youths from the Dominican Republic. Most of the youths were recent arrivals and were in the midst of difficult transitions—settling into a new city, adjusting to life within a new family context, and dealing with the normative changes that accompany adolescence. As the child of immigrants and a native New Yorker myself, I felt great compassion and empathy for the youths I worked with.

Adolescence is a difficult time, and New York City can be a tough place. Facing the challenges of adjusting to a new country and language and suddenly finding oneself trying to integrate into a new family structure can make an understandably trying transition all the more complicated. What follows are three case studies of youths whom I worked closely with during my years at the community clinic's high school satellite office. All were first-generation youths from the Dominican Republic. Names have been changed to protect anonymity.

CASE VIGNETTE: FELIX

Felix was a thin, witty, and tall 16-year-old who loved to tell jokes. I met Felix early in the school year, as he needed updated vaccinations in order to begin his classes in the English as a second language (ESL) program offered by the school. After linking him to health care services, he would often come by my office just to talk. He grew up in a rural area outside of Santo Domingo, the capital of the Dominican Republic, where he lived with his grandmother and father. Felix had been raised by his grandmother, and she and his father were the only caregivers he had ever known. Felix arrived in New York City during the summer months and was living with his mother and her husband, Felix's stepfather.

Felix was having a hard time—back home he had many friends and loved to play sports. He missed his grandmother and father terribly and often told me about the conflicts he was experiencing in his new home with his mother and stepfather. It was particularly difficult for him to take orders from his mother. "She tells me that I have to listen to her because she is my mother, but she was never around when I was young, and I am not a little boy anymore," he would say.

He had a few friends at school, most of whom were recent immigrant boys like himself from the Dominican Republic. But some of the youths who had been living in the United States for longer periods of time, or were born in New York City to immigrant parents, called him a hick and taunted him about the clothes he wore. Although Felix enjoyed classes with his teachers and the paraprofessionals who worked with him in the ESL program, he complained that he had trouble sleeping at night. He often overslept in the mornings, and because school was far from where he lived in Washington Heights, he arrived at school late, although he rarely missed classes.

Felix's experiences illustrate a common phenomenon in the immigration experience, particularly for adolescents and children living in a transnational familial context. Adolescence is a time when, normatively, youths establish independence, away from the family unit and seek counsel and identification with peers. This normative process was complicated for Felix, as he had to face the difficulty of separating from those he had formed attachments to in his younger years, his grandmother and father.

Furthermore, he was expected to automatically form an attachment and exhibit respect of authority to his mother, someone he had never lived with before, simply because she was his biological mother. It is quite possible that his mother was experiencing the guilt of not having been there for Felix when he was a boy and was trying to override these emotions by demanding that he accept her as what he referred to as a maternal figure. In terms of his education, Felix was a motivated student, but the emotional distress caused by his particular immigration experience may have led to his difficulties with sleep, and this affected his school performance. Finally, Felix was finding it difficult to fit in with his peers. His style of dress and general demeanor may have been normative back in the Dominican Republic, but it marked him as an outsider with other New York City teens.

CASE VIGNETTE: PEDRO

Pedro initially came to see me because he wanted to join the school baseball team and needed a complete physical examination before he could participate. After making an appointment for him to see the doctor at the hospital, I learned more about Pedro's background and experiences in New York City. He had moved to the United States two years prior to live with his father and stepmother and would often come by my office to talk about the difficulties he was having at home, mostly with his stepmother. Pedro's father worked long hours at a bodega, and Pedro worked there as well after school.

Back in the Dominican Republic, Pedro had a young son of his own—a toddler who lived with his mother, Pedro's ex-girlfriend. He expressed deep sadness that he was not near his son, but he felt torn. Ultimately, he agreed with his father that the educational opportunities in New York would be better for him in the long run, and his own son would benefit from this as well. But Pedro carried a secret that weighed on him heavily and caused him much emotional distress.

He shared with me that he was actually 21, but used falsified documentation so he could live in the United States and attend school. Back in the Dominican Republic, Pedro had volunteered with the local fire department and had even started taking college-level classes. He often felt like he was living a lie. He was in an ESL program, but the content of his classes was repetitive. He had already learned much of the material in school in the Dominican Republic, and he was bored. He felt out of sync with his classmates, all of whom were much younger. His hope was to get through the two years left for him to graduate, so that he could attend university and eventually get a well-paying job so that he could help support his son back home.

Pedro's immigration experience was complicated by his documentation status, which can bring additional emotional distress to an already stressful time (Jensen, 2007). Socioeconomic status also shapes the immigration experience of youths and their outcomes. As seen in this case study, Pedro and his father work long hours in order to make ends meet and send remittances back to their family members in the Dominican Republic, including Pedro's young son. Anxiety and depression are common to adolescent immigrants struggling with multiple stressors. Pedro, who had his own adult concerns regarding a son he had left behind, carried the burden of an undocumented status in addition to the stressors of reunification with a parent and entry into a new household with a new stepparent.

One case in particular is emblematic of the many stories I heard from the youth I worked with. I include the case of Judy below and then provide an overview of the literature I found dealing with depression and immigration in adolescents. I conclude with a discussion of how Judy's story fits in to the context of the literature on depression and immigration, and posit that disparities in the outcome of depression and mental health outcomes overall may be explained within the theoretical framework of secure attachment, which has been overlooked in the literature on immigrant youths.

CASE VIGNETTE: JUDY

Judy was a soft-spoken and shy 15-year-old who had been living in the United States for the past six years. Her parents had sent her to live with an aunt in Washington Heights because they felt she would have a better education and more opportunities in New York City than in the Dominican Republic. Judy understood why she was sent to live abroad, but she was a profoundly sad young woman who missed her parents deeply. Her parents remained in the Dominican Republic, as did her younger siblings. Although Judy had been living with her aunt for six years, she had not bonded with her. Judy felt that her aunt did not treat her in the same warm manner as she did her own children, Judy's cousins. She was not close to her cousins, although they shared a room and were about the same age.

Judy was having many difficulties in school—she was often absent and skipped classes. During one of the many conversations I had with her in my office, she expressed that she sometimes thought about suicide. After establishing that she did not have a plan, I linked her to mental health services, and she faithfully attended weekly sessions with a social worker. She developed a trusting relationship with this clinician, and her participation in school and her grades improved. She took part in more group activities and would attend dances that the hospital would host for our participant youth. The following summer, Judy went to visit her family in the Dominican Republic for the first time since emigrating to the United States. She did not return to school in the fall.

The experiences of these young people struggling with separation and loss highlight the complexities of the immigrant experience. When families move together to a new country as a unit, or close together in a "stepwise" fashion, the trauma of loss and separation inherent in the immigrant experience may be lessened (Suárez-Orozco, Suárez-Orozco, &Todorova, 2008).

The cases presented here highlight the challenges and complex factors at play when the family dynamic is fragmented and threatens family cohesion, with little hope of reunification. The experience of family fragmentation leads to difficult transitions, including complicated adjustment periods negotiating with new family members and shaped by class, gender, and socioeconomic status. Alternatively, these cases illuminate the resilience of youths as they face the challenges of immigration and struggle to form new social and familial networks.

FAMILY

The mediating influences of family dynamics and social networks can be either protective or harmful to individuals. The strength of the familial and social networks impacts young immigrants' feelings of connectedness and security. In the cases presented in this chapter, the family unit had been torn; youths have migrated to a new country under fragmented family circumstances, where a cherished parent, parental figure, or caregiver has been left behind.

These are traumatic losses, with consequences for both physical and mental health well-being, school attendance, and educational attainment (Suárez-Orozco et al., 2008). These young people find themselves having to adjust not only to a new urban environment, country, and language, but also to new families, peer networks, and social settings. Clashes with new family members seeking to exert authority, offer care, and to be accepted as a parental figure were common to all of the cases described here.

These points of tension between the newly arrived youths and the existing family network in the new country lead to a complicated adjustment period. Intact family contexts are critical for the healthy development and optimal functioning of youths and their continued well-being (Suárez-Orozco, Bang, & Kim, 2011). The developmental challenges of adolescence, which include exerting independence, questioning authority, and seeking out key relationships with peers, are complicated by introduction to a new family unit at a sensitive stage in development (Garcia & Lindgren, 2009).

Felix struggles with a biological mother who is not his "maternal figure" and expresses anger and resentment. In his experience, his mother was not there for him as a child, and now that he is an adolescent, he feels that it is too late for her to step in and take on this role. For him, this period is not experienced as a reunification with his mother, but rather as a separation from his beloved caregivers, as his grandmother and father represent what he refers to as his true maternal and paternal figures. Youths who experience long periods of separation from a family member, or the complete absence of a figure that is supposed to be the primary caregiver, may find it challenging to establish an intimate bond once they are reunited with the family member in the new country (Suárez-Orozco et al., 2011).

Pedro must cope with the loss of his family back home, including a young child whom he has left for what is likely to be, at best, a lengthy separation while he goes to school and works, perhaps sending remittances back home. Having lost the family members with whom he was close, he must now adjust to living with a father he does not know and a stepmother with whom there is tension. He mourns the loss of his son, as well as the loss of his identity as a young adult. His undocumented status adds another level of precariousness to his living situation and to his growing feelings of sadness. Judy is also coping with overwhelming feelings of sadness and loss. She experiences her parents as having sent her away and feels like an outsider in her aunt's home. Feeling unloved and rejected, Judy had become increasingly withdrawn.

Family reunification can mitigate the trauma of separation due to immigration. But in the cases presented, the youths have no hope of returning to or being reunited with the secure family unit. Instead, they are caught up in a new family dynamic, and they must struggle to make this new unit their own. There is no stepwise immigration in these particular cases—these youths represent the only step—the hope for a better education and future, even if it means being separated from those they most love (Suárez-Orozco et al., 2008, 2011). Though the youths in these cases cognitively understand the reasons for migration and may even have participated in the decision-making process to migrate, it does not mitigate their feelings of loss and isolation and, in Judy's case, rejection.

SOCIAL NETWORKS

In exploring the social networks that can aid in mitigating the painful process of immigration for adolescents, Jensen (2008) applies Bronfenbrenner's ecological model to the immigrant experience. Through this framework, the school community can be viewed as a proximal-level stage in which acculturation or enculturation occurs via social processes. The school environment is the setting that allows for access to and participation in social networks with peers and hopefully caring and attentive adults.

In the cases presented, the youths benefited from being in a diverse school environment that offered them access to other youths from their country of origin, as well as access to adults who were culturally sensitive, responsive, and Spanish speakers. This allowed the youths to foment resilience, possibly alleviating the less than optimal conditions of their current familial dynamics. Suárez-Orozco et al. (2008) highlight the importance of having friends from the country of origin as a source of support and a resource for information.

Unlike the experiences of youths who find themselves in a new country with little to no access to immigrant communities, the youths presented in these cases have moved to New York City where there is a large, established, and vibrant Dominican population, as well as Spanish-speaking communities from many different countries. Felix had a few friends in school that were also from the Dominican Republic, and he formed good relationships with his ESL teachers and paraprofessionals. He would willingly visit my office to speak with me about the issues he was facing and enjoyed participating in afterschool health education workshops that I facilitated.

He also joined the school baseball team and became close with his fellow teammates. Pedro also joined a sports team and eventually befriended more mature classmates from a variety of backgrounds and began to feel less isolated. Judy began to socialize with other girls from her school, attend extracurricular activities, and form trusting relationships with caring adults such as myself and her social worker. Thus, a positive protective factor for these youths stemmed from the diverse school community, with many youths from the Dominican Republic, all of whom had been living in the United States for varying periods of time.

However, the stresses of acculturation are also apparent. Felix, teased about his clothes, begins to dress differently so he can more easily blend in as a New York City teenager. Pedro has a particularly tough time fitting in—he struggles with his false identity, having to acculturate to the life of a teenager in high school when in fact he is an adult, 21-year-old male interacting with adolescents at a different developmental stage and level of maturity. Judy benefited from the intervention of a social worker to get her on track with school attendance and socialization with peers.

Immigration in and of itself does not automatically connote trauma. However, immigration characterized by fragmented familial dynamics, where strong relationships that nurture, offer warmth, and security and provide authority, which may have been torn in the process of immigration, may be quite traumatic and disruptive for adolescent immigrants. Felix, Pedro, and Judy dealt with extremely difficult and conflicted circumstances in their home environments. Although school communities can offer opportunities for immigrant youths to participate in beneficial social networks outside of the family, this support may not be enough.

Unfortunately, none of the youths presented here graduated from high school. Given the context of deep familial fragmentation, the school environment alone could not adequately provide the support necessary for improved outcomes. At the core, resilience is found within the individual. But resilience is a vital source of energy that needs nurturing during the difficult transition from childhood to adolescence and young adulthood from many levels of the environment, most notably from the family unit.

DEPRESSION AND THE IMMIGRATION EXPERIENCE

The youths whose stories were presented in this chapter, as well as immigrant youths in general, may be vulnerable to emotional and mental distress depending on the complexities of their immigration experience. Felix, Pedro, and Judy all exhibited signs of emotional and mental distress and were vulnerable to anxiety and depression. Felix was having a hard time sleeping, and at times he did not have much of an appetite and was thin. Pedro often felt anxious, worrying that he would be found out, and was bored and unmotivated in his classes.

Judy was most evidently depressed and expressed suicidal ideation. Approximately 12.4% of adolescent females and 4.3% of males in the United States have experienced depression (SAMHSA, 2009). Depression in adolescence is of vital concern, as the risk for recurring depression increases with each episode and is associated with increased suicidal ideation, attempts, and suicide rates. According to 2010 data from the National Institute of Mental Health, the lifetime prevalence of major depressive disorder/dysthymia in adolescents between the ages of 13 and 18 years is 11.2%. Lifetime prevalence for girls is twice that of boys (15.0% vs. 7.5%), and risk increases with age (7.4% for 13- to 14-year-olds, 12.2% for 15- to 16-year-olds, and 15.5% for 17- to 18-year-olds) (Ries Merikangas et al., 2010).

Racial and ethnic disparities have been noted; Latino youths have higher rates of depressive symptoms compared with their peers. Among a nationally representative sample of youths, 11.5% of Latino boys reported depressive symptoms compared with 10.3% of non-Hispanic white, and 8.7% non-Hispanic African American boys; and 32.2% of Latina teens compared with 25.7% of non-Hispanic white and 19.5% of non-Hispanic African American girls (Saluja et al., 2004).

Data from the Latino Adolescent Migration, Health and Adaptation (LAMHA) study point to the varied stressors faced by youths during the stages of immigration (premigration, migration, and postmigration), including separation from loved family members or caregivers and complicated adjustment to new family units. LAMHA is the first population-based study of mental health, migration, and acculturation among first-generation youths living in North Carolina, a state with a growing Latino population (Ko & Perreira, 2010).

Stressful events during the stages of immigration impact the family unit, resulting in conflict and fragmented social networks, as well as in individual feelings of loss, sadness, depression, anxiety, and a sense of security in the world. These feelings can be mitigated by nurturing and strong connections with others. According to LAMHA data, only 30% of caregivers report migrating with their children—the majority of parents migrate first and then send for their children afterward. Most youths in the study experienced separation from a caregiver, some for extended periods of time. Once separated, youths reported forming new bonds and networks with kin and friends who were charged to care for them in the absence of their parent or primary caregiver. These new relationships are also ruptured once the child migrated (Ko & Perreira, 2010).

Potochnik and Perreira (2010) also examined the unique migration and acculturation experiences of first-generation Latino adolescents and how these experiences contribute to mental health outcomes such as anxiety and depression, using LAMHA data. Seven percent of youths were symptomatic for depression and had been living in the United States on average for four and a half years. The investigators examined the number of years separated from the primary caregiver as a stressor, along with acculturation, documentation status, involvement in migration experience, experience of trauma during migration, dissatisfaction with migration, and discrimination, as well as the presence of social supports and optimism. In unadjusted models, the odds of depression increased significantly with the level of dissatisfaction and dissimilar documentation status (i.e., at least one parent was documented and child was not), respectively. In fully adjusted models, the most salient, statistically significant factors that protected against depression were increased *familismo*, teacher support, and length of time in the United States.

Support from the family and school environments can foment resilience in youths affected by the immigration experience (Sharabany & Israeli, 2008). *Familismo*, referring to the "importance of strong family loyalty and getting along with and contributing to the well-being of the nuclear family, extended family, and kinship networks," can be measured as an indicator of solid family ties (Ayon, Marsiglia, & Bermudez-Parsal, 2010, p. 745). Thus, more important than the stressors themselves in predicting depression is the presence or absence of supports, both from the family and school environments, after controlling for all other covariates. Support stemming from a range of social networks (such as the family, school, and community) can aid immigrant youths in dealing with the difficulties of separation, loss, and loneliness and provide opportunities for connection and resilience (Salehi, 2010).

Although not consistently found to be a significant factor in predicting depression, immigration patterns may lead to prolonged periods of separation and disrupt the family nucleus (Rivera, Guarnaccia, Mulvaney-Day, Lin, Torres, & Alegria, 2008). The family as a unit and its corresponding individuals experience upheavals in their social networks and family cohesion. The subsequent reorganization of the family structure creates a new network or system even if the same family members are involved (Suárez-Orozco, Todorova, & Louis, 2002).

Alternatively, family cohesion may protect parents from depression, which in turn protects youths, as depression of a parent increases the risk of poor mental health outcomes for their children. Leidy, Guerra, and Toro (2010) point to the centrality of the family in Latino culture and the potential role of families in promoting reliance for their children growing up in conditions of adversity. Strengthening the family fabric may be particularly important for Latino immigrant youths, as it can promote resilience in the face of the developmental challenges of adolescence, complicated by the immigration experience.

CONCLUSION: AN ECOLOGICAL PERSPECTIVE ON LATINO IMMIGRANT YOUTHS' MENTAL HEALTH

An ecological perspective of the immigrant experience allows for the examination of elements in the microsystem(s), such as the family, and the macrosystem(s), such as the school environment, the community, and society at large, that influence outcomes for the individual embedded in these systems. Using an ecological perspective, researchers have examined the role of *familismo* and experiences of discrimination on internalizing mental health symptoms among first-generation Latino parents and their second-generation offspring (Ayon et al., 2010).

The Latino Acculturation and Health Project's (cited in Ko & Perreira, 2010) data on the mental health, acculturation, and demographic information from 150 families residing along the U.S.-Mexico border provide a wealth of useful information. The majority of parents (83%) were from Mexico, and 56% of youths were born in the United States, while 22% had been residing in the United States between one and five years, and 19% six or more years. The investigators measured depression in parents and internalizing symptoms (defined as anxiety, withdrawn depression, and somatic complaints) in youths.

The results indicated that increased *familismo* predicted decreased internalizing symptoms for youths, after controlling for gender, age, length of time in the United States, and perceived discrimination, as well as parental characteristics. *Familismo* was also a protective factor against depression in immigrant parents.

Increasing immigrant generation status may be a significant risk factor for depressive symptoms, along with other factors associated with suicidal behaviors, such as substance and alcohol use by country of origin or heritage (Peña et al., 2008). This may be explained by problematic family dynamics resulting from acculturation dissimilarities between youths and their caregivers. Familial conflicts during the reunification and reintegration processes, along with acculturative dissonance (defined when youths acculturate more rapidly or take on less-traditional norms) between youths and parents, may exacerbate psychological distress and moderate the beneficial effects of family cohesion.

Cespedes and Huey (2008) frame their examination of depression in Latino adolescents from a cultural discrepancy perspective, which they define as the gap between acculturation and gender-role disparity between children and their parents. Cultural discrepancy suggests family dysfunction. Familial conflict originating from clashes over gender norms and expectations between immigrant youths and their parents or caregivers may be particularly salient for Latina adolescents compared to their male peers.

Thus, gender is also a significant factor in mental health outcomes for immigrant youths. Latina adolescents in particular may be at higher risk for poor mental health outcomes, including depression and suicide. Latinas in highly cohesive families have been found to be significantly less likely to have attempted suicide compared with those in less-cohesive families (Peña et al., 2011; Williams, 2010).

Judy's story illustrates the risk of depression in a young Latina adolescent. Judy's expectation of close family ties, emotional and physical, suggested by the concept of *familismo*, may have been violated by what she referred to as her parents sending her away, banishing her from the security, warmth, and love of home. Judy's experience of her aunt's home, where she described herself in Cinderella-like terms as being treated as an inferior to her aunt's biological children, is likely to have represented a further betrayal of *familismo*.

Judy may well have been witness to the fraying of *familismo* as a transcultural concept. Parental ambition, rather than traditional allegiance to the cultural construct of *familismo*, resulted in Judy's being sent abroad to further her education and advance her opportunities. In New York, *familismo* revealed itself to be further frayed; Judy did not experience the warm embrace of a family who would take her in as their own, but rather experienced herself as a burden, unloved and uncared for in comparison with her cousins. Judy returned to her family in the Dominican Republic that summer and failed to return to her United States high school in the fall. It is unknown whether she continued her schooling at home. We can assume that the prospect of again losing family overwhelmed Judy's and possibly her family's ambitions.

Although consideration of the role of ambition in transnational migration is beyond the scope of this chapter, it presents clear challenges to the social and cultural construct of *familismo*. Latino transnational families may well reside at the nexus of *familismo*, ambition, gender, and global migration patterns. In sending Judy abroad to study and advance her opportunities, Judy's family privileged ambition for their daughter over a more traditional trajectory that calls for staying close to home, early marriage, and family formation. This represents a change on the cultural horizon for possibilities for girls, challenging traditional expectations for women and for the role of family.

Global patterns of migration further serve to introduce change to cultural traditions sedimented in geography or land, language, and ritual. Transnational families, who move between different cultural landscapes, begin to incorporate new cultural assumptions. The tension between ambition—for oneself and for one's immediate family—and *familismo*, which assumes a broader definition of extended family, may well have found its expression in Judy's experience with her busy, financially stretched extended family, living in a cramped New York apartment.

Latino immigrant youths from transnational families may well be at the nexus of deep cultural change regarding gender, personal ambition, the meaning and place of family and language. Change contains loss; the phenomenon of depression in immigrant youths, especially in Latino youths, may signal rapid changes in family structure and cultural assumptions. Emotional well-being of immigrant youth, however, need not and should not serve as a barometer of social and cultural change.

REFERENCES

Ayon, C., Marsiglia, F., & Bermudez-Parsal, M. (2010). Latino family mental health: Exploring the role of discrimination and familismo. *Journal of Community Psychology, 38*(6), 742–756.

Cespedes, Y., & Huey S., Jr. (2008). Depression in Latino adolescents: A cultural discrepancy perspective. *Cultural Diversity & Ethnic Minority Psychology, 14*(2), 168–172.

Garcia, C., & Lindgren, S. (2009). Life grows between the rocks: Latino adolescents' and parents' perspectives on mental health stressors. *Research in Nursing and Health, 32*(2), 148–162.

Jensen, L. A. (2008). Immigrants' cultural identities as sources of civic engagement. *Applied Developmental Science, 12*, 74–83.

Ko, L. K., & Perreira, K. M. (2010). "It turned my world upside down": Latino youth's perspectives on immigration. *Journal of Adolescent Research, 25*(3), 465–493.

Leidy, M. S., Guerra, N. G., & Toro, R. I. J. (2010). Positive parenting, family cohesion, and child social competence among immigrant Latino families. *Family Psychology, 24*(3), 252–260.

Peña, J. B, Kuhlberg, J. A., Zayas, L. H., Baumann, A. A., Gulbas, L., Hausmann-Stabile, C., & Nolle, A. P. (2011). Familism, family environment, and suicide attempts among Latina youth. *Suicide Life Threat Behavior, 41*(3), 330–341.

Peña, J. B., Wyman, P. A., Hendricks Brown, C., Matthieu, M. M., Olivares, T. E., Hartel, D., & Zayas, L. H. (2008). Immigration, generation status, and its association with suicide attempts, substance use, and depressive symptoms among Latino adolescents in the USA. *Prevention Science, 9*, 299–310.

Potochnick, S., & Perreira, K. M. (2010). Depression and anxiety among first generation immigrant Latino youth: Key correlates and implications for future research. *Journal of Nervous and Mental Diseases, 198*(7), 470–477.

Ries Merikangas, He, J., Burstein, M., Swanson, S., Avenevoli, S., Benjet, C., . . . Swendsen, J. (2010). Lifetime prevalence of mental disorders in U.S. adolescents: Results from the National Comorbidity Study-Adolescent Supplement (NCS-A). *Journal of the American Academy of Child Adolescent Psychiatry, 49*(10), 980–989.

Rivera, F., Guarnaccia, P. J., Mulvaney-Day, N., Lin, J. Y., Torres, M., & Alegria, M. (2008). Family cohesion and its relationship to psychological distress among Latino groups. *Hispanic Journal of Behavioral Sciences, 30*(3), 357–378.

Salehi, R. (2010). Intersection of health, immigration and youth: A systematic literature review. *Journal of Immigrant and Minority Health, 12*, 788–797.

Saluja, G., Iachan, R., Scheidt, P., Overpeck, M., Sun, W., & Giedd, J. (2004). Prevalence of and risk factors for depressive symptoms among young adolescents. *Archives Pediatric and Adolescent Medicine, 158*, 760–765.

Sharabany, R., & Israeli, E. (2008). The dual process of adolescent immigration and relocation: From country to country and from childhood to adolescence—Its reflection in psychodynamic psychotherapy. *Psychoanalytic Study of the Child, 63*, 137–162.

Suárez-Orozco, C., Bang, H. G., & Kim, H. Y. (2011). I felt like my heart was staying behind: Psychological implications of family separations and reunifications for immigrant youth. *Journal of Adolescent Research, 26*, 222–257.

Suárez-Orozco, C., Suárez-Orozco, M., & Todorova, T. (2008). *Learning a new land: Immigrant children in American society.* Cambridge, MA: Harvard University Press.

Suárez-Orozco, C., Todorov, I. L., & Louie, J. (2002). Making up for lost time: The experience of separation and reunification among immigrant families. *Family Process, 41*, 625–643.

Substance Abuse and Mental Health Services Administration (SAMHSA). (2009). Results from the 2008 National Survey on Drug Use and Health: National Findings (Office of Applied Studies, NSDUH Series H-36, HHS Publication No. SMA 09-4434). Rockville, MD

Williams, S. M. (2010). The relationship among family cohesion, gender, level of acculturation, and depression in Latino adolescents. Ethnic NewsWatch. ProQuest Dissertation and Theses.

9

Psychological Vulnerability in Second Language Learning

Alexandra Ponce de León-LeBec and Alberto M. Bursztyn

Children who live between two language worlds experience a particular form of tension. They become attuned to the gap between the language of home and that of the external world, represented most powerfully by the language of school. This communication challenge is not simply a matter of mastering a new code; it also implies crossing a cultural divide. Although most children acquire the second language relatively easily as they seek social acceptance and academic success, some children encounter greater difficulty because of their reticence to make the cultural shift. For them, the process of learning the national language presents added psychological risk. The vignette that follows illustrates psychological and identity issues emerging from family dynamics and cultural ambivalence.

CASE VIGNETTE: SILVINA

Silvina (a pseudonym) sits at her desk and distracts herself with various objects in front of her, none of which are related to the task at hand. Her teacher approaches and asks her what she has learned about ants, the current topic of research. Silvina proceeds to read a paragraph from the book, and the teacher tells her to "put it in her own words" and walks away. As the teacher leaves, Silvina looks at her neighbor, pouts, and says, "What she say?" Later, during the whole class lesson, Silvina appears disengaged and hesitant. At times, she seems to want to answer a question, but when called on, she recoils and shakes her head, "no."

Silvina is a petite third-grader who wears her long black hair in a ponytail. She is a Spanish-dominant child in a dual-language general education class and is in many ways representative of a large number of students in her majority Latino school, for whom English is neither their first nor their preferred language. She came to the attention of the school's intervention team by her teachers who reported that she was often "zoned out" in class and gave "odd" answers, which suggests she had very little understanding of what they considered to be routine questions. She was also performing below grade level across all academic areas. Questions of speech and language problems or more significant psychiatric problems were raised, and she was ultimately referred for a formal psychoeducational evaluation.

Silvina lives with her biological mother and father. Neither parent has formal education; their English language skills are very weak. She is the only child currently living in the home; her four older siblings reside in their home country, the Dominican Republic, with the maternal grandparents. An aunt and three older cousins also reside in the home. Silvina's relationship with the family abroad is maintained via Skype and weekly telephone calls; she also travels to the Dominican Republic with her mother and spends summers with the extended family. Every year she returns to school toward the end of September. Silvina is the first of her family to be born in the United States, and despite her limited skills, she often serves as the translator for the family. However, on the days that Silvina knows class will be conducted entirely in English, she makes excuses for not going to school; she has been late or absent many times since entering kindergarten. The parents do not seem to object to her staying at home when she "doesn't feel well."

Evaluation results suggest that Silvina is reluctant to engage in English language activities and gets "annoyed" when people speak to her in English; she obtained a score of "intermediate" on the state's English language proficiency exam, which is one level up from "beginner." Either a cause or an outcome of her resistance to English, her reading and writing skills in English are very low. Her skills in Spanish are much more developed; she communicates in that language effectively and with ease. However, in English, Silvina presents as shy and gives up quickly when she cannot express herself. She also showed signs of anxiety and discomfort at being the center of attention. Her teacher reports that when Silvina broke her ankle and had to use crutches, she shunned her classmates' sympathetic overtures, feeling like she was being made fun of, rather than receiving the support that her peers intended.

The evaluation resulted in a classification of learning disability and the provision of special education support services for all academic areas, bilingually, for five periods a week.

Although often overlooked, children's native languages and cultures have profound effects on their psychological development and patterns of performance in school. In 2009, U.S. public schools registered 11.2 million students identified as speaking a language other than English in the home, representing 20% of the total student body and nearly a threefold increase from 1980. Of those 11.2 million, one-quarter spoke English with "some difficulty" (U.S. DOE, 2011). The data are unequivocal on the academic outcomes of English language learners (ELLs). On average ELLs consistently underperform on various academic measures, such as achievement tests, grade point average, dropout rates, and college attendance compared with their English-speaking peers.

Across the United States, when 70% of non-ELLs met statewide standards for math proficiency, 70% of ELLs did not (National Center for Education Statistics, 2011). In New York City, which is ranked fifth in the country by percentage of ELL students, only 39% of ELLs graduated from high school in 2009 and 19% dropped out along the way. Certainly language barriers are one component to the lower achievement noted among ELLs, but tracking procedures disproportionately affect ELLs. In secondary schools, they are often placed in lower-level remedial classes for multiple periods per day. Because remedial classes do not count toward graduation requirements, they contribute to the expanding educational gap (Koelsch, 2006)

Interrupted schooling or premature drop out in their country of origin adds complexity to immigrant students' educational needs. For example, in New York City, 10% of ELLs are classified as students with interrupted formal education (SIFE). When these students enter school in the United States, they may be placed on the basis of age, but some of them may have no school experiences or they may have had only sporadic schooling opportunities in their home countries. With little prior experience, minimal literacy, and often complicated immigration histories, they are faced with even greater challenges within the U.S. education system and achieve even lower rates of academic success than non-SIFE ELLs (Advocates for Children, 2010).

LANGUAGE LEARNING IN SOCIAL CONTEXTS

Although immigrant children often enter school with high levels of engagement, aspiration, and optimism, the pattern of achievement often falls short. Although new immigrants tend to be academically motivated, over the long term, length of residence is associated with decreases in academic achievement and aspirations, which Suárez-Orozco, Rhodes, and Milburn (2009) refer to as the "immigrant paradox." This decline is likely related to acculturation stress, including the discrimination, hostility, violence, and economic stressors that immigrant children disproportionately experience at school and in their neighborhoods. The psychological impact of negatively ascribed characteristics undermines academic achievement and emotional development.

Social mirroring, a term originally described by the British psychoanalyst D. W. Winnicott (1971), posits that the child's sense of self is deeply impacted by the way significant others in his or her environment respond to, and "reflect" back, their beliefs about him or her. For many immigrants, minority children, and adolescents, the image that is reflected back to them is dangerously negative. Young children in their elementary years are already able to pick up cues from the dominant culture that they are considered inferior. When immigrant youths were asked to complete the sentence, "Most Americans think that [people from my country] are . . . ," 82% of youngsters from the Dominican Republic, 80% of Haitians, 75% of Mexicans, 64% of Central Americans, and 47% of Chinese respondents filled in the blank with negative answers. For example, a 14-year-old boy from Mexico said, "Most Americans think we are lazy, gangsters, drug addicts that only come to take their jobs away"; a 10-year-old Haitian girl responded, "Most Americans think that we are stupid" (Suárez-Orozco & Suárez-Orozco, 2001).

The concept of social mirroring is relevant to understanding the perils of acculturation and the increasing disengagement from school. Academic experiences, when associated with negative expectations and stereotypes, may doom not only students' achievement but also their self-concept. Having teachers who resemble the children's parents and speak their languages adds credence to their desire for success. But all teachers, regardless of race and bilingual abilities, can play a pivotal role in communicating warmth, acceptance, and high expectations. In fact, the positive relationship with educators who represent the American mainstream in the eyes of immigrant children communicates the strongest message that they will be respected, accepted, and loved in the new social context.

Alternatively, schools and institutions where negative stereotypes and discrimination exist contribute to lowered expectations and patterns of academic disengagement. Schools reflect the larger society and constitute a microcosm of it; therefore, some children may face psychological difficulties in developing a healthy self-concept and internalizing expectations of mastery and competence (Bursztyn, 2003). Unfortunately, many teachers resent the fact that they have to teach children whose first language is not English. They reflect the feelings of broader society that these children are less intelligent, lazy, and unlikely to achieve much in their lives compared with their English-speaking peers. It is a great challenge for students to demonstrate their full potential in their weaker language; to do so in front of teachers who believe they simply do not have it in them leads not only to academic failure but also to psychologically destructive consequences.

Academic achievement is tightly woven with language proficiency; however, second language acquisition can be a difficult and unpredictable process that depends on many factors both within the individual and in the environment in which the learning takes place. Learning takes place at home, at school, and, importantly, in informal situations with peers. As the case of Silvina shows, some ELLs may be reluctant to learn English, because their home life and social networks are conducted largely, if not exclusively, in their native language. In certain cases, children and adolescents may resist using English in response to a feeling of not belonging and not being welcomed by the mainstream culture. In other cases, schools may not foster an environment conducive to attaining second language skills.

The idea of the social context of language learning is complex and multidirectional. The student's socioeconomic status, race, neighborhood, school, and family composition all affect this learning, and each of these factors is not easily disentangled from the next. The school is arguably one of the most important contexts in which learning takes place, and not surprisingly, the lower the quality of the school, as measured by proficiency scores on the high-stakes English language arts assessments, the lower the language proficiency of its ELL population. ELLs tend to reside in urban areas where the schools also tend to have greater numbers of students from low-income families, whose own resources and education levels affect the student's academic engagement and success settings (National Center for Education Statistics, 2011). Inequities in funding mechanisms in public education will continue to perpetuate immigrant student underachievement, thereby complicating an already difficult transition to U.S. culture.

When the environment in which the student is expected to learn English is less than ideal, many newcomers or children of immigrants will never acquire sufficient proficiency in English in order to keep pace with their English-speaking classmates. After seven years in the United States, only 7% of immigrant students in a large longitudinal study scored at or above the mean for English proficiency. Furthermore, according to 2004 data from the National Center for Education Statistics, 51% of language-minority students did not complete high school, compared with just 10% of monolingual English-speaking students (Carhill, Suárez-Orozco, & Paez, 2008). Carhill et al. (2008) concluded that 75% of the variation in standardized assessment scores could be predicted by factors such as family structure, language proficiency, and academic engagement, but language proficiency accounted for six times the variation of all other variables combined. These statistics show that not only are many immigrant children failing in school, but also that many may be doing so because of limited language proficiency, compounded by demographic variables beyond the child's control.

At the crux of immigrant self-image and social mirroring is the issue of the legal status of the student and the student's family. Though unauthorized immigrants represent only one-quarter of the immigrant population in the United States, they receive a disproportionate amount of overwhelmingly negative attention from policymakers and media outlets. Although a relatively small number of immigrants are unauthorized, more than five million students in the public school system come from unauthorized families; one million of the students are unauthorized themselves (Suárez-Orozco, Yoshikawa, Teranishi, & Suárez-Orozco, 2011).

For these millions of children, they may experience even more difficulty connecting with school, in part for fear of revealing their immigration status or that of their parents. Furthermore, research shows that unauthorized individuals endure many more challenges than other immigrants. For example, they are more likely to suffer poor working conditions, have lower levels of education, and be denied access to many resources that would promote their children's development, thereby excluding them from engaging with their children and their children's schools (Suárez-Orozco et al., 2011).

Such support is an important element in developing a child's academic skills and sense of competence. Suárez-Orozco et al. (2009) describe the importance of academic self-efficacy, or the belief that one is capable of achievement, in promoting academic success and language proficiency. However, this presents somewhat of a catch-22, because they also found that language proficiency is a crucial factor in positive school adjustment and self-confidence. What emerges is something of a vicious cycle in which language proficiency, social competence, and academic self-confidence may never fully develop.

Of course, schools play a critical role in fostering the self-efficacy that is so important to future success, linguistically and academically, starting as early as preschool. In one study, it was found that pre-school ELLs developed better social skills and enjoyed closer relationships with their teachers in classrooms in which the teacher spoke at least some Spanish. These children were also less likely to be victims of aggression (Chang et al., 2007). Appropriate language supports for ELLs can buffer against the negative outcomes of being a language minority student in an English-only classroom. Unfortunately, many schools do not adhere to well-researched and well-implemented bilingual programs, and many students do not receive the language support they need.

Where formal schooling does not advance language proficiency, research suggests that for language minority students, the greatest gains in language acquisition can be made through use of English in *informal* settings. The amount of English spoken in informal settings is positively related to English language proficiency (Carhill et al., 2008). Social relationships not only allow for opportunities to engage in English, but they also provide emotional support, a sense of community, and access to invaluable information that is shared between speakers (Suárez-Orozco et al., 2009). Social relationships have also been found to reduce behavioral problems and increase academic engagement. Children and adolescents are social beings, so this might seem like an easy fix; however, the reality is that the schools that immigrant children typically attend are plagued by racial and linguistic segregation, school violence, and limited positive and consistent role models. In these settings, ethnic and racial groups may remain segregated, with fewer opportunities to engage in cross-cultural or cross-linguistic exchange. Older children, especially, may exhibit a greater reluctance to embrace English, but as seen in the case of Silvina, this resistance is apparent in younger children as well.

Clearly there are many factors that contribute to the academic, behavioral, and socioemotional difficulties that immigrant children disproportionately endure, but there are just as many points of intervention to mitigate these influences (Korn & Bursztyn, 2002). This grim picture of the immigrant experience in U.S. schools does not represent the experiences of all immigrant students. Many thrive despite the odds stacked against them. It is as important to study these students as it is to study the institutional and societal barriers to success.

LANGUAGE LEARNING AND PSYCHOSOCIAL DIFFICULTIES

The process of learning a second language is not only about phonics, syntax, and vocabulary, but it also involves acculturation. While the social context in which learning takes place is central to linguistic and academic success, individual characteristics of the youngster, along with the circumstances surrounding immigration, also significantly affect language learning and social adjustment. In some instances, social interactions may be limited due to shyness, lack of motivation, or specific disabilities intrinsic to the student.

ELLs are often in the process of assimilating a new language and culture and may be experiencing some degree of culture shock, social trauma, and emotional predicaments (Bursztyn, 2003). For some children, their entry into the U.S. school system may be their first experience with formal education or with individuals from the mainstream culture. Not knowing the language or customs creates an understandably distressing and challenging situation. Sadness, anguish, and anger may be masked and controlled, but it is not uncommon that emotional turmoil eventually becomes a major obstacle to school success and social adjustment (Bursztyn, 2003).

For children with unauthorized status or who live in families in which one or more members are unauthorized, the inevitable recognition of the precariousness of their situation can affect their self-esteem, increase anxiety, and lead to other internalizing symptoms (Suárez-Orozco et al., 2011). These feelings of alienation and confusion may manifest as social isolation, reticence, or withdrawal, which limit the student's opportunities to engage in meaningful social interactions with their peers. Research indicates that the most successful learners of a new language are those who communicate frequently in social situations with native language speakers (Toppleberg, Snow, & Tager-Flusberg, 1999). Social and communicative difficulties may be compounded if the school environment is hostile toward minority students and devalues or negates the experiences they may have had.

In addition to coping with the stress of acculturation, children of most traditional cultural backgrounds are expected, both at home and at school, to be quiet and respectful around adults, embodying a style of being that is generally at odds with the culture in most schools in the United States. In school, they are often misunderstood as disengaged, passive, and even passively hostile and are described as excessively shy and withdrawn by their teachers (Bursztyn, 2003). As these expectations morph into self-fulfilling prophecies, these students may always remain in the back, literally and figuratively, of the class. Children who are isolated in their environment are at risk for language and social problems, becoming social outcasts, having lower self-esteem, and being perceived by their teachers as unmotivated, slow, shy, and anxious.

Language difficulties are associated with negative social and academic outcomes. Although the existing research on this topic largely deals with children with specific language impairments (SLIs), closer examination suggests that the experience of being a language minority, where linguistic comprehension and expression are affected, may mimic in many ways the experience of having an SLI. Individuals with SLIs experience difficulties in various domains of communication, either in their ability to express themselves or their ability to understand what others are trying to verbally communicate to them (American Psychiatric Association, 2013). SLI affects academic as well as social performance. For example, children with SLIs are believed to avoid social interactions that tax their communication abilities, tending to withdraw and engage in more solitary activities. They are also believed to have difficulties processing language, such that their speed and capacity to process and respond to language are compromised (Hart, Fujiki, Brinton, & Hart, 2004). These behaviors impede the child's ability to develop and engage in many social behaviors that are important to successful peer interactions.

Taking another look at the literature on ELLs, many cognitive and behavioral similarities can be noted. ELLs may exhibit withdrawn or reticent behaviors as a way to mask their lack of comprehension. Like children with SLIs, they tend to fear being called on or to read aloud in class, which would reveal their language difficulties. Like the processing difficulties described above for children with SLIs, language processing in the second language is also slower, more laborious, and not reliably effective (Bursztyn, 2003). Like Silvina, when her teacher walked away, leaving her confused and at a loss for how to continue, the ELL child may resort to tuning out and avoid academic tasks where their language skills are required and observed. Although the communication style of ELLs may resemble that of children with SLIs, it is critically important to clarify that their communication difference does not necessarily constitute a communication disorder. What it does constitute is an additional context in which learning (social, linguistic, and academic) may be inhibited as a means of mitigating anxiety and saving face.

Children who are shy or anxious tend to show less overt motivation to learn a new language, which results in less developed language skills compared with their more outgoing peers (Toppleberg et al., 1999). Silvina described situations in which people spoke to her in English to be "annoying"; her reaction may be understood as motivated by a desire to avoid difficult interactions. Selective mutism (SM) is an extreme response to situations that the child finds extremely anxiety producing and alienating. SM, as defined in the fifth edition of the *Diagnostic and Statistical Manual of Mental Disorders*, is characterized by a refusal to speak in specific social settings, despite being able to speak in other less anxiety-ridden situations (American Psychiatric Association, 2013).

Anxious immigrant and language minority children are actually more likely to develop SM compared to their nonimmigrant peers. The higher rates of SM among immigrant children is believed to be related to the higher levels of anxiety associated with acculturation and pervasive feelings of alienation. A youngster with a shy-inhibited personality type is at even greater risk (Elizalde-Utnick, 2007). International data appear to support the fact that immigrants are more prone to developing SM. Rates of SM among immigrant populations have been found to range from three to 13 times higher than the nonimmigrant average (Toppleberg, Tabors, Coggins, Lum, & Burger, 2005). SM impacts the child's ability to be successful in school, as an SM child is typically unwilling to participate in class and socialize with peers.

Elizalde-Utnick (2007) observes that SM children often stand or sit rigidly and with little expressed emotion, avoid eye contact, and stare vacantly when asked questions. Additionally, they exhibit heightened sensitivity to sensory input as well as difficulty with social routines involving expressive language. To the uninformed observer, these behaviors may be misleading, serving only to create or reinforce faulty beliefs that ELLs and immigrant students are noncompliant, lazy, less intelligent, and unmotivated. However, this disorder must be understood as an extreme response to acculturative stress, and this highlights the need for emotional supports to help the child adjust to a new and challenging environment.

LANGUAGE LEARNING AND ACADEMIC SUCCESS: MISUNDERSTANDINGS AND MISDIAGNOSES

Culturally and linguistically diverse (CLD) children may present in schools in a manner very similar to students with various learning, speech and language, and emotional disabilities. Up to now, this chapter has focused on the actual learning challenges that immigrants and ELLs encounter, and in this section, more attention will be given to the circumstances under which normal language acquisition is falsely attributed to disability (Lopez & Bursztyn, 2013).

Learning disabilities are diagnosed when the student's academic achievement in reading, writing, or math is significantly below what would be expected based on cognitive potential, years of schooling, and chronological age. If the child's level of cognitive functioning falls within the average range and the child has had access to high-quality instruction *and* the difficulties are not better attributed to limited English proficiency or other cultural factors (American Psychiatric Association, 2013), then the child may be said to be potentially exhibiting a learning disability. A central tenet in bilingual assessment of disability is to determine whether the problem persists in both the child's native language and English. If the student only experiences difficulty following directions, reading, or communicating effectively in English, and if in their home language the problems are not present, then it can be deduced that the difficulties are better attributed to language proficiency than to permanent disability. Ruling out language proficiency prior to diagnosing a learning disability is not only a clinical consideration but also a legal mandate as well.

Despite such mandates, the overrepresentation of CLD students in special education is a problem in schools across the country. Specifically, ELLs are more likely to receive classifications of mental retardation, learning disabled, and emotionally disturbed. Interestingly, ELLs in English-only classrooms are three times more likely to be placed in special education settings than ELLs in bilingual education settings (Rhodes, Ochoa, & Ortiz, 2005). This finding points to the possibility that it is the educational environment that is resulting in the *disabling* conditions under which the student is not allowed to demonstrate his true capabilities. Rhodes et al. (2005) also report that of the top-10 reasons for referral for ELLs—poor achievement, behavioral problems, expressive language difficulties, poor reading, poor written language, specific learning difficulties, socioemotional difficulties, disability diagnosis, limited attention span, inability to understand and follow directions—fully seven of these common reasons can be reasonably attributed to language or cultural differences. Too often special education services are viewed as a way to discharge students from general education programs that do not meet the unique needs of ELLs.

It is a challenge to discern linguistic differences from learning disabilities because a lack of English language proficiency impedes the ability to access and appropriately respond to the general education curriculum. Common features of ELLs indeed can be troubling to the untrained eye. It is important to recognize the key features with regard to the manifestation of linguistic, social, and academic difficulties, but rather view them as typical and understandable hallmarks of the acculturation and second language learning process. When prereferral teams are trained on these issues, the number of referrals of CLD students is significantly reduced (Rhodes et al., 2005). Unfortunately, there remains a great disparity between the number of culturally competent providers and the number of multicultural students who would benefit from their expertise.

Apparent similarities between linguistic differences, learning disabilities, and speech and language disorders certainly pose a challenge to providers attempting to explain a student's behavior. It is important to reiterate these distinctions, as communication-based difficulties may be the most obvious area of difficulty for ELLs and is therefore a common source of misdiagnosis. The ELL student may manifest as producing limited speech, using gestures or minimal words, refusing to answer questions or volunteer information, exhibiting trouble with comprehension and recall, experiencing difficulty sequencing, confusing similar words, and more that could all be misconstrued as a speech and language disability rather than language acquisition (Rhodes et al., 2005). The critical difference is that for a child to be diagnosed with a true communication disorder, he or she must have communication deficits in both the native language and English.

Behavioral problems have also emerged as a common, and commonly misunderstood, source of difficulty for ELL students and their teachers. Examples of behavioral difficulties range from passivity and withdrawal to attention and memory problems, hyperactivity, and acting out. Passivity and withdrawal are often related to social difficulties associated with limited language proficiency and the stress associated with acculturation. Apparent attention and memory problems may also be seen as the student struggles to fully understand classroom lectures and may appear to "forget" information from one day to the next. On the other hand, lacking the linguistic mastery to navigate peer interactions, some ELLs may react impulsively or aggressively in school. This is especially true for younger students who have little or no prior experience with formal education or supervised peer interactions (Bursztyn, 2003).

Finally, lower academic performance is frequently misidentified as individual disability. When students fail to master a new concept, there are a host of reasons to explain it before assuming that the student has a learning disability. First and foremost, the language proficiency must be assessed, followed by the student's background knowledge, degree of motivation, and socioemotional state, which may all be affecting the child's ability to attend to and learn in the classroom. Prior to conducting formal assessment, the social contexts of home, school, and neighborhood must be accounted for. Other critical factors include parental involvement, access to resources, and high-quality instruction prior to assessment. When it is obvious that a student is struggling in school, providers must determine whether the difficulties are better attributed to limited English proficiency or other cultural issues, so as not to add another statistic in the overrepresentation of minorities in special education.

ELLs also run the risk of being *under*identified for special education services when school personnel falsely attribute all difficulties to cultural or linguistic issues. This too is a great disservice to the student in need (Bursztyn, 2003). For students wrongly placed in restrictive special education settings and for students wrongly determined to not have a disability, their future educational successes are equally jeopardized (Bursztyn, 2011).

CONCLUSION

The relation between second language learning and academic and social difficulties is a complex and dynamic web. Multiple interconnected contextual influences interact with the child's abilities, needs, and desires. Contextually, the language acquisition process begins the moment the immigrant child or adolescent is born into, or arrives in, a place laden with cultural stereotypes and expectations about who the child is, which can affect the trajectory of the child's educational and emotional experience as a cultural or linguistic minority. Systemic barriers, such as the safety of the neighborhood, quality of the schools, and access to community resources, set the stage for the degree to which the child will or will not find the support and encouragement in school and in social relationships that foster success.

Being a member of a linguistic minority in school is a challenge that millions of youngsters face. The data overwhelmingly show lower performance on achievement tests, higher dropout rates, and a lower likelihood of pursuing higher education among this population. Many factors contribute to this education gap, with limited language proficiency at the core. With few multicultural providers and still nascent research on the needs of this vulnerable population, many students continue to be misunderstood and overrepresented in special education. The learning difficulties that ELLs experience are real, but the interventions are lagging behind the need (Lopez & Bursztyn, 2013).

ELLs need opportunities to engage in high-quality linguistic interactions with native speakers, and they need access to mental health services when they experience emotional distress. Schools have to better understand the needs of this diverse, resilient, yet vulnerable population. Too often schools try to make students fit into the programs they have, rather than create the programs they need. Silvina exhibited many typical features of a child in the process of learning a second language, such as stronger skills in the native language, avoidance of English, and anxiety in social situations. Her psychoeducational evaluation found her cognitive ability to be within the average range. She possessed average literacy skills in Spanish, but was unable to crack the code to even the most basic sound structures in English. Without this foundation, she cannot be expected to read or write with any proficiency.

Silvina's skills in math were weaker than her literacy skills and significantly discrepant from her measured level of cognitive functioning; therefore, the classification of learning disability was justified. Her individualized educational program (IEP) included recommendations for providing extra time to answer orally, additional phonics instruction in English, and access to key topics and questions before engaging in group discussions so she would have the opportunity to plan her response before being called on. These were sound recommendations, but the school overlooked the central role of social language. Silvina has participated in the dual-language program in her school for four years, yet she has not become proficient nor more engaged in the English language. She has shy and anxious tendencies, and she would benefit from organized but casual situations in which she could practice English with her peers, away from the pressures of the classroom. The IEP made no recommendations for her socioemotional development—despite its implication in language development.

Immigrant children and U.S.-born minorities live a binary existence, a constant pull between the old and the new—the country they or their parents came from and the country they now call home. They live in two worlds, with two languages, and two identities that are often at odds with each other. In many ways, Silvina embodies the tension between these worlds. She presents as a talkative and friendly girl in Spanish, but shy, and halting in English. She is the reluctant family's interpreter who prefers not to speak English. She still seeks shelter from the stressful English-speaking world in the comfort of the mother tongue and the undemanding environment of home. Her journey into English and academic competence continues to be burdened by her parents' ambivalence toward the host society and the school's apparent indifference to her lack of social engagement.

REFERENCES

Advocates for Children. (2010). More than a statistic: Faces of the local diploma: A call to create pathways to graduation for all students. Retrieved from http://www

.advocatesforchildren.org/sites/default/files/library/more_than_a_statistic_policy report2010.pdf?pt=1.

American Psychiatric Association. (2013). *Diagnostic and statistical manual of mental disorders* (5th ed.). Washington, DC: Author.

Bursztyn, A. M. (2003). Psychological vistas on pre-referral interventions for culturally and linguistically diverse students. In M. Lupi & G. Rivera (Eds.), *A monograph on prereferral intervention strategies for linguistically and culturally diverse students* (pp. 39–67). New York: New York State Education/Office of Vocational and Educational Services for Individuals with Disabilities.

Bursztyn, A. M. (2011). *Childhood psychological disorders: Current controversies.* Westport, CT: Praeger.

Carhill, A., Suárez-Orozco, C., & Paez, M. (2008). Explaining English language proficiency among adolescent immigrant students. *American Educational Research Journal, 45*(4), 1155–1179.

Chang, F., Crawford, G., Early, D., Bryant, D., Howes, C., Burchinal, M., . . . Pianta, R. (2007). Spanish-speaking childrens' social and language development in prekindergarten classrooms. *Early Education and Development, 18*(2), 243–269.

Elizalde-Utnick, G. (2007). Young selectively mute English language learners: School-based intervention strategies. *Journal of Early Childhood and Infant Psychology, 3,* 143–163.

Hart, K. I., Fujiki, M., Brinton, B., & Hart, C. H. (2004). The relationship between social behavior and severity of language impairment. *Journal of Speech, Language & Hearing Research, 47,* 647–663.

Korn, C., & Bursztyn A. M. (Eds.). (2002). *Rethinking multicultural education: Case studies in cultural transition.* New Haven, CT: Bergin and Garvey.

Lopez, E., & Bursztyn, A. M. (2013). Future challenges and opportunities: Toward culturally responsive training in school psychology. *Psychology in the Schools, 50*(3), 212–228.

National Center for Education Statistics. (2011). Fast Facts: ELL participation in education. http://nces.ed.gov/programs/coe/pdf/Indicator_CGF/COE_CGF_2013_05.pdf.

Koelsch, N. (2006). National High School Center. Improving literacy outcomes for English language learners in high school: Considerations for states and districts in developing a coherent policy framework. Retrieved from http://www.betterhighschools.org/docs/nhsc_adolescents_110806.pdf.

Rhodes, R. L., Ochoa, S. H., & Ortiz, S. O. (2005). *Assessing culturally and linguistically diverse students: A practical guide.* New York, NY: Guilford.

Suárez-Orozco, C., Rhodes, J., & Milburn, M. (2009). Unraveling the immigrant paradox: Academic engagement and disengagement among recently arrived immigrant youth. *Youth & Society, 41,* 151–185.

Suárez-Orozco, C., & Suárez-Orozco, M. (2001). *Children of immigration.* Cambridge, MA: Harvard University Press.

Suárez-Orozco, C., Yoskikawa, H., Teranishi, R. T., & Suárez-Orozco, M. (2011). Growing up in the shadows: The developmental implications of unauthorized status. *Harvard Educational Review, 81*(3), 438–473.

Toppleberg, C. O., Snow, C. E., & Tager-Flusberg, H. (1999). Severe developmental disorders and bilingualism. *Journal of the American Academy of Child & Adolescent Psychiatry, 38*(9), 1197–1199.

Toppleberg, C. O., Tabors, P., Coggins, A., Lum, K., & Burger, C. (2005). Differential diagnosis of selective mutism in bilingual children. *Journal of the American Academy of Child & Adolescent Psychiatry, 44*(6), 592–595.

U.S. Department of Education (DOE), Center for Education Statistics. (2011). *The condition of education 2011*. Retrieved from http://nces.ed.gov/pubs2011/2011033_1.pdf.

Winnicott, D. W. (1971). *Playing and reality*. London: Tavistock.

10

Immigrant Youths and the Language of Music

Angelica Ortega and Carol Korn-Bursztyn

This chapter explores the role of music programs as a buffer against acculturative stress that accompanies immigration. In the vignette that follows, a young violin student can provide the continuity and stability needed to buffer acculturative stress. Music functions as a powerful tool for Gabriela, a young immigrant, easing her transition to a new spoken language through the shared language of music. Music instruction for students in urban schools, especially immigrant and bilingual students, yields significant benefits, both emotional and cognitive. This chapter explores the lack of music programs as an issue of access in urban schools.

MUSIC, LANGUAGE, AND COGNITION: MUSIC IS A MULTIMODAL LANGUAGE

CASE VIGNETTE: GABRIELA

Gabriela[1] is a nine-year-old and a recent arrival from Mexico. Following the death of her father, she and her mother relocated to Brooklyn. She registered for school in September and was placed in a fourth-grade English as a second language (ESL) classroom. The school has an after-school violin program in which Gabriela participated. Gabriela is a talented musician who takes her violin studies very seriously, partnering up with another student who can translate for her. She demonstrates great autonomy and has no difficulty advocating for herself. However, it is noted that she gets easily frustrated if she is not able to achieve mastery easily. As the year progresses, Gabriela makes great strides, developing beautiful intonation and technique. She is one of my (the first author's) strongest students and I often ask her to model for her peers, and although hesitant, she accepts. She takes leadership roles in the group, helping her fellow musicians with a certain note or modeling her posture and bowing.

One morning in December, she stopped by my room and said, "No more Spanish Ms. Ortega. Okay?" I respected her request and began interacting with her primarily in English but (admittedly) not always. Her vocabulary in Spanish is remarkable and her limited English restricts not only how but also what she wants to say, so she learns to navigate both languages to express her thoughts.

Gabriela cannot stay for all of our afterschool sessions. She has to take the school bus home, and her bus does not come back for kids who participate in afterschool activities. Her mother attends school in the evenings to obtain her General Educational Development (GED) certificate and the bus drops Gabriela off at her neighbor's home. While she waits for the bus in the auditorium, she takes out her violin and practices.

In May, the violin ensemble put on the spring concert and Gabriela led with "Simple Gifts." As she stood in front of the ensemble, her posture and gaze reveal confidence and great intent. Only after the performance is over does she smile, revealing an overwhelming sense of pride. I congratulated her mom on having such a talented daughter and she told me that Gabriela takes after her deceased father, who was a percussionist in a band in the Mexico. Two weeks later, at the end of our rehearsal, Gabriela told me that she is returning to the Mexico. Before she leaves, she hands me a gift bag. I opened it and found a jewelry box she had made out of popsicle sticks, with the words "I love violin" outlined in red glitter. The following Monday, as I take attendance, I noticed that her name had been replaced with "discharged."

The following year, in the first week of school in September when I arrived for the afterschool program, I spotted Gabriela heading for the bus after school. She told me her mom decided to come back. I invited her back to the violin ensemble. During practice, she is hesitant. I asked her to play "Simple Gifts," and although hesitant, the notes start streaming out of her instrument. "That sounds fantastic," I remarked. She agreed, adding, "*Si pero se me olvido el Ingles.*" Yes, but I forgot English.

The following section describes the role that music plays in helping Gabriela develop emotional and academic resilience.

MIGRATION AS TRAUMA

Grinberg and Grinberg (1989) describe the trauma suffered from immigration, not only as an acute phenomenon, but as a series of events. Furthermore, trauma should not be considered in isolation, as "in any migration a constellation of factors combine to produce anxiety and sorrow" (p. 12). In the case of Gabriela, the death of her father was most likely the antecedent, precipitating her mother's decision to emigrate and to further her own education.

Gabriela again experiences trauma when she returns to Mexico, interrupting her good adjustment to school and to her music learning. Grinberg and Grinberg acknowledge that trauma may have a latency period in some immigrants, where symptoms manifest well after the initial trauma of migration. This could explain why Gabriela's mother decided to return to Mexico. Rutter (1983) observes "children typically adjust and deal with loss quicker and more effectively than adults" (cited in Jensen, 2007, p. 40). Although Gabriela seemed to be adjusting easily to her new life, her mother was facing a different reality as a new widow who had to fend for herself in a new land.

Her mother's decision to return to Mexico and then again migrate to New York perpetuates the trauma of dislocation and migration (Grinberg & Grinberg, 1989). Though this might have placed Gabriela in what Suárez-Orosco, Bang, and Onaga (2010) refer to as a liminal state between her country of origin and host country, Gabriela seems to take these changes in stride. Although death of a parent and serial migration are obvious major stressors, Gabriela's good adjustment to her welcoming school and her love of the violin are mitigating factors. Schools play a major role as a place where cultures meet and where cultural differences are negotiated (Korn, 2002). Music too fills the liminal spaces between country of origin and host country, providing a bridging function between the two. For Gabriela, whose father was an accomplished musician, the violin may have represented a link to her father, a perpetuation of the musical, holding environment (Winnicott, 1971). Additionally, Gabriela's mother's efforts at establishing and maintaining an independent household are indicative of maternal resilience, presenting a powerful model for her daughter.

MIGRATION AND RESILIENCE

Research shows that immigrant children are at risk of developing psychological distress due to stressors associated with the migration process, including the demands of acculturation. However, in spite of all the changes in her life in such a short period of time, Gabriela makes good social and academic progress.

Environment plays a large role in Gabriela's growing resilience during this period of acculturation. It is therefore crucial to consider the continuities and discontinuities between Mexico and her new home, as well as the continuities between home and school. As stated in Bronfenbrenner's (1974) bioecological model of human development, "environmental forces interact with physiological attributes to shape outcomes in individual behaviors, psychology and pathology" (cited in Jensen, 2007, p. 35). In Gabriela's case, there are continuities that allow for mitigation of trauma.

First, Gabriela traveled with her mother to New York City. Santa-Maria and Cornille (2007) find that maintenance of the nuclear family can mitigate trauma, becoming a protective agent for immigrant children. Gabriela does not experience trauma from separation of a parent or from subsequent reunification, and for this reason Gabriela is at an advantage. Furthermore, Gabriela has a strong mother, with a strong work ethic, who works weekdays and weekends and has high aspirations, as she is attending evening classes at a local community college to obtain her GED. As noted by Shields and Berhman (2004), "these strengths can help to insulate children of immigrants from various negative influences in American society" (cited in Jensen, 2007, p. 31).

Second, she has a strong social network in her new community. She lives in a community with a large Mexican population, allowing for cultural and linguistic continuity. This allows her mother to readily access nearby childcare—another Mexican mother who has children in Gabriela's school—while she attends night school three times a week. Her neighbor's kids are a valuable asset, as they provide homework support. Suárez-Orozco, Suárez-Orosco, and Todorova (2008, p. 56) observe that "these networks help with the transitioning to a new country, including linguistic and cultural orientation, companionship and a social network."

Third, in school she is able to employ her bicultural and bilingual skills because she lives in a high Spanish-speaking community (80%) and is in an ESL classroom with mostly Spanish speakers. Although Gabriela does attend a crowded, high-English language learning (ELL) school, there are diverse resources available that positively affect her academic performance. These include being taught by a highly effective ESL teacher, extra support through the ELL Saturday academy program, and participation in the violin program.

Finally, Gabriela leads a transnational life; she keeps in touch with family and friends in Mexico through social media. Gabriela's transnational life acts as a buffer for the stressor of migration and contributes to her resilience. Music, too, mediates stress and is a source of a positive outlook, serving as a source of resilience for Gabriela.

MUSIC AND ACCULTURATIVE STRESS

> It is my experience that music is one of the most important elements through which a child maintains a stable cultural identity, even when cultural traditions and associated life styles have all but disappeared.
>
> (Walker, 2006, p. 440)

Serial migration can be very traumatic for immigrant youths, as evidenced by the conclusion of the vignette. When I initially approached Gabriela in early September, she stated "I forgot my English." Her return to New York from Mexico in many ways returned Gabriela to her initial migration experience. Though she indicated that she felt like she was starting over with regard to learning English, she felt differently about the violin. When she picked the instrument up, although showing a little hesitation, the notes to "Simple Gifts" flowed with ease. The violin became the connection between the different spaces she continued to inhabit throughout her complex migration process.

Music programs can provide the continuity and stability needed to buffer acculturative stress. In the instrumental music program, Gabriela nurtures her native literacies while developing new literacies (Aprile, 2012; Bose, 2012), which act as a buffer to acculturative stress. In the following section, I examine how music functions as a powerful tool for Gabriela and the role it can play in the lives of other young immigrants.

MUSIC, LANGUAGE, AND COGNITION

Music is a multimodal language including five semiotic systems: linguistic, visual, auditory, gestural, and spatial (Antsey & Bull, 2006). A multimodal approach to teaching literacy needs to be considered when thinking about how students learn best, especially immigrant children. Immigrant children need to be recognized as literate in order to experience success in the classroom. However, they are often struggling readers and experience themselves as failures. Bourdieu (1991) argues that students experience failure as habitus, limiting the range of what they can conceive of as possible. Underachieving immigrant students are consequently at risk of developing an academic identity of failure.

Fortunately, this is not the case for Gabriela as she experiences success as habitus. Music becomes integral to her identity formation in this new context as an immigrant, emergent bilingual child. Rather than just acquiring the identity of a struggling reader, she is perceived as a talented child by teachers and peers alike. Gabriela is an exceptionally talented musician. The music classroom also has important emotional benefits for all students, not only for students who display unusual ability. It is a safe space where immigrant students can express and work through difficult emotions.

Music also has a demonstrated, positive effect on cognition, especially with regard to ELL students. Music training improves the brain's early encoding of linguistic sound (Patel & Iverson, 2007), including pitch patterns (Magne, Schon, & Besson, 2006), phonemic awareness (Lamb & Gregory, 1993), and the ability to interpret prosody (Thompson, Schellenberg, &

Husain, 2004) and decode print (Anvari, Trainor, Woodside, & Levy, 2002). A study by Slevc and Miyake (2006) found the connection between musical ability and the ability to perceive and produce subtle phonetic contrasts in a second language.

Furthermore, the role of music in facilitating language skills contributes to the development of reading comprehension (Butzlaff, 2000; Gardiner, Fox, Knowles, & Jeffrey, 1996). Language learning and vocabulary development have also been tied to music learning (Ho, Cheung, & Chan, 2003; Piro & Ortiz, 2009).

The section that follows examines the writing of immigrant students as they tell about their music-making practice. Their writing reveals that students develop resilience, both emotional and academic, within the context of their violin learning. Music is a means of expression and an important way in which children can learn to regulate their emotions. The following quotes express Gabriela's thoughts on the use of music in her life.

> Music is the only way me and my family can express how we feel and how we communicate with each other. So like if we are mad, instead of arguing with each other, we use music. For instance, my dad used to make his own music every time he would feel stressed. I also do the same. For example, when I am stressed I get my violin and start playing it and I suddenly feel calm again.
>
> Some things I can't express because my feelings come from my heart and I can't tell what my feeling is. So when I'm upset, playing "Simple Gifts" on the violin calms me down and I just enjoy the music that I play. The violin helps me express my feelings because every song has a different feeling.

Music is also a safe holding environment in which to develop inner resources that are expressed in the drive and the perseverance that results in actualization of ambitious strivings.

> I heard music from the advanced violins and I wanted to play. I asked if I can play with the advanced and got the sheet of music. I went home and practiced a lot. . . . I learned that I could do anything if I challenge myself! I practiced so much I learned to play by mind!

Music as a social domain is powerful because it is a challenging activity that allows students to feel capable and to perceive themselves as successful learners. Custodero (2012) uses Csikszentmihalyi's idea of flow to argue that music provides optimal flow because learners are challenged and feel highly capable. It is this flow that activates creativity, which is essentially how individuals learn. In thinking about one student's determination to learn a composition he regards as advanced, Custodero's explanation of creativity is that, as learning comes to mind, "we create as we accrue increasingly complex skill/knowledge through sustained inquiry" (2012, p. 370). In this context a particular student, a struggling reader and second language learner, sees himself as a successful learner. Music acts as a space where optimal flow occurs for him because he can translanguage, drawing on multiple literacies to experience himself as a capable learner.

One surprising element to the writing pieces was the strong narrative voice in student writing. Their music-making seemed to inspire beautiful writing about their process. Amy, another English language learner in the class, writes:

> When I am sad sometimes I feel like I am in a forest all alone and there is no sound. When I play, the forest has sound. There are people, birds tweeting, and music playing. Suddenly, the forest that I was in shines. And makes me happy. More than I am.

When children make music, they not only revisit their emotions, but they also call up or envision emotional states that they soon inhabit. In her writing, Amy describes a shift in mood, from unhappy to happy, which she believes is not characteristic; and yet this is how she feels, and she acknowledges her more positive frame of mind. In her succinct paragraph, Amy describes a process of self-regulation in which she moves from a sad to happy state. We can argue that music is highly salient for helping children learn to self-regulate, particularly around distressing affective states, by drawing on their capacity to imagine—or envision.

ENVISIONING AND EMOTIONAL EXPRESSION

It is not enough to have fluency in musical syntax; musicians need to be expressive when they play. Sloboda (2009, p. 305) talks about audiation, the process by which the brain gives meaning to musical sounds, and musical expression as the best evidence that a student understands what he or she is playing. There seems to be a direct connection between audiation and envisioning, as evidenced by student metacognitive writing about this process.

Amy states, "When I play music, I make a picture in my mind like when I am reading." The statement is supported by her writing around music-making, which reveals an understanding of rising and falling action of the piece when she says she pictures a boy nervously asks a girl to dance with him and the girl is saying "yes." Carina's audiation leads her to internalize the mood of the piece. She writes, "When I play *Eine Kleine*, I *see* a river go by calmly in my mind. At times when the song is rough, the river grows."

Custodero (2012, p. 371) writes, "Sinking into music becomes a sensory experience." When students of music "sink into music," they are embodying their music. Embodiment is a powerful literacy practice, because it demands the students to make connections to what they hear in order to locate themselves in the text. Karin's audiation skills lead her to make connections to other media when she writes: "Have you ever seen that movie *Ratatouille*? You know, the part where Remy bites the strawberry from the lady's house, and sparkles come to his mind? That's how I feel when I sing a song in chorus or in violin class." These students make personal connections to the characters or events they read about, which drive their reading comprehension while simultaneously making personal connections to their music-making.

CONCLUSION

Suárez-Orozco et al. (2008) point to the importance of mentoring and afterschool organizations for immigrant youths. Sadly, they find that only 9% of students in their study participated in afterschool programs or enrichment classes. Furthermore, while Chinese student immigrants were enrolled in afterschool tutoring or college preparation activities, Latino students were involved in "keep them out of trouble and off the streets" types of organizations. "Not surprisingly," the authors note, "the more scholastic activities seemed linked to more positive academic outcomes than were behavior based programs" (Suárez-Orozco et al., 2008, p. 85).

Although the arts provide higher-ordered, 21st-century skills, encouraging "problem solving, critical and creative thinking, dealing with ambiguity and complexity, integration of multiple skill sets, and the ability to perform cross-disciplinary work," they are not accessible to all demographics (President's Committee of the Arts and Humanities, 2011, p. 28). The arts continue to play a marginal role in the education of urban poor children (Korn-Bursztyn, 2012). The New York City Annual Arts Report (2014) provides a good indication of where we are regarding the arts in urban schools. That report found a 47% decline in spending to hire arts and cultural organizations to provide educational services for students. In school year 2006–2007, schools spent $25.7 million to hire arts and cultural organizations, compared with $13.7 million the previous year. In 2006–2007, schools spent $10.7 million on arts supplies and equipment, in comparison with only $1.7 million in 2012–2013—a decline of 84%. Only 8% of elementary schools in New York City are in compliance with the New York State mandates for the arts, with 38% of all elementary schools lacking even one full-time certified arts teacher.

Although there has been an increase in supplemental funding for the arts, schools have opted to divert these funds to non-arts-related areas. As a result, the report states, "many of the City's public schools are in violation of New York State Law, which sets minimal instruction requirements that schools must meet for the arts at each grade level, and deep disparities exist between school at all grade levels" (New York City Annual Arts Report, 2014, p. 1). These are also the first schools to cut the arts (U.S. Department of Education, 2013).

This is especially troubling, given the evidence of short- and long-term positive influences of the arts on students, especially immigrant students. Therefore, lack of music programs is first and foremost an issue of access in inner-city schools, not an issue of disinvestment in the arts. Music instruction for students in urban schools, especially immigrant and bilingual students, yields significant benefits, both emotional and cognitive. Music needs to again become part of schools' multilingual ecology; it has served immigrant students well in the past and should continue to do so today.

NOTE

1. All names in this chapter are pseudonyms.

REFERENCES

Anstey, M., & Bull, G. (2006). *Teaching and learning multiliteracies: Changing times, changing literacies*. Newark, DE: International Reading Association.

Anvari, S. H., Trainor L. J., Woodside J., & Levy B. Z. (2002). Relations among musical skills, phonological processing, and early reading ability in preschool children. *Journal of Experimental Child Psychology, 83*, 111–130.

Aprile, A. (2012). Music-making with young children: African Orff and rhythmic intelligence. A journey of musical collaboration. In C. Korn (Ed.), *Young children and the arts: Nurturing imagination and creativity* (pp. 173–194). Charlotte, NC: Information Age Publishing.

Bose, J. H. (2012). A journey of musical collaboration. In C. Korn (Ed.), *Young children and the arts: Nurturing imagination and creativity* (pp. 91–102). Charlotte, NC: Information Age Publishing.

Bourdieu, P. (1991). *Language and symbolic power*. Cambridge, MA: Harvard University Press.

Bronfenbrenner, U. (1974). Developmental research, public policy, and the ecology of childhood. *Child Development, 45*, 1–5.

Butzlaff, R. (2000). Can music be used to teach reading? *Journal of Aesthetic Education, 34*(3–4, Special Issue), 167–178.

Custodero, L. A. (2012). The call to create: Flow experience in music teaching and learning. In D. Hagreaves, D. Meill, & R. MacDonald (Eds.), *Musical imaginations:*

Multidisciplinary perspectives on creativity, performance, and perception (pp. 369–384). London: Oxford University Press.

Gardiner, M. E., Fox, A., Knowles, F., & Jeffrey, D. (1996). Learning improved by arts training. *Nature, 381*(6580), 284.

Grinberg, L., & Grinberg, R. (1989). *Psychoanalytic perspectives on migration and exile*. New Haven, CT: Yale University Press.

Ho, Y. C., Cheung, M. C., & Chan, A. S. (2003). Music training improves verbal but not visual memory: cross-sectional and longitudinal explorations in children. *Neuropsychology, 17*(3), 439–450.

Jensen, B. T. (2007). Understanding immigration and psychological development: A multilevel ecological approach. *Journal of Immigrant & Refugee Studies, 5*(4), 27–48.

Korn, C. (2002). Introduction: Cultural transitions and curricular transformations. In C. Korn & A. Bursztyn (Eds.), *Rethinking multicultural education: Case studies in cultural transition* (pp. 1–11). New York: Bergin & Garvey, Greenwood Press.

Korn-Bursztyn, C. (Ed.). (2012). *Young children and the arts: Nurturing imagination and creativity*. Charlotte, NC: Information Age Publishing.

Lamb, S. J., & Gregory, A. H. (1993). The relationship between music and reading in beginning readers. *Educational Psychology, 13*(1), 19–27.

Magne, C., Schon, D., & Besson, M. (2006). Musician children detect pitch violations in both music and language better than nonmusician children: Behavioral and electrophysiological approaches. *Journal of Cognitive Neuroscience, 18*, 199–211.

New York City Annual Arts Report. (2014). Office of the Comptroller. *State of the arts: A plan to boost arts education in New York City schools*. New York, NY: Bureau of Policy and Research. Retrieved from http://comptroller.nyc.gov/wp content/uploads/documents/State_of_the_Arts.pdf.

Patel, A. D., & Iverson, J. R. (2007). The linguistic benefits of musical abilities. *Trends in Cognitive Sciences, 11*, 369–372.

Piro, J. M., & Ortiz, C. (2009). The effect of piano lessons on the vocabulary and verbal sequencing skills of primary grade students. *Psychology of Music, 37*(3), 325–347.

President's Committee on the Arts and Humanities (PCAH). Reinvesting in Arts Education. Need for New Skill Sets (p. 28). Retrieved from http://www.pcah.gov/sites/default/files/photos/PCAH_Reinvesting_4web.pdf.

President's Committee on the Arts and Humanities (PCAH). (2013). Turnaround arts initiative: Interim report. Retrieved from http://www.pcah.gov/sites/default/files/Turnaround%20Arts%20Interim%20Evaluation_November%202013_1.pdf.

Rutter, M. (1983). Stress, coping, and development: Some issues and some questions. In N. Garmezy & M. Rutter (Eds.), *Stress, coping, and development in children* (pp. 1–41). New York: McGraw-Hill.

Santa-Maria, M. L., & Cornille, T. (2007). Traumatic stress, family separations, and attachment among Latin American immigrants. *Traumatology, 13*(2), 26–31.

Shields, M., & Berhman, R. (2004). Children of immigrant families: Analysis and recommendations. In R. Behrman (Ed.), *The future of children* (pp. 4–15). Princeton, NJ: Princeton University Press.

Slevc, L. R., & Miyake, A. (2006). Individual differences in second-language proficiency: Does musical ability matter? *Psychological Science, 17*(8), 675–681.

Sloboda, J. (2005). *Exploring the musical mind*. New York: Oxford University Press.
Suárez-Orozco, C., Suárez-Orozco, M. M., & Todorova, I. (2008). *Learning a new land: Immigrant students in American society*. Cambridge, MA: Harvard University Press.
Thompson, W. F., Schellenberg, E. G., & Husain G. (2004). Decoding speech prosody: Do music lessons help? *Emotion, 4*(1), 46–64.
Walker, R. (2006). Cultural traditions. In G. E. McPherson (Ed.), *The child as musician: A handbook of musical development* (pp. 439–460). New York, NY: Oxford University Press.
Winnicott, D. W. (1971). *Playing and reality*. New York: Basic Books.

11

Sex Trafficking and Migrant Youths

Jacquelin Mueller and Carol Korn-Bursztyn

Unaccompanied migrant youths are a highly vulnerable population. They face risk factors including exposure to trauma prior to or during the migration journey, homelessness, language barrier, economic need, and drug use. The social imperative of family honor in conjunction with acute personal shame increase unaccompanied minors' vulnerability to sex trafficking and exploitation. Lesbian, gay, bisexual, and transgender (LGBT) youths face the added trauma of exposure of their sexual orientation. Trafficking of youths for sexual services is a global issue in need of greater recognition. This chapter explores the phenomenon of sex trafficking of migrant youth. It draws on the vignettes of vulnerable and exploited youth to illustrate the events and experiences that contribute to the vulnerability of migrant youth to sex trafficking. All names are pseudonyms.

CASE VIGNETTE: ANA'S STORY

I was born near the Lithuania-Latvia border. Since my alcoholic parents were incapable of caring for me, social workers sent me to a state-run children's home. . . . The only person who ever visited me was a man who claimed to be my godfather. One day, when I was 13, he raped me.

. . . Shortly after my 16th birthday, a 21-year-old woman named Charlie introduced herself to me as my sister. . . . she came and inspected how my four friends and I lived. We had no idea that they had visited us to secretly decide if we were fit for prostitution. We had never heard of "human trafficking." The next night Charlie invited me and my two friends over to her apartment. When we got there, we saw three more girls our age and seven Greek men speaking in English, drinking alcohol, talking, and laughing. . . . That's when Charlie explained she'd invited us over to sell our bodies. She told us that we would be prostitutes from now on. My friends and I were shocked and refused, but my sister's friend threatened to call "the gang" if we continued to refuse to sell ourselves. She told us that the gang would beat us, rape us, and bury us alive in the woods. My friends and I started crying.

After that night I sold my body, I felt repulsed. I wouldn't get out of the shower until I washed everything away. I felt so humiliated. I heard my friends crying too. I was in prostitution from age 15 to 19. . . . My self-loathing grew, so I began injecting myself with drugs. I tried to numb myself from the pain so I wouldn't feel anything at all.

When I turned 17, the madam told us that a pimp was selling us abroad. One girl was sold in Poland, two in Budapest, and the rest of us were taken to Ravenna, Italy. After two weeks in Italy, I had an older client who understood Lithuanian. I took a risk and begged for his help. He took my friends and me to the Italian police. I was so surprised by how well the police treated us. . . .

We spent around four months in protective custody . . . a social worker worked with me a lot and helped me realize how I had been exploited. . . . Over the years, I had three other children with different men. I really love my children and I live only for them, but I do not love their fathers. I realize that I cannot keep a long-term relationship with any man, probably because I hate how men have treated me. (Equality Now, 2013, 21–23)

UNDERSTANDING ANA'S STORY

Ana's story reflects themes of pain, false hope, learned helplessness, risk, and shame as a reaction to life in the sex trafficking industry. Her story also reflects the risk factors of trauma exposure, longing for love and security, together with homelessness, language barrier, economic need, personal history of drug abuse, and roles of shame and diminished self-worth. These risk factors are repeated, and present, in the stories of many thousands of immigrant youths who were victims of sex trafficking.

Sex trafficking falls under the category of human trafficking and is often referred to as modern-day slavery by the U.S. Department of State. According to the Trafficking Victims Protection Act of 2000 (TVPA), human trafficking is defined as the "recruitment, harboring, transportation, provision, or obtaining of a person for the purpose of [labor services] or commercial sex act" (Section 103, Paragraph 9, 2000). In addition to this, TVPA defines that severe forms of trafficking involve a commercial sex act performed by any person under the age of 18. This person must have been "induced by force, fraud, or coercion" into the commercial sex act. Also illegal are the "recruitment, harboring, transportation, provision, or obtaining of a person for labor or services, through the use of force, fraud, or coercion for the purpose of subjection to voluntary servitude, peonage, debt bondage, or slavery" (Section 103, Paragraph 8, 2000).

Many young people who are vulnerable to sex trafficking networks are recruited abroad; others are recruited domestically, often among the ranks of unaccompanied, undocumented minors. These young immigrants are especially vulnerable to recruitment into the sex trafficking industry due to trauma experienced at home and during the migration journey. LGBT youths constitute another vulnerable population, at risk of recruitment and enslavement by sex traffickers. The Polaris Project (2014) estimates that there are approximately 20.9 million victims of human trafficking worldwide; 5.5 million of the victims are children. About 30% of youths in shelters and state-run homes and 70% of youths living on the streets are victims of sexual exploitation (National Center for Missing and Exploited Children, 2010).

The 2011 U.S. Department of Justice, Characteristics of Suspected Human Trafficking Incidents 2008–2010 report documented 1,016 incidents of suspected prostitution or other sexual exploitation of a child (Bureau of Justice Statistics, 2011). This appears to be the most recent statistical report published by the U.S. Department of Justice on Human Trafficking cases within the United States. However, in 2013, the National Human Trafficking Resource Center hotline received phone calls about 3,609 cases within the United States (Polaris Project, 2014). Undocumented and unaccompanied immigrant youths are at particular risk for sexual exploitation. According to the Characteristics of Suspected Human Trafficking Incident report 2008–2010 (Bureau of Justice Statistics, 2011), 460 victims of human sex trafficking were identified through their high data quality task force. Of these 460 identified victims, 284 were 17 years old or younger and 64 of the 460 victims were identified as undocumented aliens.

Young migrant youths can fall victim to sex trafficking as a result of a combination of risk factors that increase their vulnerability to violent and nonviolent coercion by traffickers. Violent coercion may include physical maltreatment including starvation, forced drug use, and rape, while nonviolent coercion refers to debt bondage, isolation, and psychological manipulation (Hom & Woods, 2013). The migrant journey provides another dangerous pathway for the exploitation of unaccompanied minors, providing multiple risks for unaccompanied minors to become victims of both violent and nonviolent coercion.

TRAUMA AND THE MIGRATION JOURNEY

Unaccompanied minors are at great risk of falling into the hands of sex traffickers and gang members. According to an anonymous U.S. border patrol officer (confidential communication to the first author) who has worked on multiple child smuggling cases, unaccompanied minors are often raped and abandoned by their smugglers to find their way alone. These children are often found stumbling about in the desert, near roads, often sexually violated. The act of smuggling is largely traumatic for migrant children even when their stories do not include kidnapping and rape, as they are concealed in small compartments in vehicles in order to make the journey (Camisa, 2010). The psychological trauma of smuggling, together with the traumatic losses that migration entails, are amplified by the physical and sexual abuse unaccompanied minors often face. In turn, this prior exposure to trauma increases their vulnerability to become recruited into the sex trafficking industry.

The sections that follow will examine how the risk factors of trauma exposure, homelessness, LGBT status, language barrier, economic need, and exposure to drug use interact with honor, shame, and diminished self-worth to increase the vulnerability of youths to international sex trafficking.

RISK FACTOR 1: TRAUMA EXPOSURE

Young people caught in sex trafficking networks often have histories of prior exposure to traumatic life events including loss of parent(s) and physical and sexual abuse, including rape. A young girl trafficked to Dubai reported: "I was twelve when my mother died" (International Organization for Migration, 2002, p. 4). A Cambodian girl reported, "My parents treated me like a house servant and frequently beat me for no reason" (Equality Now, 2013, p. 6). "I was around a lot of domestic violence as a child. I was also a victim of child abuse," reports a child who entered the sex trade in New Zealand, while another child from the United Kingdom was sexually abused by her stepfather from age six, and at age 14 reported gang rape (Equality Now, 2013, p. 39).

According to the American Psychiatric Association (2013), trauma is defined as an emotional response to a disturbing event, which over time can lead to symptoms of posttraumatic stress disorder (PTSD). The 5th edition of the *Diagnostic and Statistical Manual of Mental Disorders* (2013) lists criteria for PTSD as exposure to a traumatic event in which the event is persistently re-experienced. PTSD typically results in impaired cognition and mood changes, including heightened arousal and reactivity, often resulting in impaired social functioning. The intensity and duration of symptoms vary with exposure to recurring traumas, as well as to distressing cues. This is especially relevant to the experiences of youths who have been repeatedly traumatized in childhood. Vulnerable youths who have been victims of sexual abuse prior to entering sex trafficking reexperience the trauma of violation over and over. They are at risk of peritraumatic dissociation, an attempt to cope with overwhelming anxiety associated with the traumatic event by psychologically detaching from the experience. Often, peritraumatic dissociation occurs at the time or near the time of the traumatic event (APA, 2013).

Early childhood experiences of abuse and neglect can create vulnerability to unhealthy sexual relationships and to sexual exploitation later in life. Young people with histories of abuse and neglect are vulnerable to sex traffickers who offer the promise of love, and in a manner consistent with the youth's prior life experience, conflate violence and exploitation with love (Cecchet & Thoburn, 2014). Traffickers who exploit young, homeless, immigrant youths use nonviolent and violent coercion tactics to recruit them into the industry. Together with the pimps, madams, and johns who collude in these enterprises, traffickers take advantage of the vulnerabilities that result from recurring trauma, as part of a nonviolent coercive strategy that serves the purpose of maintaining psychological control of their victims.

A young immigrant told of how she came to be involved with a sex trafficking network, when her foster parents sent her at age 13 to live with a family in a nearby city who promptly enslaved her for $12.50 a month. Several months after she arrived, the husband raped her. She escaped to a nearby province, but reported being picked up by two men at a taxi stand who quickly discerned that she was homeless and offered her shelter and protection. This was her entry into sex trafficking (Equality Now, 2013). Prior exposure to trauma, combined with vulnerabilities of prior abuse and the need to feel loved and accepted, can motivate vulnerable youths to run away from home. The section that follows explores the related risk factor of homelessness in the recruitment of youths into domestic and international sex trafficking networks.

RISK FACTOR 2: HOMELESSNESS

Homelessness presents youths with sharply increased vulnerability to exploitation. Homelessness has multiple causes; it may result from placement, running away, escape, or abandonment by family. A young girl from Canada reported placement in government care prior to her 13th birthday where she was preyed upon by sex traffickers who sought out vulnerable children in group and foster homes. Another typical story is of sexual abuse by a family member or mother's boyfriend, leading to running away and homelessness (Equality Now, 2013).

Running away from negative and aggressive home lives increases the likelihood of introduction into prostitution for adolescents (Clarke, Clarke, Roe-Sepowitz, & Fey, 2012). Young, homeless youths are an open system in high entropy. In order to minimize entropy, young, homeless immigrant youths will search for stability, leaving them vulnerable to sex traffickers who typically offer false promises of jobs, shelter, and safety. LGBT youths are especially vulnerable to homelessness and to subsequent entry into the sex trafficking industry.

RISK FACTOR 3: HOMELESSNESS AND LGBT YOUTHS

Homelessness in LGBT youths often occurs following disclosure of sexual orientation, when the child may be evicted from the family home. Dale (2012), a journalist for the *Washington Times*, reported on a young boy who became homeless after his father discovered his sexual orientation. The boy's search for stability and support increased his vulnerability to sex traffickers, and he was violently coerced into prostitution in Chicago and neighboring Michigan.

The National Coalition for the Homeless (2009) reports that young, homeless, LGBT youths are at high risk for manipulation, psychological illness, and exposure to sexually transmitted diseases. Additionally, they report that 58.7% of LGBT homeless youths have been sexually victimized compared with 33.4% of heterosexual homeless youths. Further, immigration status increases the risks that LGBT youths face. The 2014 Trafficking in Persons Report asserts that not only do LGBT immigrants face the same vulnerabilities that local LGBT individuals face, including homelessness, fear of exposure of sexual orientation, but they also face the traumatic sequelae of the migration experience, often further complicated by undocumented status (U.S. Department of Justice, 2014). The report further estimates that LGBT homeless youths comprise 20% to 40% of the homeless youth population.

International sex trafficking of LGBT victims is typical. Caribbean and Latin American LGBT individuals are often trafficked to Western Europe; LGBT Africans are trafficked to Europe, specifically Scotland, and to trafficking rings for the wealthy in the United Arab Emirates, Qatar, and Saudi Arabia. LGBT immigrants recruited into sex trafficking often fear deportation and exposure of their sexual orientation to their family, thus reinforcing their motivation to remain with the pimp (Martinez & Kelle, 2013). The U.S. Department of Justice's Trafficking in Persons Report (2014) notes that the threat of exposure of sexual orientation is a powerful means of control that sex traffickers exert over their victims. Additionally, LGBT victims are at risk of the contraction and spread of sexually transmitted diseases. Sex trafficking has also been linked to the spread of AIDS (Martinez & Kelle, 2013).

Trauma, exposure and history, and homelessness—and the intersection of actual or feared exposure of sexual orientation and homelessness for LGBT youths—are all recognized risk factors for vulnerable youths. Migrant status presents an added risk factor of language barrier, thus increasing the vulnerability of the young to fall victim to sex traffickers.

RISK FACTOR 4: LANGUAGE BARRIER

Traffickers often take advantage of the inability to speak the foreign language, exploiting the vulnerability that comes with not understanding or speaking the language to coerce the young into prostitution. The language barrier prevents undocumented youths from communicating to health care providers when brought into the emergency room and from seeking help. Unable to communicate with service providers without the presence of a translator, young victims must rely on the accomplice who accompanies them to the hospital ostensibly to translate. Often the accomplice presents as a concerned family member, whereas the actual identity may be that of pimp. Hom and Woods (2013) recommend that service providers learn how to identify trafficking victims. In addition to language barrier serving the aim of traffickers and their accomplices to maintain control over their victims, a language barrier also hinders young victims from understanding their rights and the laws in the host countries.

R. Contarino, director of Love True, a nonprofit organization, observes that a language barrier prevents youths trafficked into the United States from understanding how the federal law protects them (personal communication, November 19, 2014). Under U.S. federal law, immigrant, sexually exploited youths are typically eligible for a T-visa. A T-visa allows immigrant victims of severe trafficking, defined as labor or sex, to remain in the United States on condition that they comply with law enforcement in the investigation and prosecution of their traffickers (U.S. Citizenship and Immigration Services, 2013).

As a result of inadequate training for law enforcement in sexual exploitation of youths and limited rehabilitation resources for young victims, exploited youths are often wrongfully prosecuted as criminals. This leads to lost opportunities to help young victims exit sex trafficking and prostitution. It is critical that youth victims be identified as victims of sex trafficking in order to qualify for a T-visa (U.S. Citizenship and Immigration Services, 2013). The U.S. Citizenship and Immigration Services (2013) Department reports that victims who qualify for T-visas may legally work in the United States and are eligible for a four-year extension of their status, with the option of applying for permanent residency and federal refugee benefits.

Language barriers significantly increase the vulnerability of immigrant youths to sex trafficking. Dire economic circumstances present an additional major risk factor that increases the vulnerability of the young. Unaccompanied immigrant youths must fend for themselves economically in order to survive; the need to make money is a compelling factor that increases the vulnerability of the young.

RISK FACTOR 5: ECONOMIC NEED

Economic need often serves as a motivator for immigrant youths to enter the sex trafficking industry in order to support themselves and their families or to pay off debt bondage. For example, a young girl living in New Zealand reported, "The first time I sold my body I was scared and disgusted, but relieved that I made $100 in five minutes because it meant I could pay my board and survive" (Equality Now, 2013, p. 3). Another young girl from Nigeria, schooled until 10th grade, was sent away by her impoverished parents ostensibly to support the family. A family contact subsequently provided her with a counterfeit passport and plane ticket to Germany, where she was coerced into sex trafficking. She reported: "Once I arrived, I was told that my debt was 50,000 euro [around US$67,000] which I realized would take a very long time to repay. My family's contact then told me that to pay the debt, I would be working as a prostitute in brothels" (Equality Now, 2013, p. 3).

Youths born into poor families are often compelled to work at an early age to help the family survive. Young girls are especially vulnerable to sexual exploitation. A young girl from Bangladesh describes herself as born into a poor family with eight brothers and sisters. She recounts her understanding of leaving with an older man, who promised her "that he could make me into a famous singer one day" (Equality Now, 2013, p. 2). She also observed, hinting at her current understanding of how gender intersects with family economics to the detriment and vulnerability of girls, and specifically to her own trajectory: "It is very common for girls to marry early in rural India. . . . The older a girl gets, the more her family will have to pay for her dowry" (Equality Now, 2013, p. 2).

The desperation of sex trafficking victims to survive leaves them vulnerable to disease. Their traffickers intentionally neglect their health in order to keep profits constant and to avoid the potential scrutiny of medical workers. A young Nigerian girl reported: "The women here are so desperate for money that they don't care about AIDS—people here are ready to die. This is blood money, and it was killing me too" (Equality Now, 2013, p. 3). Several months later, the police raided the brothel, noticed her papers were forged, and took her to an immigration detention center, where she was later hospitalized with AIDS. Another young girl who was trafficked to Dubai highlighted the dangerous intersection of greed and intentional neglect. She reported: "Once I got so sick that I could not even move, but the pimp wouldn't pay attention to me and keeps sending clients to me. . . . I told the pimp that I needed to see a doctor, but she said that it was very expensive and I could not afford it. The next day I was so weak that I could not even stand" (International Organization for Migration, 2002, p. 5). Another young girl internationally trafficked as an escort for influential national leaders was forced to have unprotected sex. She commented, "I didn't feel like I deserved to live or not get a disease" (Equality Now, 2013, p. 4).

The lives of youths caught up in global sex trafficking quickly take a despairing and desperate turn. Vulnerability to drug abuse is an added risk factor in the lives of these young people. Although all of the risk factors discussed in this chapter intersect, economic need, history of family drug abuse, forced drug use, and personal drug use are clearly connected.

RISK FACTOR 6: EXPOSURE TO DRUG ABUSE

Youths who are coerced into global sex trafficking often report exposure to drug use in the home, by family members, or through personal use in order to cope with trauma. For example, a 13-year-old girl, trafficked to Dubai, reported: "My father and uncle had been using drugs for many years. Soon after my father was imprisoned. . . . My uncle sold everything in our house to buy drugs" (International Organization for Migration, 2002, p. 4). Youths involved in prostitution report higher rates of drug and alcohol abuse by parents (Kramer & Berg, 2003). Additionally, traffickers exert coercion by inducing sedation and addiction through repeated drug use. Dependence on and access to drugs are powerful means of control of vulnerable youths by sex traffickers; chemical dependency is a motivator for prostitution and hence a vehicle for control by traffickers (Hom & Woods, 2013). For example, a young, poor, and homeless Cambodian girl was violently coerced into drug use so she would have sex with clients. She reported: "[He] ordered me to have sex with a man on video but I refused. He said: 'You cannot refuse. You must do this for me.' He ordered someone to inject me with drugs. Then I could no longer refuse because I had no control" (Equality Now, 2013, p. 3).

This pattern of violent coercion through involuntary introduction of drugs is consistent with violent techniques of sex traffickers both internationally and closer to home. In 2012, the *Washington Times* reported on the violent drugging of a young gay boy in Chicago. "[H]is first pimp snuck up behind him, put a rag laced with sedatives over his mouth to knock him out, and literally dragged him off the street. . . . His pimp later introduced him to cocaine by blowing it in his mouth and forcing him to ingest it" (Dale, 2012, p. 2).

Kidd and Kral (2002) report that youths who are forced into prostitution often rely on drugs to dull the pain of the traumas they have endured and to escape the feeling of enslavement. The end result is addiction to the substances that bring transient relief. Addiction serves the purpose of escape from reality, but also creates a new, powerful economic need to fuel drug habits and to avoid painful and dangerous withdrawal symptoms. The economic need immigrant youths face when forced into sex trafficking is further complicated by addiction. Prior exposure to drugs is a risk factor in vulnerability to sex trafficking, an industry that is heavily reliant on the coercive use of chemical substances. Finally, the cluster of social roles of honor, virtue, shame, and diminished self-worth constitutes a final risk factor implicated in vulnerability to sex trafficking.

RISK FACTOR 7: HONOR, SHAME, AND DIMINISHED SELF-WORTH

The roles of honor, shame, and diminished self-worth present a cluster of socially rooted phenomena that greatly increase the vulnerability of youths to sex trafficking. Many of the youths sex trafficked across international and domestic borders hail from traditional homes and cultures where gender roles, especially regarding the role of women, parent–child relationships, deferential attitudes toward authority, and religion are fixed. Traffickers will often exploit the vulnerable young person's deeply ingrained loyalty to family, even where families have knowingly or unwittingly sent their children—usually daughters—into sexual slavery.

It is not uncommon for desperately poor families to sell daughters to sex traffickers in order to generate income. The shame of prostitution is then shouldered by the young people who have been sold, whereas the family maintains its honor. The young girls, mindful of not bringing shame or dishonor upon the families that sold them, quietly accept their fates. When a young girl trafficked to Dubai was asked why she did not reach out for help, she remarked that she hadn't thought to do so, but suggested that shame prevented her from doing so. She observed: "After all, what was I going to do after that? How could I return home? What would I say to my parents?" (International Organization for Migration, 2002, p. 4). A young girl trafficked from Nigeria to Germany similarly reported:

> My family's contact told me that to pay the debt I would be working as a prostitute in brothels. It was then that I realized that my family's contact was a madam. I refused and called my parents to explain what was happening, but they told me to obey her and do whatever she told me to do. I didn't have any papers and didn't know my rights. She said that if I asked anyone for help, I would be deported. (Equality Now, 2013, p. 29)

Caught in a bind, trafficked youths experience feelings of shame, dishonor, and low self-worth. Yet failure to fulfill the wishes and needs of their families, even those who sold them to sex traffickers, also results in feelings of shame, dishonor, and low self-worth. Youths with histories of abuse and neglect prior to sex trafficking are at enhanced risk of not only entering the realm of sex trafficking, but also of remaining there. These children, unloved from an early age, are vulnerable to the attentions and ministrations of their traffickers and abusers.

Ominously, sex trafficking networks work internationally through unregulated seemingly legitimate venues. A young girl, trafficked into the United States from Georgia (former USSR), reported that her family contacted a "well-known and reliable mediating agency, and arranged for [her] a study tour to New York" (International Organization for Migration 2002, p. 15). After this 17-year-old girl arrived, two Georgian representatives from the agency picked her up and brought her to the college. She was forced by the representatives to sign a contract holding her responsible for working while studying in exchange for their financial support. After a few months, when she turned to them for additional funds, they refused and tried to recruit her into prostitution. When she refused and asked to return home, "they said they would beat up my family members or even gas them, and me too, and that I had no choice here on the other side of the ocean" (International Organization for Migration, 2002, p. 15).

CONCLUSION

Unaccompanied migrant youths face risk factors including exposure to trauma prior to or during the migration journey, homelessness, language barrier, economic need, drug use, and the social constraints of family honor, and personal shame increase their vulnerability to sex trafficking. LGBT youths face the added trauma of exposure, or fear of exposure, of their sexual orientation. Trafficking of youths for sexual services has become a global issue in need of greater recognition by those in the frontlines of identification, such as educators, medical and mental health providers, as well as law enforcement officers.

On November 20, 2014, President Barack Obama presented a series of executive orders that permits undocumented immigrants to come forward, exonerated from deportation, and apply for the Deferred Action for Childhood Arrivals, and the Deferred Action for Parents of Americans and Lawful Permanent Residents (U.S. Citizenship and Immigration Services, 2013). However, LGBT equality advocates have raised concerns about the failure to clarify whether LGBT immigrants and their families are included in the president's executive order (Immigration Equality, 2014). This may be of great significance to sex trafficked immigrant youths, as many young undocumented victims of sex trafficking fail to come forward to apply for T-visas that they are eligible for under federal law.

Clear protocols for identifying youths who have been or who may be at risk of victimization are critical. Currently, too few treatment options exist for traumatized immigrant youths, including youths who are victims of sex traffickers. Language barriers often prevent young victims from seeking help; often barriers of trauma, invisible to the eyes of others, prevent those in a position to help from recognizing the need. Clearly more attention needs to be paid to developing treatment approaches that help young victims cope with their complex histories of trauma and abuse.

It is critical that schools and other community-based organizations that work with young people from diverse backgrounds integrate mental health support within the educational and social activities that they promote. Development of out-of-school programs offers an opportunity to thread a mental health component through the everyday activities offered in these informal settings. Additionally, safe, high-quality residential programs for deeply traumatized young people are needed in order to help them cope with their traumatic histories and transition to new possibilities for their futures.

REFERENCES

American Psychiatric Association (APA). (2013). *Diagnostic and statistical manual of mental disorders* (5th ed.). Washington, DC: Author.

Bureau of Justice Statistics. (2011). *Special report: Characteristics of suspected human trafficking incidents, 2008–2010*. Washington, DC: U.S. Department of Justice.

Camisa, R. (2010). *Which way home*. (Motion Picture). GOOD & White Buffalo Entertainment.

Cecchet, S. J., & Thoburn, J. (2014). The psychological experience of child and adolescent sex trafficking in the united states: Trauma and resilience in survivors. *Psychological Trauma: Theory, Research, Practice, and Policy, 6*(5), 482–493.

Clarke, R., Clarke, E., Roe-Sepowitz, D., & Fey, R. (2012). Age of entry into prostitution: Relationship to drug use, race, suicide, education level, childhood abuse and family experiences. *Journal of Human Behavior and the Social Environment, 22*, 270–289.

Dale, Y. (2012, June 18). Chicago: A survivor of gay sex trafficking speaks up about his ordeal. The Washington Times Communities. Retrieved from http://communities.washingtontimes.com/neighborhood/rights-so-divine/2012/jun/18/chicago-survivor-gay-sex-trafficking-speaks-about-/.

Equality Now Survivor Stories. (2013, March). Retrieved from http://www.equalitynow.org/sites/default/files/Survivor_Stories.pdf.

Hom, K. A., & Woods, S. J. (2013). Trauma and its aftermath for commercially exploited women as told by front-line service providers. *Issues in Mental Health Nursing, 34*, 75–81.

Immigration Equality. (2014, November 21). President Obama's executive order stresses family ties, fails to mention LGBT families. Retrieved from http://immigrationequality.org/president-obamas-executive-order-stresses-family-ties-fails-mention-lgbt-families/.

International Organization for Migration. (2002, January 1). Trafficking from Caucasus. Retrieved from http://publications.iom.int/bookstore/free/Trafficking_Caucasus_ENG.pdf.

Kidd, S. A., & Kral, M. J. (2002). Suicide and prostitution among street youth: A qualitative analysis. *Adolescence, 37*, 411–430.

Kramer, L. A., & Berg, E. C. (2003). A survival analysis of timing of entry into prostitution: The differential impact of race, educational level, and childhood/adolescent risk factors. *Sociological Inquiry, 73*(4), 511–528.

Martinez, O., & Kelle, G. (2013). Sex trafficking of LGBT individuals: A call for service provision, research, and action. *International Law News, 42*(4).

National Center for Missing and Exploited Children. (2010). Child sex trafficking. Retrieved from http://www.missingkids.com/CSTT.

National Coalition for the Homeless. (2009). LGBTQ homeless. Retrieved from http://nationalhomeless.org/wp-content/uploads/2014/06/LGBTQ-Fact-Sheet.pdf.

Polaris Project Human Trafficking Combating Human Trafficking and Modern-day Slavery. (2014, January 1). Retrieved from http://www.polarisproject.org/human-trafficking/overview.

U.S. Citizenship and Immigration Services. (2013). T and U visa changes. Retrieved from http://travel.state.gov/content/dam/visas/policy_updatesT_and_U_Visa_Changes_June_2013.pdf.

U.S. Department of Justice. (2014). Trafficking in persons report. Retrieved from http://www.state.gov/documents/organization

Victims of Trafficking and Violence Protection Act (TVPA). (2000). 22 U.S.C. 106-386.

12

You Learn When You Fall Down: Experience and Adaptation in a Program for Court-Involved Youths

Parvoneh Shirgir

> People make mistakes all the time. Even if you don't make that one, you'll make another one, but that's how you learn. You can't learn by looking in someone else's mirror. You learn when you fall down.
> —Jennifer, age 18, pre-High School Equivalency student[1]

Just as our lives are too complicated to split into binaries like work/home or personal/political, students' lives do not fit tidily into only the school environment nor do their home selves live only in apartments, streets, or houses. Fortunately for those of us who call teaching in the adult education world our "work," this complexity has been acknowledged and embraced for some time. Our students often split their time between being a student, head of household, parent, laborer, and caregiver, to name just a few roles. Or perhaps split is the wrong analogy—adult learners are simultaneously all of these things and all of these roles are constantly shifting. Educators and mental health professionals have typically highlighted this very skill—adaptation—when creating programs, environments, and curricula for use with adult learners. Adaptation is an invaluable trait that learners bring with them to their classrooms and their lives. Immigrant youths, especially, become skilled at adapting, given their experience with shifts in surroundings, language, and culture.

High School Equivalency (HSE)[2] programs would not survive if we expected learners to split themselves and leave substantial parts of who they are at home, or at work, or outside of our classrooms. Instead, most quality programs do not consider the HSE exam and a rigid sense of academic achievement the only measures of success, but rather weigh students' goals and hopes with many kinds of achievement that speak to many parts of a person's life (being able to successfully fill out job applications without assistance, reading a full book, understanding current events, and being able to assist younger family members with homework are but a few tangible goals). Likewise, much of the adult education world actively engages students' roles outside the classroom, embracing these experiences explicitly and implicitly in curriculum design in order to make lessons relevant and engaging. Students may be reluctant readers or voracious readers; they may be returning to school for the second or seventh time. Much like K-12 students, they are dynamic and diverse. As Jennifer explained, programs must also recognize that mistakes are a necessary part of the learning process; this attitude toward mistakes can encourage educators to inspire perseverance and self-reflection for these dynamic learners.

> I wasn't thinking about the future. I never thought I would get older, I thought my mother would always take care of me.
> —Michael, age 21, pre-HSE student

As a teacher in a New York City community-based organization focused on formerly incarcerated or court-involved individuals, I also witness students navigate complex public bureaucracies, the criminal (in)justice system, the shelter system, and various court-mandated drug treatment, anger management, and child welfare programs. Many students—especially immigrants, trauma survivors, emerging bilinguals, and those who have been diagnosed with disabilities—have often been treated by schools as deficient when in actuality these students and their pasts call attention to how bright, strong, and resilient people can be, especially with some support.

Instead of trying to disentangle young adults' multiple backgrounds, current roles, and hopes for the future in an attempt to create concrete, fixed models for support, I wonder if we might approach young adult learners (and perhaps all students) with a more adaptive approach. Given that we ask students to adapt their ways of engaging with the world in order to learn new approaches and techniques in classrooms, educators, too, must trust that students are savvy and informed individuals who know a great deal about themselves and our world.

As such, I aim to engage various scholars who explore language, culture, and disability in school settings, and I intend to connect these thoughts with lived experiences (those of my students, as expressed to or interpreted by me, as well as my own experiences) in a pre-HSE[3] class environment where change and adaptation are constant and constantly shifting. Although the program serves a diverse group of students, I focus particularly on immigrant youths in order to explore how external and internal motivators, cultural and lingual acclimation, legal and social services systems, family responsibilities, educational settings, disability labels and accommodations, and relationships and emotional ties all intersect, shift, and impact immigrant youths' development.

EDUCATIONAL INFLUENCES, MOTIVATIONS, AND GOALS

> What am I an expert at outside of school? I'm an expert at people. Being in jail I had no choice but to deal with people. I know I'm good at it because everybody says I'm a good people person. I get to practice in school when my teacher makes me speak in front of people.
> —Michael

This group of 17- to 24-year-old students meets twice a day—two hours for reading and writing in the morning and one hour for math in the afternoon—for five days a week. All students have been court involved, though only about half are currently court mandated to participate in an alternative to incarceration or drug treatment program in the agency. For many mandated students, participation in the education program seems favorable for court reports and court appearances, and some judges may even indicate that students must be enrolled in classes by their following court date. Indeed, many influential people in a young person's life outside court environments may hope that the young adult earns his or her HSE, oftentimes based on arbitrary timelines.

Parents, grandparents, child welfare programs, and judges often ask the student to achieve their HSE certificate within a year (in the case of court-mandated students, this timeline is even shorter—during the six months they have been mandated to the program). Given that so many students leave school during the eighth, ninth, or tenth grades and that most of these students were not performing at the same level as their peers and have been out of school environments for anywhere between two months and six years, attaining a HSE certificate in six months is a rather speedy timeline. Some students certainly continue in education classes after they have completed their mandated program, but several also begin to attend irregularly or stop coming at all in order to focus on work or because they never really wanted to join the program. Other students elect to be in the education program because they believe the HSE will assist them in their careers or educational goals or because education is a pervasive expectation for young adults.

> I'm motivated on my own. Education ends the crime cycle. It's the key to success. You can get a higher income, pay your bills, give your kids what you missed.
> —Jennifer

In addition to the varied, student-specific enrollment and attendance practices mentioned above, classes have rolling admission during each 11-week cycle, so it is unlikely that students in the classroom have attended classes for equal amounts of time before arriving at our program or while at our program. Similarly, students may vary in the exact periods of time they have been in the class (some may start in January, leave for the summer, and return in the fall, while others may join at any point in between or return after a year's absence or longer). Although this range proves challenging in building momentum and successfully scaffolding the group, this situation is not entirely unique to high school equivalency programs. Students from public K-12 schools may also move geographically (countries, neighborhoods, schools, grades, and teachers' classrooms) and into and out of different academic environments (honors, advanced placement, vocational, or other tracks, English language learner programs, special education, and mainstream programs). Indeed, it is clearly a common misconception that schools follow a singular, linear path. Likewise, we may find that students' progress and needs are not so simple to fulfill.

Students have an educational counselor for our class as well as other counselors and staff in wraparound programs throughout the agency. Thus, no one student will be typical, but it is exactly that atypicality that allows their stories to speak to the diverse experiences of students in K-12 schools and in the adult education world.

As students reenter educational environments, various identities and experiences begin to surface, and students also begin to glimpse new possible identities and roles. According to student interviews at intake and subsequent formal and informal conversations, members of our group are enrolled in classes because they believe having an HSE will help them enroll in the armed forces (Pedro),[4] because the HSE is required to get into college and later become a corrections officer (Lashonda) or in preparation for an unknown career (Steven, Alexander, Chantel, Claude), because their parents want them to finish this stage of schooling (Michael, Tyrell, Said), because they need a place to spend the day and stay out of trouble (Michael, Melissa), because they are on house arrest and want to leave the house to socialize as well as advance their studies (Juan and Cristian), and because their judge deemed education necessary and the student has aged out or been expelled from public school (Montell, Leonardo, Tyrell), among many others.

> Coming out of jail, I became a better person. I did three years and it changed me because I realized this isn't how I want to live my life, being told what to do the way they did it in jail. No. So as soon as I got out I told my parole officer to send me to this

> program because I wasn't doing too good in school or on the streets or in jail, but our program helped me.
>
> —Michael

Each individual's circumstances and goals influence student involvement and interest in class activities, but if the teacher is aware of these circumstances and other students are also aware of their friends' circumstances, the class community is better able to check in and revisit these circumstances when motivation seems lacking. Of course, lessons and the design of the curriculum also play a part in student engagement, and so our class foregrounds what we are doing and why on a daily basis through the use of an agenda as well as verbal explanations to the group and one-on-one conversations with individuals. For our class, hands-on projects, structure, repetition, and recall reinforce students' exposure to and mastery of skills. In addition, I aim to speak only enough to guide students during class and use my voice and presence to act as facilitator and questioner in order to encourage students to teach one another and (re)discover their own skills while accomplishing some common goal. Whenever possible, students are directed to their peers to get answers to their clarifying questions.

EXPLORING CLASSROOM ROLES AND IDENTITIES

It is additionally helpful to recognize that students shift roles and identities during literacy activities, just as they grow and develop (nonlinearly) in their lives outside school environments. Indeed, language is increasingly understood as "action," meaning that is developed through meaningful and engaging activities across the curriculum with appropriate supports (Bunch, Kibler, & Pimental, 2013; van Lier & Walqui, 2012; Walqui & vanLier, 2010). Because different activities and roles will click for different individuals, it is useful to expose students to many hands-on activities as well as many ways to engage in those activities. Literacy involves both cognitive and social processes, consequently reading, writing, and other forms of meaning-making, imply activity in which students have multiple purposes, often beyond those planned by teachers, and participants take on various roles and identities (Hull & Moje, 2012). Although teachers might not anticipate all of the possible roles students may encounter in a learning activity, they can support students as they navigate these possibilities by designing activities and environments where exploration (including making mistakes) is welcome and encouraged. Such activities aim to give students opportunities to try many kinds of engagement and also witness many ways of processing information in order to connect with something familiar or comfortable or to stretch and take on new ways of engagement.

When actions for the group task have not been preassigned, students tend to self-regulate, though patterns do emerge. Typically, students who have had positive experiences in the past feel more secure in tasks like reading aloud or attempting a math problem at the board. This dynamic in many ways illustrates Vygotsky's (2012) peer mentorship, where a student can teach others how and where they see connections and actions that can be made. I do see potential for harm in this self-selection process, however, as some students may build reputations as "experts" in certain areas. This expert status is excellent for students who once experienced stigma, as they are able to demonstrate to themselves and the group (including the teacher) that they have achieved deeper understanding. These students are often eager to share with others how they came to this point as well, as was the case with Pedro, who had a newfound love for math, and Michael, who struggles to focus during math activities but prefers a peer's assistance rather than the attention of the teacher.

At the same time, this "expert" identity can also reinforce the false notion that some individuals have innate skills that others can never achieve. If Pedro is seen to be *the* student who is "good at math," others may imagine that they themselves cannot fill that role, or at least not as well, and in doing so may limit their own achievement. Furthermore, students who view others as inherently "good" at some skill or topic might misidentify or even ignore the process that got the individual to the seemingly masterful level. If we remind ourselves and our students that learning involves acting, reacting, revising, working, and achieving these skills, we might avoid deficit models where some students "can do" art, math, or science and others "cannot."

Students certainly come with prior knowledge from K-12 educational environments, but unfortunately that knowledge often includes rigid ideas of disciplinary tasks that are often memory based rather than engaging, complex, thought-provoking ideas about topics with which students are more familiar. Many students wish to rush past seemingly basic skills and question the need to understand foundational concepts. Oftentimes these students have internalized the idea that math must be confusing and complicated, and that reading is about being able to pronounce multisyllabic words fluidly, quickly, and only once. The patience needed for a deeper, more conceptual approach is especially challenging for those who view themselves as "ready for the test" in reading or writing and feel anxious to move on from literacy lessons in favor of math. These students tend to have a fairly traditional idea of what reading is, which is reinforced by a testing culture that emphasizes being able to bubble answer sheets after reading a short passage over reflection, conversations, or projects that engage reading materials in a variety of ways. In addition, they have preconceived notions of what math is, which is typically polynomials and equations for volume or circumference.

Part of the teacher's role, then, is to ask students to reimagine what mathematical thinking is—to move the focus from rote procedures to the kinds of deductive, translation, and construction skills students regularly employ in their daily lives. Students also engage in areas in which they feel they have some security; with academic support, such as scaffolding, students may envision what they will be able to do in the future that they cannot currently do (Walqui, Bunch, Kibler, & Pimentel, 2013). This envisioning is one of the most challenging elements of teaching, as it asks that teachers piece together complex histories and then make predictions about the future. Scaffolding requires a critical transition as the learner begins to gain mastery. This handover/takeover requires both effort and support (Walqui et al., 2013). In some ways, this is exceptionally tricky, as students enter with different skill sets and interests, but in other ways, this system is very forgiving, as all students are welcomed to contribute to the task. Students like Pedro may also lead in the process of handover or takeover, until the student mentors and their peers all have a key understanding for the task at hand. Again, variety may exist, but students feel empowered to make connections and mistakes in an active process of learning.

PRIOR KNOWLEDGE, ACCLIMATION, AND SYSTEM INVOLVEMENT

As mentioned earlier, adult education programs are especially attuned to students' prior knowledge and experiences and purposefully design environments and curricula that speak to students' expertise and refocus when previous experiences may have been negative or confused. This makes sense, especially considering the overlap between English for speakers of other languages' environments and adult basic education environments and the unique academic and social methods that support English learners (ELs). Since all learning builds on prior knowledge and experiences, instruction for ELs must adequately assess what ELs bring to the classroom and expand knowledge from that foundation (Walqui & Heritage, 2012). ELs most certainly bring knowledge they may be eager to share, but previous school experiences have often made students tentative to share, either because of stigma or because environments simply neglected to address and give space for their knowledge. Psychological issues beyond issues of ability may hamper second language acquisition, as students are tasked with multiple kinds of acclimation, such as new family structures and roles, new locations, new peers, and unfamiliar cultures, in addition to language.

One student in our program, Jennifer, joined the class with relatively strong math skills but slightly lower literacy skills. Jennifer had moved to New York City from Mexico four years prior and she expressed embarrassment about her accent and reading abilities. In addition to being relatively new to her geographic home, Jennifer struggles with her home in terms of family life.

> If I could change one thing about my life I would change the decision of running away from home. I would deal with my sadness, responsibility, and new life of being a teen mom. The moment that I ran away I put myself in the jungle, like I knew how I got there but I didn't know how to get out.[5] The moment I started being independent is the moment I put myself in jail.

Jennifer often makes insightful comments about her life and the lives of her peers, challenging expectations and assumptions about the decisions young people make. Because Jennifer turned herself in to the court, after having violated parole by running away from home, she faced "the worst, eating fruit all of the time because the nasty food in jail just makes you throw up, but the best thing happened—feeling the relief of no warrants, no cops, no courts." At a young age Jennifer realized that she had decision-making power and that she could find or shape positive changes in her life even in seemingly negative situations.

Today Jennifer is involved with social service programs for herself as well as for her baby daughter. Clearly she is tasked with a great deal as she works to address acculturation, home life, language, court, and school requirements. As a very driven young woman, she has also bumped heads with other students at times. In private, Jennifer often expresses frustration that other students do not focus as much as she does or that they make poor life decisions. In a case conference, Jennifer explained that she believes she is the smartest in the class, and she relayed a moment where she told a friend that she is the smartest in class and the friend is the smartest after her and together they will be first to attain their HSE certificates. Jennifer's friend struggles with self-described low self-esteem, so this moment demonstrates positive development in Jennifer's academic confidence, but also a potentially damaging moment for her friend and their relationship.

After teasing in class escalated to name calling and verbal threats, Jennifer and two other students were asked to take a weeklong break from class. Jennifer was upset during the counseling meeting that led to this decision and, since our class counselor is bilingual, Jennifer switched between Spanish and English as she expressed her frustration. If our counselor had not allowed Jennifer to speak in her first language or if we did not have staff with such capabilities, Jennifer would experience what many ELs experience—an additional barrier to understanding during a moment of conflict. Months after, Jennifer brought up the suspension again, as she is interested in fairness and how she has been treated compared to others on a small scale and also how groups are subject to injustice on a large scale.

> Jennifer: It was unfair. It was my first suspension, I had never been suspended before. We had been playing in class and then the next week [another student] just took it too far. I don't play with him like that, I told him to stop, and then I told Ms. Parvoneh and I got suspended, too.
> Michael: Yeah, that seems unfair, if someone's bullying you and then you get in trouble.

Although it can be challenging to revisit these moments, we should not consider Jennifer deficient or troublesome for being concerned with her academic participation, reputation, and interpersonal relationships with peers and staff. Instead we can attempt to understand the situation from her perspective and better explain the thought process that led to our decision. The counselor and I agreed that all students involved in the initial incident should take a break from school given that the original horseplay seemed to lead to the later incident. In order to have some space from one another and reflect on their academic goals, we gave each student a week off. Students' reactions have sparked some doubt in our process, however, and we have started to debate whether to utilize suspensions at all in the program. Students' attention to justice can be informative and poignant. At the very least, this attention is understandable given students' previous experience with the legal system, and we do not want to reinforce the idea that school environments and other formal institutions turn to broad and simplistic disciplinary measures in the face of community conflict.

As she nears the end of her required program mandate, Jennifer expressed that she's excited and happy to be successfully completing her program, stating with exasperation that she has gone through "All of this over one shirt, can you believe that?" Though she did not elaborate in detail, Jennifer explained that she had become immersed in the legal system and various programs because of an initial minor theft charge. Being told where to live, how to live, and what to do for several months seems to have been a plan made for Jennifer's best interests, but these decisions may also seem punitive. "It's their job," she explained, noting that court and mandated program staff have little autonomy. "No matter how you feel, you don't get to express yourself. They have to do the paperwork, they don't ask you what you want." Jennifer's tone implied forgiveness toward the individual worker but also frustration with the larger system.

This lack of control or influence over major decision making is especially out of synch with the needs and desires of young people, who have values, goals, and unique perspectives on the world, but experience confusingly generalized systems and institutions that subject them to adult consequences for adult actions without providing room for their voices in the process. Students like Jennifer have especially shone when given the opportunity to voice their perspectives. Even in our organization, however, contractual obligations and policies within and outside the agency severely limit individual agency and self-determination. Jennifer is very bright and motivated and has shown that she can persevere in many learning experiences. I do fear, however, that the extreme involvement of the legal system in her life will limit her possibilities not only in terms of employment, housing, and higher education, where a criminal record is outrageously detrimental to a person's prospects, but also that the legal system's warped version of justice and punishment may influence Jennifer's and her peers' sense of what is permissible and possible in her life and the lives of others.

Although she has some growing and new challenges ahead of her, Jennifer typically channels her energy into academic achievement. She is extremely focused and motivated, and her test scores have risen steadily throughout her time in the program. She has taken on leadership roles in after-class projects and has become familiar with staff and participants in many departments throughout the organization. She led the class in a community justice project, speaking to our senior executive staff about the agency's outdated "No Hats" rule and convincing the group to change the policy.

Jennifer also traveled to Albany with members of our class and several partner organizations in order to advocate for reentry bills. Although she has momentary anxiety, like most do with public speaking, Jennifer always communicates with passion and eagerly articulates facts and opinions that might inform others about injustices and how these injustices can be remedied. Although spare moments of difference have caused conflict in the classroom, Jennifer has also utilized moments of difference to share and expand our community. When a fellow student explained the importance of basketball in his life, for example, Jennifer talked about her love of soccer. Her explanation was welcoming and informational in tone, as if she noted this cultural difference but hoped that both parties could share their enthusiasm together. Indeed, a Puerto Rican student pointed to Jennifer's shirt and said that he rooted for the same team featured on her jersey.

As she has taken on new challenges, Jennifer has also articulated new and updated goals for herself. Inspired by Harriet Tubman and her subsequent success with our intra-agency activism, Jennifer expressed interest in becoming a lawyer. When we visited Albany to speak with legislators on reentry issues, she expressed interest in becoming a judge. Clearly as students engage in educational environments, their experiences, interests, and hopes shift. Thriving classrooms and programs will not only acknowledge but also encourage these changes by creating opportunities for students to pursue new interests with ample time and support.

CULTURAL DISSONANCE AND YOUTH DECISION MAKING

Though we do not have sports or many formal school extracurriculars, these kinds of activities and interests impact students' sense of self academically and socially. In a class application essay,[6] Claude explained that he was a volleyball star in his home country of Trinidad and he was unhappy when he learned that his family would be moving to the United States during his final years of high school. Once here, he found that volleyball is not a popular sport in New York City high schools (though not explicitly stated, this seems especially true for a young man). Claude picked up basketball for a while, but he explained that he was teased for his accent and never felt as if he fit in.

He explained that he "fell in with the wrong crowd" back home and had switched from government school to private school. Once in New York, Claude attended a high school where he got into a fight during his first week and was consequently suspended. After a week, Claude returned to school, but he got into another fight and was given another suspension. Eventually he dropped out of high school altogether because he sensed that he would continue to encounter more trouble in school than he would outside of school. Though sports and other so-called extracurricular activities are often deemed irrelevant, at least by policymakers, Claude experienced a specific delegitimization of his experience and interest when he arrived in an environment where volleyball was not offered by his school and not valued by his peers and the larger culture he was attempting to grasp.

In addition to this cultural shift, Claude also shifted academic and living environments repeatedly. Although he seems to have a strong network of family support (I have received calls from his mother as well as his uncle about Claude's participation and progress), schools must also make an effort to recognize and address the needs of young adults, specifically immigrant youths. Suspending Claude repeatedly, just as with many of our students, left Claude and his family frustrated. Such suspensions additionally contribute to the school-to-prison pipeline that further disrupts young people's educations.

Claude has often expressed regret about this series of events, explaining that he could have been done with high school at this point in time had he not dropped out. Nonetheless, Claude is very motivated and helpful, and he has read several books from the "Bluford High" series during his time in the class. Most recently, he explained that he went home, cleaned in anticipation of his mother's return from a trip to Trinidad, took a late afternoon nap, then stayed up until 2 a.m. to finish reading his book. Although he can be a bit playful in class, Claude often asks clarifying questions and enlists the participation of neighboring students. As with many immigrant and adult learners, Claude has learned to be a master of adaptation.

Claude is not alone in his tendency to self-shame, which is particularly apparent when students write their application essays, calling out "bad decisions" or "screwing up" their lives. The status quo is unspoken yet ever-present—these students miss their homecoming dances, proms, and graduations, while their peers participate in such milestone events. Students like Lashonda have mentioned that younger siblings are sometimes studying similar topics or doing similar work, which can also feel demoralizing to our pre-HSE students. The very idea of "screwing up" one's life implies that there is a right way to live one's life, and these students take on responsibility for not fitting that mold.

Indeed, schools are often where students first encounter the police and experience suspensions, expulsion, and other kinds of official punishment and discipline. This culture of compliance results in a culture of fear, and also shame, for those who do not or cannot comply due to language, culture, or disability dissonance. As Michael explained, "In my house nobody tells you what to do, but school did. Or tried to. They tried to tell me what to do but I didn't listen. They'd say 'I'm going to call your mother,' but I didn't care, I didn't listen. I knew she wouldn't really be bothered herself." He admits that he sometimes feels regret, but he also notes "There's nothing you can do about it. I mean, you can make a change by doing things here at school, but you can't go back in time, back to high school. Other people talk about prom, graduation, how they wish they were going, and I'm kinda mad, too. But there's nothing you can do about it."

Individuals change, and I believe that much of the potentially harmful self-shaming that students put to paper in their application actually stems from a hopeful belief that while they cannot change the past, they can learn from their experiences, and in some ways then they can change. Ogbu and Simons (1998) suggest that we can identify group adaptation patterns based in past experiences and how those experiences influence expectations for the future. Much like scaffolding, positive outcomes require that students and staff both have some understanding of background and also share a trust that the future can build positively from that base. Systems have some influence, but individuals also have agency in this process:

> More specifically, to understand why minority groups differ among themselves in school performance we have to know two things: the first is their own responses to their history of incorporation into U.S. society and their subsequent treatment or mistreatment by white Americans. The second is how their responses to that history and treatment affect their perceptions of and responses to schooling. Structural barriers and school factors affect minority school performance; however, minorities are also autonomous human beings who actively interpret and respond

to their situation. Minorities are not helpless victims. (Ogbu & Simons 1998, p. 158)

When students do not adapt to the norms of their environment, it may be because they have experiences that do not support this kind of behavior, but it may also be because they *choose* not to adjust based on their prior knowledge. The young adults in our class have often been labeled defiant, disruptive, or hostile, but these attitudes are not arbitrary, nor do they point to any kind of inherent deficiency. A great deal of this labeling comes from adults who have rigid expectations for youths and who view student struggles as efforts to undermine the instructor or class rather than an expression of discontent or discomfort. In fact, students theorize their own lives very well; what they sometimes lack are the literacy and numeracy skills to engage in more formal educational environments. If we aim to understand how students carry and respond to their histories, we might ask students to adapt to our classroom structures and expectations, rather than ask students to conform to unfamiliar or even irrelevant educational expectations.

NAVIGATING FAMILY RESPONSIBILITIES AND EDUCATIONAL SETTINGS

Walqui et al. (2013) explain the centrality of scaffolding to build on students' prior knowledge and language skills to create the conditions for productive and meaningful learning and language development. This is challenging for teachers, certainly, and also for students. For language and acculturation purposes, many immigrant children have near head-of-household status in their families, especially as young adults. Even when not head of the household in the wage-earning sense, these students may serve as translators or interpreters for parents who need to engage with English-dominant agencies and offices. Alexander, a student who joined our class with a backpack full of supplies and a rather high skill set, openly shared about his arrest for selling drugs, specifically pills. He regretted the arrest but took pride in his sales and math skills and seemed to value his knowledge of pharmaceuticals and their effects (a kind of scientific thinking that we did not engage directly in during our class sessions, but which is indeed notable).

Alexander's mother, an immigrant from Colombia, has a steady job cleaning, and, according to Alexander, has been disappointed by her son's trouble in high school and his arrest. When I called Alexander's home to check in after absences from our class, his mother was always extremely cheery and apologetic about her English. At times she would pass the phone to a younger sibling who would take a message, giving the impression that Alexander, as the eldest child, likely fills a similar role when he is home. Although

Alexander was born in the United States, his family's immigration continues to influence his life, and he rises to this familial responsibility while pursuing his individual scholastic goals.

> Cultural-ecological theories argue that the resources in children's families, schools, and neighborhoods influence their lifestyles, daily experiences, and outcomes. Because migration exposes children to unique developmental demands and stressors associated with acculturation, it reshapes their normative development. To adapt, immigrant children and their families choose different combinations of acculturation and enculturation strategies. (Perreira & Ornelas, 2011, p. 197)

Students like Claude and Alexander were presented with multiple instances to interpret and act in order to protect their individual and family interests while also weighing systematic expectations. These are rather snarly situations for such young people to try to assess; that they feel they have made mistakes, or that they have done their best given the circumstances is understandable. Alexander eventually tested out of our class's literacy range and was moved to a higher-level class, but his on-and-off employment took precedent and his attendance slipped over time. Alexander asked to take the GED before the 2014 cutoff, and although he did not meet our program requirements (we ask that students successfully pass all five sections of the practice test before finding a testing date on their behalf), he was computer savvy and found an application online. He recruited my assistance to map out testing sites and mailed his application independently to secure a seat. At the end of 2013, Alexander passed the GED and, after we reached out to him, he returned to our facility and agreed to meet with our college advisers.

Alexander has a young aunt who is in college and lends him books she has enjoyed, but Alexander otherwise lacks role models who have navigated the college system. When he revisited our program, he explained that he was partway through the enrollment process for a predatory trade school nearby, but he was deterred after meeting with a college adviser. At that point, Alexander shared a story that is unfortunately quite common with adult learners—he had already taken out a good deal of loans with another predatory college that promised he would earn his GED on his way to achieving an associate's degree. After accumulating several thousand dollars of debt at that college and little tangible progress, Alexander left to pursue full-time employment at a bank.

Alexander leaves jobs after short stints somewhat regularly (another common, understandable occurrence with our students who juggle caretaker roles as well as legal, interpersonal, and bureaucratic duties), so he joined our education program and earned his HSE certificate within a year. Alexander also came to our program with a burgeoning student identity, demonstrating skills such as note-taking and habits like sustained pleasure reading. Alexander explained that his mother required he carry certain markers of educational involvement such as his book bag or homework, markers that have often been maligned in students' previous educational experiences as "corny" or perhaps even useless. In fact, he explained that when he did not carry a book or papers home, his mother doubted that he had been at school at all, so carrying work was for his own benefit and also a performance of his student identity for family audience. Court involvement, immigrant family duties, and lack of educational guidance impacted Alexander's journey, but he has also been able to utilize these experiences, including positive elements of these experiences, in order to become an adaptive young person who is prepared and motivated to accomplish his goals.

YOUTH'S NEEDS AND APPROACHES TO AMBIGUITIES

Wright, Taylor, and Moghaddam (1990, p. 998) write about the deaf culture, but their framework holds for many immigrant students in New York City, as "individual attempts at social mobility will be maintained as long as the advantaged group appears open and as long as entry is dependent solely on individual performance. However, when a disadvantaged-group member is prevented from gaining entry into the advantage group and perceives the system as closed, individual social mobility will be abandoned in favor of collective action."

Indeed, many students in our program have been gang involved at some point, and many of our staff trainings emphasize the needs that are met in gang membership (housing, community, security, money, feeling part of something, and gaining status, to name but a few). Although we do not often speak openly about specific gang activity in class in order to minimize conflicts between students, young people are fairly open about the presence of gangs in their communities, and an understanding of students' proactive choice to meet their needs through an organization greatly informs the work my colleagues and I do with students. It is instructional to note the ways that students have psychological and other needs met through gang involvement, as these needs might also be addressed through supportive and adaptive educational settings.

Fortunately, managing multiple roles, interpreting past events, and making intuitive decisions can actually equip students well for learning actions. Walqui et al. (2013) note that the most effective second language learners tolerate ambiguity and make educated guesses. Students in our class have become masters of ambiguity, whether it be in housing and homelessness, public benefits' bureaucracy, documentation processes, incarceration and court delays, abrupt relocation, loss of friends and loved ones to gun violence or HIV or diabetes, or custody and new parenthood. Many, like Jennifer, balance many ambiguous moments and go even further to seek moments to push themselves, to strive for excellence. "I'm an expert at soccer and maybe math. I know that I am an expert at soccer because most of the time my team wins when I play, and also my friends, family, and my boyfriend tell me that I am good at it. Math, I practice all the time, school, home, and anywhere. Math is everywhere, and also I told myself I am good and I show it to my teachers." Every student faces intersecting challenges and also complex, joyous triumphs. Supportive school environments should recognize students' navigational abilities and celebrate processes as well as more traditional progress milestones.

When it comes to literacy, teachers must then interpret where struggles or delays might be and which delays occur in which languages (oral as well as written) in order to facilitate student growth, especially when working with ELs or immigrant students. We might even apply this approach to speakers of Standard Black English (SBE, or African American Vernacular English), who are often asked to "code switch" between SBE and Standard American English (SAE) as SAE is treated preferentially in most academic environments.[7] Indeed, SBE has grammatical rules and structures like any language, but it is marginalized in educational institutions, especially on standardized tests. Consequently, most students of color in urban schools must learn to navigate language ambiguity in school settings.

In our young adult class, students obviously recognize when they are using SBE during editing sessions, and I often hear them self-shaming as they change SBE to SAE, calling certain terms or spellings "hood" or "ghetto" (or, less racially charged, "text speak") and implying that this language is lesser or improper in our environment. One 20-year-old black student, Michael, insists that his name should be pronounced "the way white people say it," and he often inquires about racial difference, at times ascribing certain positive characteristics like friendliness or proper manners to whiteness. The way that Michael expresses this socially inherited racism outright is perhaps unique to his personality, but many students share these self-deprecating tendencies, especially when discussing their written language. As an instructor, I always express that I understood the student's first draft and attempt to validate his or her knowledge by repeating the idea in my own words. Students have a deep understanding of their culture, however, and also take pleasure in explaining slang and insider language to those who are not as informed. As mentioned earlier, when students are given space to make connections and activate their prior knowledge, they demonstrate great skill and resilience.

DISABILITY AND COGNITIVE DIVERSITY

At times I hear from students that they once had an individualized education plan (IEP) that addressed a learning disability in their former schools. Because the adult education world is not part of the New York City public schools network (with a few exceptions), I rarely see these documents myself. Janelle, a 21-year-old Caribbean young woman who rejoined our program after a year doing odd jobs, brought her IEP after a few months in class in order to see if she might qualify for extra time on the TASC exam. The IEP document was incredibly vague, however, and made no mention of extra test time, though Janelle recalls having additional time in high school. Aside from recommending small class sizes, the document only conveyed a general message that Janelle was below her peers on academic tests.

It is not clear if the preparer knew Janelle before writing the IEP; there were no descriptions of assessments used to make these claims. Ultimately, we found the document to provide little insight about Janelle's educational abilities. Instead, the existence of this paperwork provides insight into Janelle's mostly negative experience in K-12 schooling environments. Indeed, Janelle would often tremble in class when she first joined, seemingly suffering from anxiety about being in class. She explained her low self-esteem openly and often made self-deprecating remarks in our lessons. Nonetheless, Janelle has been an eager participant from the start. This kind of resilience is striking at times, but also makes a lot of sense given the responsibilities Janelle has taken on at home and her desire to succeed formally and build positive informal relationships.

Thus, while a student's feelings about or account of disability and special education labels can be informative for work together in our program, for the most part these delineations are hazy at best. Instead, our class attempts to include methods for addressing a variety of abilities in the structure of our curriculum. Several students have referred to an attention deficit hyperactivity disorder (ADHD) diagnosis, for example, which could call for hands-on activities, structure, and individual check-ins from the instructor. These practices benefit most students in our program, so I attempt to include plenty of manipulatives, group tasks that may involve movement, and a great deal of instructor circulation during class. Some students, like Christopher who is often chatty or impulsive, can be proactive about their needs once this dialogue exists—he might request a break to get water when he starts to feel he is losing focus, or he can request individual attention during a task. Similarly, instruction methods for autism involve visual, auditory, and kinesthetic activities that benefit many kinds of learners. Rather than differentiate instruction or attempt to diagnose students, classes may build skills using methods that could benefit students in any classroom.

Adult education students thrive with structure and clarity while simultaneously living complicated, adaptive lives. In order to survive, students make choices and change to respond to their environments. Many ADHD symptoms match behaviors exhibited by trauma survivors and, as a teacher, I am not equipped to determine whether a student has a disability or is coping with trauma (in fact I do not believe these are necessarily separate or that prior diagnoses are necessarily founded or accurate). What I can do as an educator is encourage students to bring their experiences to our class, and I can also foster a validating atmosphere for students to employ the skills they have developed during their lives thus far—be it at home, in another country, at work, as a parent, as a child, or in some other environment or role. Rather than shirk from the personal as private, I aim to view students as people whose personal lives inform their scholarly pursuits.

In feminist epistemologies, the concept of cognitive diversity suggests that human intellectual capacities are manifested in multiple ways of organizing the production of knowledge and there is no justification, scientific or philosophic, to reduce them to the small numbers that have been privileged at particular times and places (Harding, 1998). Classrooms that organize and value knowledge along strict academic standards cannot adequately serve students who are so diverse and adaptive. In fact, cultures comprise both continuity and change; the identities of a societies survive through changes. A society that ceases to change is bound to die (Appiah, 2006). If we apply this analysis of culture to educational cultures, we may see that educational models that resist or stifle students' adaptive natures cannot survive without ejecting those who cannot or choose not to conform.

MISPERCEPTIONS AND EMOTIONAL OPENNESS

Students not only adapt, they also tolerate misunderstandings and misperceptions, even from well-meaning support figures such as myself. In writing this chapter, I emphasized categorical identities based in age, culture, immigration, and other socially ascribed group categories. It seemed obvious that certain changes in students' lives—shifts in language, home, environment, legal standing—would have an impact on their educational journey. While discussing the chapter with students, two students packed up their belongings while discussing love and heartbreak, asking each other and me about our struggles with love. When I asked, tentatively, if I should include heartbreak in the chapter, they emphatically supported the topic. "Yes! It f***s up my school when I'm thinking about this female," one student said. "I guess between your heart and your brain, your feelings are gonna win," the other mused.

Just as students adapt in literacy activities and between various identities and environments, all the while regulating emotions related to these shifts, they are also asked to adjust their emotional lives less explicitly. I was shocked at how much I value emotion and the personal on an abstract level, how much this thinking informs my feminism, and yet completely ignored the complexities of love when it came time to examine the struggles and triumphs of the young adult learners. Indeed, I believe romantic love and even family relationships are often treated, with good intentions, as private or personal and so are carefully sidestepped when in fact these personal emotions can actually greatly impact engagement, focus, and the overall well-being of both students and staff. Though we do not always ask students to split their home selves from their school selves, we tend to ignore certain kinds of relationships due to societal conventions and norms. Perhaps openness about love (joy, heartbreak, and all) might encourage us to expand our thinking about education and challenge us all to better understand our capacities and choices. Although this may seem an idealistic task, such considerations may have more tangible, practical consequences as well. As one student pointed out, "Young people don't go to school sometimes because they want to be with their boy or their girl. I missed a lot of school from that, meeting during class somewhere outside."

Luckily, just as students are adaptive, so too are educators and mental health professionals (despite protestations to the contrary). Thus, we might pursue Appiah's (2006) cosmopolitanism, wherein we embrace the philosophical notion of fallibilism—a recognition that our knowledge is imperfect, provisional, subject to change when confronting new evidence. It is shortsighted and uneven to expect students to adapt without calling for educator counterparts to adjust, engage, and revise—to be active learners. Instead, educators and mental health professionals may revisit traditional narratives of youths' deficiency and reorient to focus on adaptability, specifically for immigrant youths who have started their lives in other cultures (including, at times, other languages) and continue to navigate multiple cultures throughout their lives. Surely we must ask for students to adapt at times, but if students choose not to, we must also pause to understand why—instead of insisting on compliance, we might adapt ourselves, questioning the impulse to ask youths to discard their prior knowledge.

Many immigrant youths carry with them complex histories and nuanced ways of interpreting experience. Appiah's (2006) cosmopolitan embrace of change is likewise informative for educators and mental health professionals who aim to support these young people. Appiah argues that to preserve a wide range of human conditions in order to allow free people the best chance to make their own lives, enforcing diversity may in fact trap people within those categories they long to escape. Through attitudes, policies, and everyday practices, we can aim to support students as dynamic individuals rather than short-term test-takers or clients. While students approach their work with openness from below, those above can make choices that encourage flexible goal setting, individualized timelines, and varied academic approaches. Though it means our work is unending, my hope is that educators and mental health professionals, especially those who work with immigrant youths, will be flexible enough to support students when their experiences and desires differ from our preconceptions, and that we will push ourselves to be this protean—this free—as well.

NOTES

1. Pseudonyms have been used throughout to maintain students' privacy.

2. HSE is the preferred terminology in the adult education field today, as the General Educational Development (GED) exam is a trademarked term and New York State no longer officially endorses the GED as of January 2014. HSE testing across the United States has changed, according to policymakers, in order to align to the Common Core State Standards and ensure that HSE recipients are college ready. New York State's Board of Regents put out a call for proposals and decided to pursue McGraw-Hill's Test Assessing Secondary Completion (TASC) exam for 2014.

3. Pre-HSE students generally score between a fourth- and eight-grade reading level on McGraw-Hill's Test of Adult Basic Education (TABE). My program also uses a writing sample, a one-on-one oral reading assessment, and an interview between the new student and a staff member in order to determine class placement. Class enrollment caps at about 20 students.

4. The students listed here have not all attended during the same time period but rather represent a few students from each cycle of classes in 2013.

5. When I mentioned that Jennifer's "jungle" metaphor was very evocative, Jennifer explained that the jungle was a major setting in the last novel she had read. This self-motivated application of new knowledge demonstrates students' constantly changing skills, interests, and goals—the very act of learning brings about a changed and ever-changing student.

6. Our youth classes require a 500-word application essay before students are officially admitted, as these classes involve a slightly higher commitment and the potential for internships halfway through each class cycle. The prompt is to describe "A moment or situation that either demonstrates your character or helped shape it."

7. For more on the history and linguistics of SBE/AAVE, see Geoffrey K. Pullum's "African American Vernacular English Is Not Standard English with Mistakes," in *The Workings of Language: From Prescriptions to Perspectives*, ed. by Rebecca S. Wheeler, 39-58. Westport, CT: Praeger, 1999.

REFERENCES

Appiah, K. A. (2006, January 1). The case for contamination. *New York Times*.

Bunch, G. C., Kibler, A., & Pimentel, S. (2013). *Realizing opportunities for English learners: Common core english language arts and disciplinary literacy standards*. American Educational Research Association annual meeting.

Harding, S. (1998). Women, science, and society. *Science, 281*(5383), 1599–1600.
Hull, G., & Moje, E. B. (2012, January). *What is the development of literacy the development of?* Paper presented at the Understanding Language Conference, Stanford, CA. Retrieved from http://ell.stanford.edu/papers/language.
Ogbu, J. U., & Simons, H. D. (1998). Voluntary and involuntary minorities: A cultural-ecological theory of school performance with some implications for education. *Anthropology & Education Quarterly, 29*(2), 155–188.
Perreira, K. M., & Ornelas, I. J. (2011). The physical and psychological well-being of immigrant children. *The Future of Children, 21*(1), 195–218.
van Lier, L., & Walqui, A. (2012, January). *How teachers and educators can most usefully and deliberately consider language.* Paper presented at the Understanding Language Conference, Stanford, CA.
Vygotsky, L. (2012). Imagination and childhood. Quoted in Smagorinsky, P. Vygotsky, "defectology," and the inclusion of people of difference in the broader cultural stream. *Journal of Language and Literacy Education, 8*(1), 1–25.
Walqui, A., Bunch, G. C., Kibler, A., & Pimentel, S. (2013). *Postscript: Key reconceptualizations for ELA teachers in enacting effective instruction for ELLs in the Common Core.* American Educational Research Association annual meeting.
Walqui, A., & Heritage, M. (2012, January). *Instruction for diverse groups of English language learners.* Paper presented at the Understanding Language Conference, Stanford, CA
Walqui, A., & van Lier, L. (2010). *Scaffolding the academic success of adolescent English language learners: A pedagogy of promise.* San Francisco, CA: WestEd.
Wright, S., Taylor, D., & Moghaddem, F. (1990). Responding to membership in a disadvantaged group: from acceptance to collective protest. *Journal of Personality and Social Psychology, 58*(6), 994–1003.

13

Narratives of Immigrant Community College Students

Stacey J. Cooper and Carol Korn-Bursztyn

Formal education can ease the transition to immigrant life for newcomers into a new land; however, educational experiences can also complicate this process. To many immigrants, school provides a secure pathway to social mobility. According to research, schooling is also associated with beneficial developments like better health and greater economic security. Schooling is believed to be particularly important for immigrant youth, as it is often the first sustained, meaningful, and enduring participation in an institution in their new society (Suárez-Orozco, Suárez-Orozco, & Todorova, 2010). This chapter presents the reflective accounts of immigrant college students' memorable schooling experiences. These narratives show that despite coming from different cultural backgrounds, these immigrant students shared similar dispositions toward school, felt that relational supports were important, and believed that graduation was valuable.

Children and youths spend a majority of their time in school environments where they interact with teachers and peers. It is in school that immigrant youths are introduced to new cultural norms, both officially and unofficially, by faculty and peers. Developing and maintaining school relationships can help students in the acculturative process. By building friendships and social networks, immigrant students can acquire the required academic, linguistic, and cultural knowledge that will help them to navigate this acculturative transition.

The narratives in this chapter are culled from the first author's work as an instructor in an introductory psychology course at a local community college. The school has an ethnically, culturally, and racially diverse student population; about half the student population was Latino; 25% were African American; 19% were identify as other. Only half were U.S. citizens, although about 80% had completed high school in the United States. Nine percent of the students were enrolled in English as a second language course; 14% were taking an English development course. A quarter of the students were enrolled in developmental math courses.

I asked the students to reflect on their experiences in school, specifically those that made the deepest impressions on them, and how they thought these experiences helped them to grow. They spoke about graduation, participation in clubs and activities, interacting with friends, doing and learning new things, and overcoming fears, shyness, and loneliness. Upon further examination, it became clear that these memories clustered around themes of overcoming difficulties, the importance of relational support, and graduation as an achievement. Moreover, these narratives highlight the important role that peers, friends, and teachers played in shaping the school environment for these immigrant students. Surprisingly, the students' narratives became a starting point for examining not only the difficulties they experienced as young immigrants, but also increasingly emphasized their triumphs.

In the sections that follow, narratives of students will be presented, followed by a brief discussion of each vignette, followed by the contexts that amplify the concepts raised by these student writers. The first vignette, Alex,[1] presents a triumphant, heroic narrative. English is the chief obstacle Alex had to hurdle in the quest of his goal, graduation. High school graduation, the golden apple of pre-K-12 education, is only the first of several epic feats he must accomplish in his continued academic quest. True to heroic trope, Alex tells a story of self-reliance and perseverance, despite the forbiddingly high walls that the English language presents.

CASE VIGNETTE: ALEX

> One of the most memorable experiences I had in school was the day I graduated from high school. I was so happy, glad and proud of myself because in just four years I got to accomplish one of my goals, which was to learn English. Thanks to this experience I am able to understand what a non-English speaker have [has] to go through in this country and also that no matter how high a wall is, I can go over it and reach my goals. This experience helped me to grow as student because I learned not to give up with the English language. I know it is not an obstacle [and] to keep going with my life and dream.

Graduation

Graduation represented a rite of passage, signaling hard-won maturity borne of perseverance in the face of challenge. Additionally, graduation was a ritual to be shared with family and friends. A good deal of the literature on immigration has focused on exploring and understanding student academic performance and success (Fuligni, 1997, 1999; Suárez-Orozco, Suárez-Orozco, & Todorova, 2010). Many of these sources agree that academic performance and academic trajectories are determined by not only the student's own efforts but also the contexts in which they develop (Suarez-Orozco et al., 2010).

Student motivation is believed to be central to student achievement and typically involves task and performance goals. Although motivation is typically conceptualized as an individual endeavor, research suggests that like student engagement, it too is subject to the influence of peers, family, and community (Trumbull & Rothstein-Fisch, 2011). The following narrative also invokes the epic challenges that the English language presents as an obstacle to feeling at home, to self-expression, and to communication with others. The heroic trope is tempered by the more nuanced account that Alicia introduces.

CASE VIGNETTE: ALICIA

> Migrating to America and going to school as a foreign student wasn't easy. It [is] a new school, new language I couldn't understand at all. I cried every single day because it is hard when you [are] trying to express yourself and could not. Thanks to my teachers, family and friends [and] also my motivation I was able to focus on my study. I started ESL [English as a second language class]. I learned, asked for help, read aloud and memorized. As a person, I learned a lot about that experience, now I know a language. [I am] able to translate for someone who [is] new to America. I am not where I am supposed to be but I am getting there little by little.

Alicia opens her narrative with a description of despair at feelings of otherness (i.e., "foreign student") but quickly moves into her central narrative of successfully facing and surmounting obstacles. Significantly, Alicia positions herself in relation to other helpful figures and envisions herself as reciprocating or giving back the help she received to others. She first acknowledges the role of others in her achievement, "teachers, family and friends," and secondarily her own intrinsic motivation and self-directed initiatives, including "asking for help, reading aloud, memorized."

Alicia's imagined future-directed prosocial behavior—"translate for someone"—is clearly intended to benefit others, reflecting Alicia's aim of reciprocity. Reciprocity, a prosocial behavior that emerges from healthy relationships between parents and children, typically generalizes to cooperativeness among peers and among identified group members, including immigrant groups.

RELATIONAL ENGAGEMENT AND SUPPORT: THE DILEMMA OF HELP

In order to navigate the trials of daily life, immigrant students often find themselves reliant on many people for support and assistance. This presents a developmental dilemma for young immigrants who are chronologically and developmentally well beyond the early childhood years. The developmental push for autonomous functioning has its roots in toddlerhood but finds its fullest expression in adolescence. When assistance is experienced as a regression to the dependency of early childhood, resistance and refusal of help are psychologically consistent with the tasks of adolescence. Alex deals with this dilemma in his narrative by omitting the contributions of others and focuses on his own determination and self-directed efforts to achieve his goals. This is consistent with the developmental task of late adolescence and early adulthood to engage in goal-directed behavior, to persevere through difficult situations, and to demonstrate capacity to tolerate frustration in order to achieve one's aims.

Alicia takes a slightly different tack. Her narrative is also one of perseverance and strength; like Alex she is the author of her own life. Her narrative opens with a similar heroic structure: she opens with the travails of her new situation—alone, bereft, and despairing. Predictably, her story takes a turn toward action and activity. Her story, though, includes helpful others. She acknowledges the support she received but also emphasizes that she sought this help. The help received, therefore, did not render her dependent; on the contrary, it was through her own efforts at seeking help that she was able to grow. Alicia further underlines her sense of initiative by noting that she intends to return the help she received by helping others.

Alicia notes that support from teachers and friends was an invaluable resource. By making connections with others, immigrant students develop what is termed *relational engagement*, which describes the extent to which they feel connected to teachers, peers, and others in their school. Immigrant students who forge meaningful and positive relationships have a higher likelihood of adapting to school life. Moreover, building these kinds of relational supports can provide students with a sense of belonging, emotional support, information, guidance, role modeling, and, sometimes, tangible assistance (Suárez-Orozco et al., 2010). Further, maintaining school relationships fosters socially competent behaviors, academic engagement, and even academic success.

Attitudes toward help may reflect gender differences. Traditional masculine roles call for singular independence and fearlessness in the face of daunting challenges. Accepting help—especially from women—may signal to adolescent boys, in particular, childish regression to dependence on female authority. This presents far more of a dilemma for immigrant boys than for girls. Added to the dilemma of accepting help is the fact that those helpers are likely to be adult females; women, it should be noted, are overrepresented in the helping professions, including teaching and mental health. The threat of dependence, especially dependence on older female authority figures, is likely to be less pronounced among girls.

In her book *In a Different Voice*, Carol Gilligan (1982/2003) posits that an ethic of care, based on relational transactions, is consonant with female development. This position likely reflects greater social comfort with female emotional expressiveness in relational exchanges and a social inhibition communicated early in life to boys regarding self-expression. Immigrant boys may well be reluctant to accept help, even when offered, as relational exchanges often assume emotional expressiveness and the possibility of relational vulnerability. Actively seeking help, while not inconsistent with female development, is likely inconsistent with patterns of traditional approaches to raising boys.

FRIENDS

Although family plays a significant role in the adjustment of immigrant youths, relationships with friends and age peers are salient. They provide a sense of belonging and acceptance and can offer help to their age peers that is more easily accepted than similar offers by friendly professionals. Age peers offer concrete help with homework, language skills, translation, and school orientation. Most important, friends help immigrant students feel less lonely.

In many cases, peers play a larger role in immigrant youths' adjustment than their parents do. "Youths see and compare themselves in relation to those around them, based on their similarity or dissimilarity with the reference groups that most directly affect their experiences" (Rumbaut, 2005, p. 8). In this regard, immigrant youths' social identities, inclusive of their ethnic identifies, are based on contrasts with others and on how they define themselves and the situations in which they find themselves. Rumbaut contends that youths in ethnically dissonant contexts, where their ethnic, racial, or other social markers place them in a minority status position, may deal with this dissonance by seeking to reduce conflict by assimilating to the relevant social context.

Few of the narratives specifically cited parental support or involvement. Friends, however, were high on the list of both male and female writers as important influences. In the narrative that follows, Cinthia describes how her friends helped her to gain social confidence by enveloping her in their vitality and warmth.

CASE VIGNETTE: CINTHIA

> The most memorable experience in school I had was when I first attended a talent show with a group of friends. I was shy and get easily nervous when in front of a large crowd, but I overcame that fear once I had fun with the dance, especially with my friends. This stood out for me 'cause this was the day I overcame the fear of stage frights and [I] actually couldn't do it without my friends helping me out. That's how this experience helped me out as a person. I was a loner but with a small group of friends, I overcame my fear.

Theater, in the form of talent shows and multicultural fair skits, offers immigrant youths an opportunity to access less-inhibited parts of themselves—their at-home or premigration selves. For both male and female participants, theater in any of its guises offers socially sanctioned opportunities for self-expression (Korn, 2004; Korn-Bursztyn, 2003). Such opportunities are in short supply for immigrant youths whose focus must be on the tasks at hand, with the added challenge of inhibiting emotional expression.

CASE VIGNETTE: JOSHUA

> One of the best experiences that happened to me as a student was in my freshman year of high school. This experience was in the multicultural fair. Everyone knows that as a freshman it is a little hard to get friends and talk to people. So when one of my teachers offered me an opportunity to play the role of John Travolta from *Grease* on stage I took it. I did his role to the best of my abilities. At the end of the show I had to dance Salsa with a partner on stage, and me being a freshman was the main reason why I was so nervous, but at the end of the show 98% [of the audience] was up and clapping for me. It was then that my high school experience changed and I decided to do the show for the rest of high school. This experience showed me how expressing yourself can help you out in the end.

Extracurricular activities play an important role in the emotional lives of immigrant students. Basketball, in Antony's example, offers the opportunity to take a bold initiative in a new environment, building the kind of confidence he is not yet developing in his academic classes. Marisol was grateful for elective classes and clubs. These likely provided more informal sites for interacting and learning from peers.

CASE VIGNETTE: ANTONY

> The most memorable experience I had in school was being on the middle school basketball team and leading them to [the] championship as a starting point. It stood out to me because I was doing something I love which was playing basketball. This experience helped me to build confidence.

CASE VIGNETTE: MARISOL

> The most memorable experiences I had in school were the clubs and electives I was able to participate in. I am a shy person and these classes and clubs helped me to be more involved and to learn new things. The things I learned helped me to understand and open my mind in new ways. It also taught me to solve problems and be positive. These classes and clubs also helped me to be thankful for what I have and for the lessons I am grateful.

Although peers can provide a buffer against negative influences like violence and drugs, too prevalent in low-income communities, Suárez-Orozco, Suárez-Orozco, and Todorova (2010) point out that many students experience being pulled into instances of negative peer interactions, an example of which is presented below.

CASE VIGNETTE: JOSE

> I guess I would love to say being in two plays where I was the lead. It broke me out of being shy and built my confidence. I was really shy in junior high school. In a way it was good and at the same time it was bad. Once I came out of my shell, everything turned around in my life. I started running around with the wrong people and it turned my whole life around. I lost interest in school and the rest is history. I finally [ended] up in the navy so I guess my experience wasn't totally a disaster. I got the structure and discipline that I needed.

Jose's vignette presents a number of paradoxes. Most educators and mental health clinicians would agree that increased confidence is desirable. For Antony and Marisol, this was indeed the case, and increased confidence led to stronger academic achievement and identification with academically motivated peers. Jose, however, presents his isolation or "shell" as a protective covering, shielding him from harmful affiliations, even at the cost of loneliness. An increase in confidence suggests only confidence to act and to make choices; the motivations for the choices adolescents—immigrant or native-born—are considerably more complex.

SCHOOL AND RISK

School characteristics,[2] family characteristics,[3] and individual characteristics[4] are associated with different trajectories of academic performance. Because immigrant families typically settle in poor, inner-city neighborhoods, their children tend to attend poorly performing, underfunded, and highly segregated inner-city schools (Suárez-Orozco & Suárez-Orozco, 2001; Xie & Greenman, 2005). As a result, these youths encounter difficulties within the educational system. In reality, a larger numbers of immigrant students perform poorly on several academic indicators, including achievement tests, grades, and college attendance, and these students also have high levels of attrition.

Poorly performing schools place immigrant students at higher risk of acculturating into oppositional youths' cultures or to assume adversarial outlooks found among their native minority peers (Ogbu, 1991; Portes & Rumbaut 2001). The cultural values found in underperforming schools tend to discourage high academic achievement and school engagement, negatively impacting immigrant students' chances at upward mobility. In difficult learning settings, Portes and Rumbaut (2001) suggest that maintaining the culture of origin can have a protective effect for immigrant children, two examples of which are family cohesion and segmented assimilation, characterized by strong family cohesion and parent involvement.

The immigrant community may be able to reinforce the achievement-related and behavioral norms that parents try to teach their children and thus help immigrant youths avoid the pitfalls of poor neighborhoods. A problem arises as immigrant students assimilate too fully into the surrounding social environment. They may experience dissonant acculturation, which may lead to loss of access to the social and cultural resources of the ethnic community, including parental support. In this regard, the segmented assimilation framework would predict that in disadvantaged contexts, segmented acculturation and the deliberate preservation of the immigrant community's culture and values, accompanied by economic integration, would be most beneficial (Xie & Greenman, 2005).

Age is another factor in immigrant student academic success. Immigrants who arrive as adults seldom lose their original linguistic allegiances or accents, even while learning English. Immigrant adults arrive with more or less fully formed identities and personalities. Adult immigrants are often nostalgic for their lost homes and often desire to impart their cultural heritage to their children. The parental group may actually strengthen their own identification with their countries of origin as their children display rapid Americanization (Rumbaut, 1999). Immigrant youths raised in the United States may experience identity development as a complicated process, mainly as a result of intense acculturative and generational conflicts, as they adapt to American contexts that, according to Rumbaut (1999), may be racially and culturally dissonant. These students may experience strained relations with their parents and family members as a result of differing rates of acculturation.

Suárez-Orozco et al. (2010) identify that nearly half of newcomer youths arrive sometime during their secondary education, and that they often face multiple stressors in acclimating to their new school environments. Early adolescence is a time of increased risk of "downward educational spiral" (p. 500) among new arrivals. Moreover, newcomer immigrant students who enter new school systems midway through their academic trajectory find themselves facing overwhelming hurdles in adjusting to life in a new land, including learning a new language.

THE PSYCHOLOGY OF SECOND LANGUAGE LEARNING

As second language immigrant students enter school, they encounter apparent differences in their functional use of language, which may provide instances of incongruity. Because students come into classrooms already socialized to language in culturally specific ways, Lovelace and Wheeler (2006) believe that their discourse structure and communication styles may be dissimilar to that of their teachers and peers, resulting in dissonance between home and school (Portes & Rumbaut, 2001; Suárez-Orozco, Bang, & Onaga, 2010), or what Lovelace and Wheeler (2006) term *cultural discontinuity*.

In the book titled *Lost in Translation*, Eva Hoffman (1989), who emigrated from Poland to Canada in adolescence and subsequently became a journalist and writer (in English), depicts her confused feelings about her English language competency. In the following excerpt, she expresses feelings of hesitation, second-guessing, and withholding when it comes to speaking. This is common among newcomer second language students who grapple with the subtleties of the English language simultaneously with the norms of host culture life.

> But these days, it takes all my will to impose any control on the words that emerge from me. I have to form entire sentences before uttering them; otherwise, I too easily get lost in the middle. My speech, I sense, sounds monotonous, deliberate, heavy—an aural mask that doesn't become me or express me at all. This willed self-control is the opposite of

real mastery, which comes from a trust in your own verbal powers and allows for a free streaming of speech. For those bursts of spontaneity, the quickness of response that can rise into pleasure and overflow in humor. (Hoffman, 1989, p. 118)

ENCULTURATION, LANGUAGE, SCHOOL, AND MENTAL HEALTH

Enculturation of the newcomer to the knowledge, skills, and practices of the host culture and the process of language socialization are intertwined developmental processes. Drawing on cultural psychology and neo-Vygotskian sociocultural approaches, Patricia Duff (2007) considers development in light of second language socialization.

> Culturally situated, as mediated, and a replete with social, cultural and political meanings in addition to propositional or ideational meanings carried or indexed by various linguistic, textual and paralinguistic forms. The core theoretical premise of language socialization is that language is learned through interactions with others who are more proficient in the language and its cultural practice. (p. 172)

Decades earlier, in 1983, Heath argued that "all language learning is culture learning" (p. 5). Similarly, Agar (1994) claimed that because language and culture are interwoven, it is impossible to study them in isolation without distorting them. Language learning involves both linguistic and sociocultural knowledge, with language being the primary mode through which cultural knowledge is communicated, reproduced, and transformed (Garrett & Baquedano-Lopez, 2002). Language teaching and learning take place through social contexts, interactions, and practices. Newcomers' socialization through language occurs in relation to the social beliefs, values, and expectations that are socially accepted and organized within cultural practices (Ochs, 2002; Shi, 2006).

All learners experience primary language socialization during childhood but continue to experience secondary language socialization throughout their lives, mainly as they enter into new sociocultural contexts or join new communities of practice (Lave & Wenger, 1991). This has particular meaning to immigrant students. As they engage in learning practices in their new school environments, they can be expected to assume new roles and to take on new activities as they learn the dominant language. The task of the immigrant student is ostensibly to achieve mastery in school communities of practice, learning from the old-time members and becoming members of the community (Lave & Wenger, 1991). Although it is clear that schools include practices like academic work, knowledge and skill acquisition, and navigating school environments, what is more significant is that school contexts require students to negotiate school-based interpersonal relationships (Shi, 2006).

Nowhere is the importance of culture more relevant or evident than in students' interactions with the language and social practices of higher learning. From a symbolic capital theory perspective, schools allow for social relationships that lead to institutional support, including social ties, access to knowledge-based resources, coursework, and career guidance (Bourdieu, 1977). Second language learners in schools learn the values and rules of learning in a new culture (Ochs, 2002). Although it is understood that students as members of cultural practices must come to grips with the cultural expectations about how people are to act, feel, and think in specific situations (partially conferred as explicit instructions, but otherwise inferred from performances of conventional socially coordinated activities), it is unclear how or whether immigrant students actually come to internalize these cultural values for themselves and what it takes for them to do so.

Duff (2007) claims that newcomer learners who use contextual language appropriately often gain several other types of cultural knowledge about relevant beliefs, identities, affective orientations, and practices that are valued in the particular community. In classrooms, students are socialized in and through discourses and practices that are seemingly explicit; for example, showing respect, self-control, and decorum (to teachers and to others and to the subject matter itself). In reality these practices reflect socialized ideologies of respect as well as patterns of social stratification, in response to which learners may internalize, resist, or oppose.

FAMILY TIES, ACCULTURATION, AND MENTAL HEALTH

In their study of the different modes by which immigrants interact with and become incorporated into the host society, Portes and Rumbaut (2001) identified family structure as the relevant background factor that shapes the experience of the first generation. Family structure, they posit, is central to the outcomes of the second generation, too. They identified two types of parent–child acculturation: consonant and dissonant acculturation. When parents and children acculturate at a similar pace and in similar ways, their acculturation is considered consonant acculturation. However, when children acculturate faster or more completely than parents, this is considered dissonant acculturation. Dissonant acculturation leads to parent–child conflicts and to a breakdown in communication between the generations. It decreases parental ability to guide and support their children and is viewed as a major risk factor for downward assimilation among the second generation. Thus, the relation between parent acculturation and children acculturation is considered important because it influences the family and community resources available to support children, who confront numerous challenges in adapting to life in the host society.

For many minority and working-class youths, supportive ties are typically found outside the family, that is, in school settings and community organizations (Stanton-Salazar & Dornbusch, 1995). Although parents can and do provide support for their children, when it comes to schooling, teachers and other institutional agents, including peers, can often provide more appropriate help. Suárez-Orozco, Bang, and Onaga (2010) suggest that parents often are ill-equipped to help their children navigate the complex, foreign, and sometimes forbidding educational system.

According to Rivera et al. (2008), family cohesion, characterized by strong emotional bonds, may also act as a protective factor that can mitigate stress for immigrant students. However, high levels of family cohesion are related to low levels of acculturation, while low levels of family cohesion have been found among immigrants who adapt mainstream tendencies. Unfortunately, low levels of family cohesion are associated with elevated levels of psychological risk for immigrants (Rivera et al., 2008).

High levels of cohesion in families, coupled with parents' limited access to appropriate resources or cultural capital, can sometimes negatively affect their children's academic trajectory (Rumbaut, 2005). On the other hand, parents who arrive with high levels of education and strong language skills tend to access better occupational and economic opportunities and are better able to create stable home environments and navigate a complex school system.

CONCLUSION: IDENTITY, LEARNING, AND IMMIGRANT STUDENTS

Immigrants develop identities that are representative of their social positions in both their home cultures and the receiving culture. Yet in the case of second language immigrant youths, it still remains unclear how this takes place; it forces us to ask, Where is the individual in all of this? Wenger (1998, p. 215), in examining the connections between learning and identity, claims that "because learning transforms who we are and what we can do, it is an experience of identity. It is not just an accumulation of skills and information but a process of becoming."

Accordingly, identity is a negotiated experience in and across social communities where learning occurs. Osterlund and Carlile (2003) believe that we do not solely learn facts about the world. Rather, as we learn, we develop the ability to act in the world in socially recognizable ways that simultaneously define how others perceive us and how we see ourselves. Subsequently, this process implies a mutual recognition that results in an identity that in turn promotes a sense of belonging, which is also based in the individual's appropriation of relevant sociocultural practices (Falsafi & Coll, 2010).

How do individuals, specifically second-language immigrant beginning college students, form identities in practice, beyond simply appropriating certain practices? Vagan (2011) argues that this approach to identity development cannot comprehend the multiple identities and different identification opportunities that open up to learners in the process of learning and doing. Also, although many psychologists, sociologists, and educators agree that achievement and underachievement are products of a society that differentially structure access to resources (Freire, 1970; Giroux, 1997), they also argue that issues of underachievement can only be addressed by implementing significant changes in societal and school organizations (Nasir & Hand, 2006).

Although culture can be reproduced, it can also be transformed by individuals actively responding to their social circumstances as they encounter them (Stetsenko & Arievitch, 2004; Willis, 1977). This approach introduces the important role agency plays in shaping cultural reproduction in individual lives. The immigration narratives that opened this chapter follow closely to the idea of personal agency and transformation. The narratives of the young immigrant college students centered in agency and revealed an emotional investment in crafting life stories of perseverance and overcoming of obstacles. The narratives that they told about their own lives suggest pride in agency and a developmentally appropriate rejection of a storyline of dependence and neediness borne of dejection.

The stories presented here were written by immigrant students who had successfully completed high school and had enrolled in college. A recurring theme in the students' stories and in the literature is the role that relationships play in helping young immigrants, particularly those in adolescence and into emergent adulthood, navigate the shoals of the passage to adult autonomy. Gender and developmental differences in how helping relationships might be accessed bear further consideration. This is of particular salience to educators and to mental health professionals who work with immigrant youths in schools and in other community venues.

NOTES

1. All names in these vignettes are pseudonyms.
2. For example, the school segregation rate, school poverty rate, and student perceptions of school violence.
3. For example, separation from mother and father, maternal education, paternal employment.

4. For example, academic English proficiency, academic engagement, psychological symptoms, and gender.

REFERENCES

Agar, M. (1994). *Language shock: Understanding the culture of conversation.* New York: Morrow.

Bourdieu, P. (1977). *Outline of a theory of practice.* Cambridge: Cambridge University Press.

Duff, P. A. (2007). Second language socialization as sociocultural theory: Insights and issues. *Language Teaching, 40*(4), 309–319.

Falsafi, L., & Coll, C. (2010). La identidad de aprendiz. Una herramienta educativa y analytica [Learner identity. An educational and analytical tool]. *Revista de Educacion, 353,* 211–233.

Fuligni, A. J. (2007). Family obligation, college enrollment, and emerging adulthood in Asian and Latin American families. *Child Development Perspectives, 1*(2), 96–100.

Giroux, H. (1997). *Pedagogy and the politics of hope: Theory, culture, and schooling, a critical reader.* Boulder, CO: Westview.

Freire, P. (1970). *Pedagogy of the oppressed.* New York: Continuum.

Garrett, P. B., & Baquedano-López, P. (2002). Language socialization: Reproduction and continuity, transformation and change. *Annual Review of Anthropology, 31,* 339–361.

Gilligan, C. (1982/2003). *In a different voice: Psychological theory and women's development.* Cambridge: Harvard University Press.

Heath, S. B. (1983). Ways with words: Language, life and work in communities and classrooms. Cambridge: Cambridge University Press.

Hoffman, E. (1989). *Lost in translation: A life in a new language.* New York: Random House.

Korn, C. (2004). Art education, critical thinking and the arts. In D. Weil (Ed.), *Critical thinking and learning: An encyclopedia* (pp. 57–62). Westport, CT: Greenwood.

Korn-Bursztyn, C. (2003). The arts and school reform: Case study of a school in change. *Teaching Artist Journal, 1*(4), 220–227.

Lave, J. W., & Wenger, E. (1991). *Situated learning: Legitimate peripheral participation.* Cambridge, Engl.: Cambridge University Press.

Lovelace, S., & Wheeler, T. R. (2006). Cultural discontinuity between home and school language socialization patterns: Implications for teachers. *Education, 127*(2), 303–309.

Nasir, N. S., & Hand, V. M. (2006). Exploring sociocultural perspectives on race, culture, and learning. *Review of Educational Research, 76*(4), 449.

Ochs, E. (2002). Becoming a speaker of culture. In C. Kramsch (Ed.), *Language acquisition and language socialization: Ecological perspectives* (pp. 99–120). New York: Continuum.

Ogbu, J. U. (1991). Cultural diversity and school experience. In C. E. Walsh (Ed.), *Literacy as praxis: Culture, language, and pedagogy* (pp. 25–50). Norwood, NJ: Ablex.

Østerlund, C., & Carlile, P. (2003). *How practice matters: A relational view of knowledge sharing.* Retrieved from http://www.socio-informatics.net/fileadmin/IISI/upload/C_T/2003/Osterlund-Carlile.pdf.

Portes, A., & Rumbaut, R. G. (2001). *Legacies: The story of the immigrant second generation.* Berkeley: University of California Press.

Rivera, F. I., Guarnaccia, P. J., Mulvaney-Day, N., Lin, J. Y., Torres, M., & Alegria, M. (2008). Family cohesion and its relationship to psychological distress among Latino groups. *Hispanic Journal of Behavioral Sciences, 30*(3), 357–378.

Rumbaut, R. (1999). Assimilation and its discontents: Ironies and paradoxes. In C. Hirschman, P. Kasinitz, & J. DeWind (Eds.), *The handbook of international migration* (pp. 172–195). New York: Russell Sage Foundation.

Rumbaut, R. (2005). Sites of belonging: Acculturation, discrimination, and ethnic identity among children of immigrants. In T. S. Weisner (Ed.), *Discovering successful pathways in children's development: Mixed methods in the study of childhood and family life* (pp. 111–164). Chicago: University of Chicago Press.

Shi, X. (2006). Intercultural transformation and second language socialization. *Journal of Intercultural Communication, 11,* 2–17.

Stanton-Salazar, R. D., & Dornbusch, S. M. (1995). Social capital and the reproduction of inequality: Information networks among Mexican-origin high school students. *Sociology of Education, 68,* 116–135.

Stetsenko, A., & Arievitch, I. (2004). The self in cultural-historical activity theory: Reclaiming the unity of social and individual dimensions of human development. *Theory and Psychology, 14*(4), 475–503.

Suarez-Orozco, C., Suarez-Orozco, M. (2001). Children of immigration: The developing child. Cambridge: Harvard University Press.

Suarez-Orozco, C., Suarez-Orozco, M., & Todorova, I. (2010). *Learning in a new land: Immigrant students in American society.* Cambridge: First Harvard University Press.

Trumbull, E., & Rothstein-Fisch, C. (2011). The intersection of culture and achievement motivation. *School Community Journal, 21*(2).

Vagan, A. (2011). Towards a sociocultural perspective on identity formation in education. *Mind, Culture and Activity, 18*(1), 43–57.

Wenger, E. (1998). *Communities of practice: Learning, meaning and identity.* New York: Cambridge University Press.

Willis, P. (1977). *Learning to labor: How working class kids get working class jobs.* New York: Columbia University Press.

Xie, Y., & Greenman, E. (2005). *Segmented assimilation theory: A reformulation and empirical test.* Population Studies Center Research Report (05-581). Retrieved from http://www.psc.isr.umich.edu/pubs/pdf/rr05-581.pdf.

14

Undocumented Latino Youths Reach for College: Coming of Age in a Time of Uncertainty

Sally Robles

The United States leads the world in the number of immigrants who move to its shores. Thirteen percent of the U.S. population in 2013—or 41.3 million people—were immigrants. The current wave of immigrants is primarily from Latin America (50%) and Asia (27%). Of these, an estimated 11.1 million are unauthorized immigrants (Pew Research, 2013) and 2.1 million are undocumented adults brought to the United States as children (Gonzalez, 2011). Many of these young adults were hopeful that a path to citizenship for them would be possible through the DREAM Act of 2001 (Development, Relief, and Education for Alien Minors).

The defeat of the DREAM Act and the passage instead of DACA in 2012 (Deferred Action for Childhood Arrivals) has left undocumented college-age students in a state of limbo (U.S. Department of Homeland Security, 2013). DACA defers deportation for two years (subject to renewal) for those who arrived in the United States "illegally" and allows for legal employment and other rights. However, U.S. citizenship continues to be denied, and young adults who have been in the United States since childhood and were educated in a school system that emphasized acculturation into the English-dominant culture are facing a wall. They often graduate from high school bilingual but functionally illiterate in their native language. Nonetheless, the country whose behavior, mores, and language they have adopted gives them limited options. Although a K-12 education is provided by law, higher education is not.

States vary in how they treat undocumented college students: some charge them out-of-state tuition, some require proof of citizenship for attendance, some charge in-state tuition. In all states, they are prohibited from receiving federally funded aid. There are few private scholarship options. Most important, they are considered to be in the country "illegally" and must maneuver the ever-changing legal landscape to avoid deportation. The stress of an uncertain citizenship status is in addition to other known challenges that Latino college students face: acculturation conflicts, family obligations, and financial limitations. This chapter focuses on undocumented Latino college students who were brought to the United States as children by their parents.

This chapter explores—through a case study and a review of the relevant literature—the various psychological, sociocultural, and legal challenges encountered by undocumented Latino college students. In addition, the chapter presents a preliminary framework for conceptualizing the identity development of undocumented young adults. It proposes an Undocumented Adult Identity Development Model that can be used to understand the varied emotional trajectories experienced by undocumented youths and young adults who wrestle with a marginalized immigration status.

CASE VIGNETTE: ANDRES

Andres Garcia[1] is an undocumented 19-year-old Mexican American college student who was seen in the counseling center prior to the passage of DACA. Unlike some other undocumented college students, he eschewed online and on-campus activist Dreamer groups and did not reveal his immigration status. He has resided in the United States since the age of 10. His immigration to the United States coincided with his father leaving the family; he also left his beloved grandparents in Mexico. In counseling, Andres complained that his grades had slipped from A's to an occasional B. In addition, he spoke in a devaluing way of his interdependent, collectivistic family who constantly sought out each other's company and were constantly asking for favors and money: "How many times is my mother going to lend my sister money? All she does is party. I'm not giving a penny!" He had an aloof, judgmental, slightly superior air when discussing the interdependency his mother and two brothers had on one another. It seemed that Andres' own early separation from his father and grandparents left him profoundly threatened by his own dependency.

He disowned his dependent longings for his collectivistic Mexican extended family and his father; instead he projected those longings onto his family, viewing them with disdain and anger. The early family separation and loss of important caregivers left him vulnerable; on a deeper level he felt unlovable, otherwise how could his father have left? He also felt unable to rely or depend on others; his early life taught him that even those most reliable and caring can be taken away at a moment's notice. In sum, Andres faced challenges in maintaining a stable sense of self-esteem and a stable identity and struggled to balance autonomy and intimacy.

To compensate for the feeling that he had not been good enough (or else his father would have stayed) and in the hope of being part of a more reliable (albeit symbolic) family, Andres acculturated rapidly into American culture. And no venue offered him more opportunities to shore up his shaky sense of identity and self-esteem than the school system. Good grades and excellent written and oral English language skills would provide him with the validation of his worth that separation from his homeland, from his father, and from his extended family had taken away. This compromise (i.e., rapid acculturation and stellar academic performance as a compensation for core feelings of abandonment, low self-esteem, anger, and sadness) helped Andres cope at some cost: he had a distant relationship with his family who viewed him as cold. Moreover, the intensity of his disowned feelings came through in the form of periodic passive suicidal ideation whenever his class or academic performance was criticized. For example, when a professor gave him a C on a term paper that was described as weak on substance, Andres had recurrent thoughts that it would be better if he wasn't around. This would then mobilize him to devalue the professor or precipitate his flight into denial of any problems or emotional distress.

In counseling, Andres was very gently shown his tendency—in the here and now relationship with the therapist—to deny any sad or angry feelings. Initially, he devalued the counselor for so erroneously reading his emotional state. The devaluing and dismissing tendencies were also explored. Andres was eventually able to trust the reliability and consistency of the counselor enough to reveal his "legal limbo" status. Only then could the negative impact of his undocumented status be understood as adding (and paralleling) the sense of loss, low self-worth, and estrangement he felt as a result of his family life.

LATINO COLLEGE STUDENTS

There has been a fivefold increase in the enrollment of Latinos in postsecondary education in the United States. Latino student enrollment rose from 350,000 in 1976 to 1.9 million in 2007 (Fry, 2009, p. 7). This encouraging increase in the number of Latino college students has been tempered, however, by the strikingly lower rates of degree completion for Latinos. National data show that by the age of 26, less than 25% of Latinos who enter college obtain a bachelor's degree. This is close to half the rate of white students, 47% of whom receive a college degree after enrolling in a college or university (Fry,

2004, p. 2). Traditionally, and perhaps intuitively, these disparities were thought to be due to the inadequate academic preparation provided to Latinos in low-income areas. However, recent longitudinal data research has suggested that "the best prepared Latinos fare worse than white youth of equal preparation" (Fry, 2004, p. 4), and there has been an attempt to look at nonacademic factors that impact graduation rates.

IMPORTANCE OF FAMILY

Current research suggests that the impact of familial cultural mores on sobering economic realities is an obstacle to graduation for many Latinos. When a cross-section of college noncompleters were asked why they did not complete or attend college, the factor that was endorsed twice as often by Latinos as by whites was the need to be close to their family. Fully one-third of the Latinos said they needed to be close to their families. Although all groups endorsed economic obstacles to college completion, the need to be close to family was disproportionately endorsed by Latinos (Fry, 2004, p. 12). And indeed the research suggests that being part of a close-knit, mutual caregiving, family-oriented culture can be both a benefit and a burden for some college-age Latinos hoping to attain a college degree.

College students often present to the counseling center with issues concerning identity and establishing their autonomy from their families of origin (Chickering & Reiser, 1993); Latino students born or raised in the United States often have similar concerns. However, these goals may be nonexistent or ambivalently held, unacknowledged, or repudiated by Latino students who often see their identities as embedded within a network of family relationships. Moreover, the family relationships are hierarchically structured, and obedience and respect for parents are highly held values. These patterns contrast with the American culture, which emphasizes individualism and equality (Zayas, Bright, Alvarez-Sanchez, & Cabassa, 2009). Latino college students often present with conflicts between the (often internalized) cultural norm of seeing identity as embedded in the family versus the (also internalized) American norm of seeking independence and self-fulfillment. Specifically, three family-influenced sociocultural factors have been identified as stressors for Latino late adolescents and young adults: *familismo* or the importance of family ties, the stress of acculturation, and—for females—the self-sacrificing *marianista* as an internalized feminine ideal.

Familismo

The term *familismo* (or familialism) is used to describe the deep sense of unity, loyalty, mutual obligation, and attachment that characterizes Latino families (Marin, 1993; Torres & Solberg, 2001; Tseng, 2004). It creates a strong attachment between members of a Latino family (immediate and extended). There is the expectation in many Latino families that support will be given and the obligation to support family members when they are in need. Socialization, therefore, is not necessarily seen as ushering in personal autonomy, but as a time to take on more adult-like tasks in order to help the family survive. Youths may be relied on more, and they may feel increasingly encumbered with family obligations. For example, Andres, the client cited above, distanced himself from his Latino family so he would not incur obligations by keeping closely connected to them. *Familismo* is closely related to another culturally related family value often seen in Latino families: *marianismo*.

Marianismo

Marianismo is believed to derive from the Catholic veneration of the Virgin Mary. As both a virgin and mother, she is exalted for her purity and nurturance of the son of God. She is an archetypal role model of the eternally giving, pious woman who puts the needs of her family before her own. Some researchers have suggested that the impact of *familismo* falls disproportionately on daughters, since attending to others' needs before one's own dovetails so neatly with *marianismo*. *Marianismo* and *familismo* are cultural guideposts that—like behavioral norms of any culture—are subject to change. The process of migration to the United States often accelerates this change process.

ACCULTURATION

The change in the original cultural patterns of a group that has come into continuous firsthand contact with a different cultural group is termed *acculturation* (Redfield, Linton, & Herskovits, 1936, p. 147). For Latinos, adolescence and young adulthood are often when the struggles with acculturation and biculturalism begin. Raised to see their identities as embedded within a network of family relationships that are hierarchically structured, the concomitant socialization into the American culture that emphasizes individualism, personal fulfillment, and equality may present personal and familial conflicts (Zayas et al., 2009). Socially conservative parents may try to restrict their children's more liberal behavior, and the young Latino themselves may struggle to find a standard of behavior that reconciles their bicultural perspectives. Similarly, Latino youths may wrestle with balancing family obligations with the seemingly "selfish" goal of individual success, gain, and fulfillment. Often this struggle peaks during a developmental phase termed *emerging adulthood*. Contrary to many Latino students, Andres, the client discussed above, was notable and unapologetic in her single-minded quest to separate from her family and to achieve occupational success. His family found him "cold" and odd; his quick and eager acculturation made him a cultural outsider in his own family.

EMERGING ADULTHOOD

The developmental stage of emergent adult occurs from about age 17 to 21. It is a time when certain youths take a hiatus from the practical realities and burdens of adulthood (such as rent and mortgage, childcare, or eldercare responsibilities) to explore their career options and life plans (Arnett, 2000). Research on family obligations and Latino young adults suggests that the developmental path into emerging adulthood for Latinos is almost the opposite of the path taken by mainstream college students. Sy and Romero (2008) state convincingly that emerging adulthood is not a hiatus for Latinos; instead, it is a time when many are given (or take on) *increased* adult responsibilities to help the family survive. Many Latinos do not have an expectation that their needs are primary or separate from the good of the family.

What does research have to say about the impact of increasing family obligations for Latino college students? Sanchez, Esparza, Colon, and Davis (2010) conducted a qualitative study on Latino students transitioning to college students and found students often considered the family needs as more important than their own personal goals. The multiple responsibilities typically described by first- and second-generation Latino students include child rearing, financial support, eldercare, and household chores. College attendance was sometimes delayed or onerous work schedules were taken on while in college in order to help the family financially. Sanchez et al. describe one participant who strongly rejected a coworker's view that she (the participant) should be in college instead of taking on the provider role in her family. The participant was clear that her primary obligation was to her mother and siblings; her individual achievement could not be pursued in the face of such pressing family needs. Looking at the parental perspective, Phinney and Haas (2003, p. 709) found that the parents of first-generation college students often have not attended college and do not understand the burden multiple family obligations place on students already facing considerable academic pressures. This may lead to additional interpersonal familial conflicts, which only adds to the students' stress.

LEGAL STRESSORS

On August 15, 2012, the DACA act was passed by U.S. legislators. DACA is not a path to citizenship; rather, it is a temporary reprieve from the consequences of having an undocumented legal status. Specifically, it is a two-year hiatus from the threat of being deported and it enables undocumented young adults to legally obtain work permits. DACA defers "the removal action of an [undocumented] individual as an act of prosecutorial discretion." In most states, it also means being eligible for a driver's license and in-state college tuition rates. According to the U.S. Citizen and Immigration Services, as of June 2013, there have been a total of 557,414 DACA applications received, of which 400,562—the vast majority—were approved.

In order to be eligible for DACA, an undocumented immigrant will have to meet several requirements:

- Being under age 31,
- Arrived in the United States before the age of 16,
- Be currently in school, having graduated or obtained a certificate of high school completion OR being an honorably discharged veteran of the coast guard of the armed forces of the United States.

Although met with jubilation and relief by many, DACA is not a permanent solution. It is a temporary (though renewable) timeout that allows youths to pursue academic and employment goals for at least two years.

DACA differs significantly from the DREAM Act, which is the namesake of the so-called "Dreamers." Legislation for minors is envisioned as a path to citizenship; it has gone through various iterations, beginning with the DREAM Act in 2001, and DACA in 2012. Undocumented youths and young adults are granted six years of "conditional" legal status in the United States during which time they must complete two years of college or have served in the U.S. military. During the six years, they would not qualify for federal college grants but could apply for work study and student loans. The DREAM Act also allows Dreamers to pay in-state tuition. Similar to DACA, the Dreamers would have to have arrived to the United States before the age of 15, have been in the United States continually for five years, and be of good moral character.

For undocumented college students, the DREAM Act was a path to citizenship and a hopeful, welcoming message that they were going to be fully accepted as Americans. DACA, as a temporary reprieve from deportation, is generally interpreted as a step in the right direction and leads to cautious optimism and lingering feelings of being in a marginalized group.

The impact on the identity and aspirations of undocumented Latino college students is significant. According to Gonzalez, Suárez-Orozco, and Dedios-Sanguineti (2013), typical developmental models do not capture the ways in which identity development proceeds for undocumented youths. Undocumented youths' reactions to their legal limbo status tend to occur upon high school graduation when the pragmatic consequences of their status separate them from their peers. Much of what has been seen clinically and in the literature parallels many elements of the identity development stages described for other (often marginalized) groups. However, the sociolegal context of their nationality also makes their adult identity unique. Incorporating elements of the original and more recent African American identity development models, an Undocumented Adult Identity Development Model is proposed that describes the process many undocumented young adults go through as they gradually accept their legally marginal status.

MINORITY IDENTITY DEVELOPMENT MODELS

Cross (1971, 1991) developed the most well-known theory of minority identity development, the Cross Model of Nigrescence. It originally proposed a five-stage model in which initially black Americans have low self-esteem, identify with whites, and unconsciously devalue black Americans. After an "encounter" that shocks them into confronting the reality of prejudice and bias, black Americans enter a phase of immersion in their black identity and hold anti-white feelings. After internalizing a secure black identity, black Americans will have a more flexible view of racial and ethnic groups and commit themselves to activities that reflect their commitment to social justice.

Similar to Cross's original model for undocumented youths, the first stage of the Undocumented Adult Identity Development Model is the *pre-encounter stage*. They may not be aware of their undocumented status or may be unaware of the limits placed on them due to their status (Ellis & Chen, 2013). There is identification with the immigrant American Dream, that is, that hard work and a good education will open the doors of prosperity denied to their parents in the ancestral homeland.

This perspective changes during high school when their "encounter" with their marginalized immigration status takes the form of being excluded from many late adolescent rites of passage such as driving and working legally and qualifying for college financial aid. As stated by Gonzalez et al. (2013, p. 2), the inability of undocumented youths to join their peers in age-appropriate milestones triggers further discoveries about what undocumented status means, leading to feelings of fear, anxiety, uncertainty, and guilt. The realization of the consequences of their undocumented status is often an abrupt shattering of their sense of who they are in the world (Ellis & Chen, 2013).

The next stage in the Undocumented Adult Identity Development Model for undocumented youths is *identity disintegration and alienation*. Similar to gay and lesbian students in conservative settings (Cass, 1979), undocumented youths are often "closeted," that is, unable to share their frustration with friends due to stigma and fear of deportation. For undocumented youths, the "secret" of their undocumented status may lead to a forced distance from their social circle as they fear trusting the wrong person or the stigma of their undocumented status. In addition, they may compare themselves unfavorably to their peers who are not hindered by an "illegal" immigration status. They feel increasingly disconnected to others who do not share their struggle and cannot easily be trusted. This social estrangement as well as the inability to call the United States home often results in a sense of alienation. Moreover, the lack of citizenship in the country they feel is their home causes fear and uncertainty as well as identity incoherence (Gonzalez et al., 2013). The idealism and hope of the pre-encounter stage is replaced with pessimism about their personal life possibilities. The previous (seemingly naïve) acceptance of the American Dream being within their grasp is replaced by an anxious, often angry, confusion about their limbo immigration status.

The next stage of the Undocumented Adult Identity Development Model is *mourning*. In this phase, the youths' idealized image of their future selves—unfettered by sobering immigration realities—is mourned. They grieve for the loss of their identity, which is the basis of their sense of belonging (Gonzalez et al., 2013). Similar to an unexpected death, their status is a very unpleasant reality they must accept and over which they have no control. However, unlike a death—in which the loss is final—this type of loss is ambiguous and the outcome is uncertain; this makes the completion of the mourning process much more complicated and, at times, protracted and unresolved (Boss, 1999; Gonzalez et al., 2013).

For those unable to complete the mourning process, the feelings of anger, frustration, hopelessness, and low self-worth are dealt with as externalizing and internalizing symptoms. Gonzalez et al. (2013) found undocumented youths using drugs and alcohol in an attempt to self-medicate and chronically depressed youths who sometimes attempt suicide as a result of their sense of powerlessness and hopelessness regarding their futures. Psychological symptoms and externalizing behaviors, when chronic and extreme, suggest that the youth is unable to progress past the mourning phase of their identity development and has been unable to mobilize social, personal, or intellectual resources in order to begin to rebuild their lives (Ellis & Chen, 2013) and to rethink their life plans in light of their undocumented status.

The ability to begin to plan a life within the confines of an uncertain immigration status is the final stage of the Undocumented Adult Identity Development Model: *adaptation*. This stage differs from the internalization phase of Cross's model, which emphasizes a cognitive shift in how an African American views him- or herself. Although this may also occur with undocumented youths, it is the verbal expression of realistic academic or employment plans for the future as well as actions that implement these plans that are the hallmark of a shift into adaptation. In the adaptation phase, the process of mourning is largely accomplished or it is eclipsed and repressed. The youth has intellectually accepted his or her undocumented status as well as the financial, academic, and employment limitations inherent in that status. Their status, while important, is not an aspect of their identities, which hinder their ability to engage the world or plan their futures. They are able to engage in adaptive actions that move them closer to realistic goals.

In addition, the adaptation stage is influenced by many of the person- and context-specific factors detailed in the Multidimensional African-American Identity Development Model (Scottham, Sellers, & Ngyen, 2008). Specifically, the following five factors—adapted to apply to undocumented youths—will account for individual variations within the adaptation stage:

1. The centrality of their undocumented immigration status to their self-concept;
2. How they regard the undocumented immigrant community;
3. How they think the country regards the undocumented immigrant community;
4. Their ideology regarding how they think undocumented immigrants should engage the world. There are four options: nationalist, oppressed minority, assimilationist, and humanist;
5. How salient their undocumented status is to their self-concept based on the specific situation and at a specific time.

Another way the stages differ from the original identity development models is that they are not rigidly linear or mutually exclusive (Carter, 1995; Helms, 1995, p. 183). After the pre-encounter and encounter stage, the stages are fluid, and a youth's social context and psychological defenses can impact the sequence of steps. Emerging adults can skip stages or have characteristics of several stages at once.

In the case study cited at the beginning of the chapter, we can see that Andres is an example of a student who relies on his ambition and considerable intellectual prowess to reach the adaptation phase. Ellis and Chen (2013) observe that some youths are able to call upon defense mechanisms in order to protect themselves from intrapersonal conflicts related to their undocumented status. Andres projected his self-doubts about his ethnicity and undocumented status onto his (devalued) extended family. This freed him from the threats to his self-esteem that being part of a rejected group may entail. He gave low centrality and low salience to his undocumented status. In addition, he had a low regard for his family members and was heavily assimilationist in his ideology. This allowed him to personally dis-identify with the negative stigma associated with an undocumented immigrant status. Similarly, his dis-identification from his family gave him a precocious sense of independence and self-reliance. He was consequently able to use his intellectual gifts to fashion a long-term career path that accounted for his undocumented status.

Andres' period of mourning, with its anticipated sense of resignation and defeat, was seemingly short-lived. He almost immediately reviewed career options that were not bound to his citizenship. Although as teachers we often hear of the importance of having our college students become global citizens, Andres was ahead of this thinking. In some ways I was in the defeated and resignation phase (or projectively identified with that disowned aspect of his experience) while he was exploring career options in his native Mexico and other countries where his Mexican citizenship was not an obstacle. He changed majors to appeal to a career he thought more amenable and marketable abroad and changed colleges to get specialized training in that field.

He conceived of himself as a boundary-less, global worker, where, ironically, the United States—where he had spent half his life—considered him illegal and ineligible to work. He would move on. He researched opportunities in the high-end travel industry and focused his studies in that direction. Indeed, we can surmise, that on a deeper level, Andres is hoping that this geographic cure will distance him from his profound and denied longing for his Mexican cultural world and from the American acceptance that he thought would be his reward for such diligent acculturation. His solution to become a sort of permanent expatriate was an adaptive and creative solution that was a testament to his intelligence, resilience, and a coping style that emphasized adaptive action rather than raging rumination. It remains to be seen if Andres, in the future, will be able to integrate his feelings of loss, anger, abandonment, dependency, and rejection so as not to wall off major aspects of both his cultural identity and his family connections. It is likely when facing a future significant life stressor that he will cycle back to the mourning stage (perhaps blended with the disintegration and alienation phases) and grieve for the U.S.-American identity he worked so hard to earn.

Interestingly, from a psychodynamic perspective, his quick adaptation to his undocumented status would suggest a reliance on narcissistic defenses, that is, his fragile self-esteem is precariously balanced on the backs of those he can devalue (e.g., Latinos) and on his ability to feel validated by his academic achievements. Any threat to his narcissistic supplies, as the grade of C on a paper was, and he is plagued by suicidal thoughts. For Andres, "success" was needed for his psychological survival. One can anticipate, however, that this brittle and unreliable defense will be tested by the ordinary trials and tribulations of life. However, as long as he is able to mobilize his gifts to fuel his "success," as long as he continues to market himself not as an "illegal alien" but as a fully bilingual and bicultural potential employee who would be an asset on the global stage, he may outwardly adapt quite well.

Undocumented youths will vary on the path they follow to reach adaptation and on how adaptation is defined. Andres' assimilationist ideology as well as the low salience and regard he gave to his undocumented immigrant identity led him to make grand individual (though doable) plans. Other undocumented youths, who have an oppressed minority ideology and give high salience to their undocumented status, may band together with other undocumented youths to form supportive, empowering Dreamer groups that break the stigma and alienation of their immigration status. These groups will give them access to information regarding their legal, occupational, and educational options, thus breaking the hopelessness they may feel. In addition, these groups may engage in political activism and advocate for a change in the policies that exclude them from full citizenship and provide invaluable social support. We could infer that these students would be integrating, rather than dis-identifying with, their cultural identities as a positive attribute that bonds them to others. They would adapt to their undocumented status while feeling progressively empowered and connected to peers rather than feeling estranged and stigmatized.

In addition, there are students who may be particularly at risk. These are students who cannot connect socially or do not have an anchor ethnic group in their school or neighborhood. They appear to be at higher risk for internalizing society's rejection and are consequently at higher risk for depression. Rather that leaping into adaptive action to protect their self-esteem, they may begin a downward spiral of self-loathing and bitterness.

IMPLICATIONS FOR COUNSELORS

Undocumented Latino youths present a clinical paradox. The goal is to help clients establish a stable identity when their citizenship—a core aspect of identity—is unclear and out of their control. Gonzalez (2013) notes that a priority for these youth is to strengthen their ability to build narrative identities that include—their undocumented status. In order to achieve this goal, awareness of the normative stages of undocumented identity development, as well as the varied course it may take, will help. Awareness of the stage a youth is going through will inform the types of interventions that may be needed.

In the encounter and mourning phases, the counselor should be attentive to the issues of shock and sadness that students experience when they realize the practical effects of their undocumented status. It is common for anger, sadness, resignation, and hopelessness to surface. The counselor has the multifaceted role of:

- Helping process the client's emotional reactions,
- Assessing for risk in particularly vulnerable students,

- Imparting accurate education and career information tailored to undocumented students (see Appendix), and,
- Referring to or starting groups that impart a sense of empowerment (e.g., Dreamers groups).

Although not all the roles will be used with all students, it is important for the counselor to have a diverse "tool box" when addressing the struggles of undocumented youths. If the counselor is able to impart accurate information regarding career and college options during the early stages of the undocumented identity development, it is less likely a student will become "stuck" in the mourning phase.

The interventions cited above have the goal of ameliorating the sense of resignation and hopelessness that often stymies undocumented youths. Access to accurate information regarding college admission and financial aid can help youths develop a plan for college completion. Similarly, accurate information about the limits of DACA and how to discuss it during an employment interview is empowering. For other students, connecting to a strong online or school-based group of activist Dreamers may be needed to counteract their internalization of a rejected, marginalized identity. The group may decrease alienation and provide a sense of agency as political activism empowers them to take steps in improving their own lives.

Although it is necessary for the counselor to be attuned to the students in front of him or her, it is often the case that the undocumented student does not self-identify. In order to reach these students, academic institutions and youth organizations can distribute and advertise information for undocumented students in ways that do not require them to self-identify. This can include, for example, handouts, website addresses printed on more general literature, and links on the school website.

Finally, high schools and colleges are increasingly reaching out to families as allies in the educational process. The culturally encapsulated paradigm that currently guides many college student affairs policies stresses the need for parents to let their children adopt adult roles. This needs to be supplemented with information and resources for undocumented students and families as well as parental orientation sessions held in Spanish that discuss culture-specific patterns that impact educational success. For example, the potentially negative impact of family obligations on college retention can be discussed. The need to decrease—rather than increase—Latino youths' adult responsibilities may be more salient than for other groups. Moreover, undocumented parents need to be explicitly informed of the educational and career options available to their children and to be reassured that their undocumented status is not a barrier to receiving parental orientation.

APPENDIX: RESOURCES

Life After College: Guide for Undocumented Students: http://www.e4fc.org/images/E4FC_LifeAfterCollegeGuide.pdf

Educators for Fair Consideration—their mission is to support undocumented students in realizing their academic and career goals: http://www.e4fc.org/

Education Not Deportation: A Guide for Undocumented Youth in Removal Proceedings: http://www.e4fc.org/images/E4FC_DeportationGuide.pdf

Young Lives on Hold: The College Dreams of Undocumented Students: http://professionals.collegeboard.com/profdownload/young-lives-on-hold-college-board.pdf

City University of New York Immigration Centers—The centers offer free immigration services to all members of the community—CUNY students and nonstudents: http://www.cuny.edu/about/resources/citizenship/about-us/contact.html

The College & Financial Aid Guide for AB540 Undocumented Immigrant Students: http://www.eric.ed.gov/PDFS/ED498734.pdf

Mexican American Legal Defense and Educational Fund—scholarships for ALL students regardless of residency status: http://www.maldef.org/assets/pdf/Scholarship_List_2010_2011.pdf

Financial Aid and Scholarships for Undocumented Students: http://www.finaid.org/otheraid/undocumented.phtml http://www.e4fc.org/resources/scholarshiplists.html

Resources for Students Interested in DACA: http://www.e4fc.org/resources/deferredaction.html

Community College Consortium for Immigrant Education: Dreaming Big: What Community Colleges Can Do to Help Undocumented Immigrant Youth Achieve Their Potential: http://cccie.org/images/stories/DREAMING_BIG_CCCIE_Report_9-2012_final_version.pdf

NOTE

1. All names are pseudonyms.

REFERENCES

Arnett, J. J. (2000). Emerging adulthood: A theory of development from the late teens through twenties. *American Psychologist, 55*(5), 469–480.

Boss, P. (1999). *Ambiguous loss: Learning to live with unresolved grief.* Cambridge, MA: Harvard University Press.

Carter, R. (1995). *The influence of race and racial identity in psychotherapy: Toward a racially inclusive model.* Hoboken, NJ: Wiley.

Cass, V. C. (1979). Homosexual identity formation: A theoretical model of homosexuality. *Homosexuality, 4,* 219–235.

Chickering, A. W., & Reisser, L. (1993). *Education and identity* (2nd ed.). San Francisco: Jossey-Bass.

Cross, W. E., Jr. (1971). The Negro to black conversion experience. *Black World, 20*(9), 13–27.

Cross, W. E., Jr. (1991). *Shades of black: Diversity in African-American identity.* Philadelphia: Temple University Press.

Ellis, L. M., & Chen, E. C. (2013). Negotiating identity development among undocumented immigrant college students: A grounded theory study. *Journal of Counseling Psychology, 60*(2), 251–264.

Fry, R. (2009, December). *Between two worlds: How young latinos come of age in America.* Washington, DC: Pew Hispanic Center Report. Retrieved from http://www.pewhispanic.org/files/reports/117.pdf.

Fry, R. (2004, June 23). *Latino youth finishing college: The role of selective pathways.* Washington, DC: Pew Hispanic Center Report. Retrieved from http://pewhispanic.org/files/reports/30.pdf.

Gonzalez, R. G. (2011) Learning to be illegal: Undocumented youth and shifting legal contexts in the transition to adulthood. *American Sociological Review, 76*(4), 602–619.

Gonzalez, R. G., Suarez-Orozco, C., & Dedios-Sanguineti, M. C. (2013). No place to belong: Contextualizing concepts of mental health among undocumented immigrant youth in the United States. *American Behavioral Scientist, 57*(8), 1174–1199.

Helms, J. E. (1995). An update of Helm's white and people of color racial identity models. In J. G. Ponterotto, J. M. Casas, L. A. Suzuki, & D. M. Alexander (Eds.), *Handbook of multicultural counseling* (pp. 181–198). Thousands Oaks, CA: Sage.

Marin, B. (1993). The influence of acculturation on familism and self-identification among hispanics. In M. E. Bernal & G. P. Knight (Eds.), *Ethnic identity: Formation and transmission among Hispanics and other minorities* (pp. 181–196). Albany: SUNY Press.

Pew Research Hispanic Trends Project. (2013, January). *A nation of immigrants: A portrait of the 40 million, including 11 million unauthorized.* Retrieved from http://www.pewhispanic.org/2013/01/29/a-nation-of-immigrants/.

Phinney, J. S., & Haas, K. (2003). The process of coping among ethnic minority first-generation college freshmen: A narrative approach. *Journal of Social Psychology, 143*(6), 707–726.

Redfield, R., Linton, R., & Herskovits, M. J. (1936). Memorandum for the study of acculturation. *American Anthropologist, 38,* 149–152.

Sanchez, B., Esparza, P., Colon, Y., & Davis, K. (2010). Tryin' to make it during the transition from high school: The role of family obligation attitudes and economic context for Latino-emerging adults. *Journal of Adolescent Research, 25*(6), 858–884.

Scottham, K. M., Sellers, R. M., & Ngyen, H. X. (2008). A measure of racial identity in African American adolescents: The development of the multidimensional inventory of black identity-teen. *Cultural Diversity and Ethnic Minority Psychology, 14*(4), 297–306.

Sy, S. R., & Romero, J. (2008). Family responsibilities among Latina college students from immigrant families. *Journal of Higher Education, 7,* 212–227.

Torres, J. B., & Solberg, S. V. (2001). Role of self-efficacy, stress, social integration, and family support in Latino college student persistence and health. *Journal of Vocational Behavior, 59,* 53–63.

Tseng, V. (2004, May–June). Family interdependence and academic adjustment in college youth from immigrant and U.S.-born families. *Child Development, 75*(3), 966–983.

U.S. Department of Homeland Security. U.S. Citizenship and Immigration Services. (2013). Consideration of Deferred Action for Childhood Arrivals Process. Washington, DC. Retrieved from http://www.uscis.gov/portal/site/uscis/menuitem.eb1d4c2a3e5b9ac89243c6a7543f6d1a/?vgnextoid=f2ef2f19470f7310VgnVCM100000082ca60aRCRD&vgnextchannel=f2ef2f19470f7310VgnVCM100000082ca60aRCRD.

Zayas, L. H., Bright, C. L., Alvarez-Sanchez, T., & Cabassa, L. J. (2009). Acculturation, familism and mother-daughter relations among suicidal and non-suicidal Latinas. *Journal of Primary Prevention, 30*(3–4), 351–369.

15

Conclusion: Beyond Psychopathology and Toward Resilience

Alberto M. Bursztyn and Carol Korn-Bursztyn

When we initially imagined the text for this book, we considered addressing the mental health needs of immigrant children and adolescents along accepted and standard categories of psychopathology. Our original table of contents covered a spectrum of diagnosable conditions, including the usual list of woes, such as anxiety, depression, posttraumatic stress disorder (PTSD), and oppositional defiant disorder. This volume could have been a companion to the fifth edition of the *Diagnostic and Statistical Manual of Mental Disorders*, focusing on psychopathological risks to young newcomers and the children of immigrants. However, as we delved into the project, our thinking shifted from psychopathology, and we began to describe the psychological processes of migration and resettlement, focusing on the human capacity for resilience. The travails of migration give rise to emotional responses to hardship; depression, anxiety, and PTSD are common and recur in the narratives presented in many chapters. We acknowledge the pain and sorrow that accompany many of these migration stories, but choose to underline the flexible strengths and capacity for adaptability that characterize this new generation of Americans.

Cultural transitions present psychological risks; they inevitably strain every aspect of the child's and youth's coping capacities, yet in most cases the strain subsides as adaptive mechanisms and new competencies emerge. Thus, zeroing in only on young immigrants' risk for psychopathology obscures the potential for coping, development, and emotional growth, as documented in the preceding chapters.

There is a substantial body of literature on immigrants, much of it sociological in nature, focusing on demographic trends, academic achievement, and utilization of services. This book has done much to situate immigration as an important contemporary phenomenon. It is our hope that this volume will complement this body of work by offering insight into the particular lived experience of young immigrants and children of immigrants. Case vignettes in each chapter provide educators and mental health practitioners with real-life examples of the experiences of child and youth migrants and provide nuanced descriptions of emotional distress and coping. A narrative approach complements the review of the professional literature by providing a textured account of human experience; for the practitioner, these vignettes provide an entry point into empathic understanding of immigrant youths.

In the context of unprecedented global migrations and cultural crossings, the immigrant journey ceases to be exceptional. In effect, all modern societies are requiring their members to adjust, adapt, and master new tools and technologies in their everyday lives. New technologies engender new vocabularies, new ways of interacting, and new ways of doing business. Cultures are undergoing tectonic shifts, challenging assumptions of basic cultural competence. For the young of all backgrounds, gaining access to technological knowledge and competence is a path toward developing community and potentially a major equalizer in terms of social status. Technology also figures prominently in contributing to social isolation and emotional stress; it opens the door to cyber-bullying and harassment and encourages detachment from one's immediate social surroundings.

Although prior generations of immigrants typically were fairly cutoff from friends and families by virtue of the distance between them and the difficulty of staying in touch by letter or phone, contemporary immigrants can sustain greater dialogue and remain interconnected through videoconferencing and social media. Additionally, at least for those who are documented, frequent air travel blurs the line between migrants and immigrants. In an equalizing and perhaps ironic way, some of our poorer residents share the experience of the very rich—living in the United States with seasonal accommodations abroad. The forced choice that was so familiar to older generations of immigrants is relaxed for new, documented immigrants, and it is increasingly possible to live between places and between cultures. Undocumented immigrants, however, continue to live a forced choice between their pre- and postmigration lives. For many children and adolescents, documentation status has an added consequence of traumatic separation from their parents.

As we consider and reflect on a more fluid and dynamic social framework, one that demands lifelong adaptability, interconnectivity, and innovation, the static structures described by psychological theory in the 20th century no longer seem to fit. Early work on human development, for example, suggested that identity is a process that leads to a stable and grounded view of the self, a somewhat immutable self-concept. "Achieved identity" was the untroubled ego's address, a permanent structure built on a strong foundation, resistant to floods, storms, and earthquakes. And it was to be completed at the end of adolescence (Erikson, 1950, 1959, 1968). Over the past 50 years, the understanding of human identity has expanded greatly, first by recognizing that the initial model was overtly androgenic, white, and middle class, and later by focusing on the dynamic nature of personal adjustment to life circumstances by virtue of age and social status. Views of identity development continued to expanded further to include a wide range of possible ways of identifying, including race, ethnicity, gender, sexual orientation, (dis)ability, health status, nationality, religion, and others.

Some researchers have sought to describe the assumedly orderly patterns by which individuals progress toward specific identities, for example, racial identity (Helms, 2007). But data to validate those conceptual models are generally inconclusive. In a postmodern world, identities are actively constructed, fluid, flexible, contested, and temporal. It seems as though many teens cannot be bothered with the old categories and traditional census boxes. The music young people listen to and the way they dress offer windows into their identities; yet their music choices shift, and their closets may contain multiple identity signifiers.

Immigrant youths are particular examples of active "identity crafters," their experience between cultures requires them to find ways of adapting to binary or multipolar social worlds. The short essay below is an excerpt from a contribution to a school publication made by a 16-year-old arrival from Hong Kong.

TWO CULTURES

> When I first came to this country from Hong Kong I had some problems with this culture. When I was in the ninth grade in Hong Kong, every student had to study until 10 p.m. at school and take special tests in order to go on to high school. In this country students don't study hard. Some students study very hard, but most students don't. When I was in Hong Kong I studied hard. But I'm not studying as hard now as I was in Hong Kong. . . . I will mix the two cultures together to make a better culture for my life. But I will never take everything from both cultures. I will take just the good points.

In his essay, Henry[1] expresses misgivings about American culture, including still having strange (strong?) feelings, probably implying that he has reservations about American ways. The contrast between the two cultures is in regard to study requirements and academic expectations. Perhaps he now sees Hong Kong norms as excessive, or maybe he is referring to those norms with pride, but what is apparent is that he now has a contrasting frame of reference. He can now see Hong Kong education, not as part of an inevitable and normative childhood experience, but more as an approach among many that can be subjected to scrutiny and judgment. Henry, by his own admission and not knowing why, is "not studying as hard now," but he is gaining a worldly sense of perspective on education systems and cultures. He is not ready to commit to becoming an American, maybe in 10 years he will decide, but even if he were to return to Hong Kong, he would be different for having made a conscious effort to choose what he considers the "good points" from each culture.

A more interconnected and dynamic world offers new possibilities for expanded engagement and individual self-determination, but it is not necessarily a kinder world for children and youths. The ability of children to overcome difficulties and meet developmental challenges hinges on a number of factors, primarily the nature of their internal resources, the networks of emotional support available to them, and the nature and severity of the contextual pressures. This book has focused primarily on internal resources and networks of emotional support, but the larger environment plays a critical role as well. The degree to which society understands and welcomes the immigrant child plays a pivotal role in acculturation outcomes.

Immigrant children and youths who are identified as members of racial minority groups have additional unfair and burdensome hurdles to navigate. Concern about addressing immigrant children's mental health must therefore recognize that members of racial minority groups may encounter hostile attitudes and rejection, not only for their stranger status but also because of prejudices based on local stereotypes about the children's county of origin and their skin color. For example, Suárez-Morales and Lopez (2009) found that perceived discrimination and a sense of a "closed society" was predictive of youths' reports of concentration problems and worrisome thoughts. The authors suggested interventions, such as promoting adaptive and coping skills and involving family in the process, and they suggested school and family practices to prepare young immigrants to deal with discrimination. They also recommended group therapy utilizing culturally adapted folktales or heroic role models. Although these are all sound suggestions, mental health professionals should also advocate for cultural change at the local and national levels to diminish prejudice and marginalization of immigrant and minority groups.

Sad and defensive, Marie's essay for her high school's magazine tells of her pride in her country. But more telling, her words betray a longing for a time when she would blend in with everyone, when she was happy and carefree, a time when what she wore did not provoke teasing or humiliation. Most of all, she misses those she loves, who are far away now. Her sadness is evident in her having ceased to sing. Marie, a 15-year-old new arrival, has lost much in leaving Haiti; but despite it being a poor and derided country, it is home for her, where she feels she belongs.

MY COUNTRY

> What I miss most of all of my country is my friends, my family, my school, and my church. In my country, Haiti, you can go anywhere you want at any time without being afraid that somebody will hurt you. People over there are very friendly. In school you find more friends, they all speak the same language as you. It doesn't matter how you dress. If your colors don't match, people won't bother you. I used to sing, in my church. Now I don't sing anymore, I don't go to church. I miss my grandmother, my mother, and my best friend. It is hard to be away, it is hard to replace them. I don't care what people say about my country, I miss it, and I think Haiti is the best place to be.

Marie is not feeling welcome in America. Beyond the acute sense of loss she is experiencing due to separation from family and friends, she is hurt by a perceived rejecting stance from those around her. Mental health work with immigrant children and youths, to be effective, cannot be limited to individual treatment. It must encompass a broader agenda to promote greater awareness of emotional risks and advocacy within institutions and society at large (Lopez & Bursztyn, 2013).

Immigration and acculturation are profoundly trying experiences, the trauma of leaving is compounded by the stress of displacement, but for most children and teens, the journey is as much about discovering the new social milieu as it is an internal process of self-exploration and identity formation (Korn, 2002). The host society's receptivity to its new members is a critical dimension that complicates the psychological developmental path for many immigrants, particularly those who may be ascribed racial minority status (Waters, 1990). In a racialized and stratified society, acculturation is more stressful and complicated for those children and adolescents confronting prejudice against their group (Ogbu & Simons, 1998). Psychological risks increase as families struggle with poverty (Raphael & Smolensky, 2009), undocumented status (Ellis & Chen, 2013), trauma and separations (Gonzalez, Suárez-Orozco, & Dedios-Sanguineti, 2013), and disability (Bursztyn, 2011).

Adolescence is by nature a time for transition and change. Immigration and acculturation during adolescence complicate the process by requiring youths to deal not only with the normative issues of identity formation and emerging autonomy, but also to do so in a context devoid of the familiar peer group, in a challenging new social setting, and often in a language that is foreign and confounding. Adolescence is a period of self-discovery (Laser & Nicoleta, 2011), but immigration changes the rules of the normative process;

self-discovery, while acculturating, is fraught with the danger of loss of competence and confidence and may lead to alienation.

The known self is suddenly less capable, isolated from childhood peers, and awkwardly more tied to family. Some teens may begrudge their being uprooted from their social lives and emerging autonomy, and they may subsequently intensify their struggle against parental authority in the adopted country. The struggles for independence and differentiation from family may need to wait as the challenges of adapting to a new setting demand greater family cohesion and mutual support. Acculturation extends the moratorium period; it calls upon all the internal resources young immigrants have to cope, adapt, and evolve, but it also may enrich and expand their internal worlds, competence in the external world, and their sense of possibility within it.

NOTE

1. All names in this chapter are pseudonyms.

REFERENCES

Bursztyn, A. M. (2011). *Childhood psychological disorders: Current controversies.* Westport, CT: Praeger.

Bursztyn, A. M., Afonso, A. G., & Black, K. (2013). Through a cultural lens: Psychopathology within and across borders. In T. Plante (Ed.), *Abnormal psychology through the ages* (pp. 217–230). Westport, CT: Praeger.

Ellis, L. M., & Chen, E. C. (2013). Negotiating identity development among undocumented immigrant college students: A grounded theory study. *Journal of Counseling Psychology, 60*(2), 251–264.

Erikson, E. (1950). *Childhood and society.* New York, NY: Norton.

Erikson, E. (1959/1980). *Identity and the life cycle.* New York, NY: Norton.

Erikson, E. (1968). *Identity: Youth and crisis.* New York, NY: Norton.

Helms, J. E. (2007). Some better practices for measuring racial and ethnic identity constructs. Journal of Special Issue: Racial and ethnic identity theory, measurement, and research in counseling psychology: Present status and future directions. *Counseling Psychology, 54,* 235–246.

Gonzalez, R. G., Suárez-Orozco, C., & Dedios-Sanguineti, M. C. (2013). No place to belong: Contextualizing concepts of mental health among undocumented immigrant youth in the United States. *American Behavioral Scientist, 57*(8), 1174–1199.

Korn, C. (2002). Crossing the Brooklyn Bridge: The geography of social and cultural transitions. In A. Bursztyn & C. Korn, *Rethinking multicultural education: Case studies in cultural transition* (pp. 64–79). New York, NY: Bergin & Garvey, Greenwood Press.

Laser, J. A., & Nicoleta, N. (2011). *Working with adolescents: A guide for practitioners.* New York, NY: Guilford.

Lopez, E., & Bursztyn, A. M. (2013). Future challenges and opportunities: Toward culturally responsive training in school psychology. *Psychology in the Schools, 50*(3), 212–228.

Ogbu, J. U., & Simons, H. D. (1998). Voluntary and involuntary minorities: A cultural-ecological theory of school performance with some implications for education. *Anthropology & Education Quarterly, 29*(2), 155–188.

Raphael, S., & Smolensky, E. (2009). Immigration and poverty in the United States. *Focus, 26*(2), 27–31.

Suárez-Morales, L., & Lopez, B. (2009). The impact of acculturative stress and daily hassles on pre-adolescent psychological adjustment: Examining anxiety symptoms. *Journal of Primary Prevention, 30*(3), 335–349.

Waters, M. C. (1990). *Ethnic options: Choosing identities in America.* Berkeley, CA: University of California Press.

About the Editors and Contributors

ALBERTO M. BURSZTYN, who chairs the Department of School Psychology, Counseling and Leadership at Brooklyn College, is professor of urban education at the City University of New York Graduate Center. Previous publications include *Childhood Psychological Disorders: Current Controversies* (Praeger, 2011) and *The Praeger Handbook of Special Education* (2006). He also coedited *Teaching Teachers: Building a Quality School of Urban Education* (2004) and *Rethinking Multicultural Education* (Praeger, 2002). Bursztyn is a licensed psychologist who received his doctorate in counseling psychology from Columbia University. He also holds graduate degrees in science education (Brooklyn College), school psychology (Brooklyn College), and organizational leadership (NYU).

CAROL KORN-BURSZTYN is professor of education at Brooklyn College and in the Ph.D. program in urban education at the Graduate Center, City University of New York. Korn-Bursztyn developed and led the School of Education's lab school from 1991 to 2007 and currently directs the graduate program in play therapy. She is the editor of *Young Children and the Arts: Nurturing Imagination and Creativity* (2012); coeditor of *Rethinking Multicultural Education: Case Studies in Cultural Transition* (2002); series editor of *Making Sense of Psychology* (Praeger); and author of numerous articles. Korn-Bursztyn is a New York State licensed psychologist and holds a doctorate in clinical child/school psychology and postdoctoral certification in psychotherapy and psychoanalysis from NYU. She maintains a private practice with diverse youth and families.

GABRIELA SANTANA BETANCOURT is a doctoral candidate in the Public Health Program at the City University of New York, specializing in epidemiology. She also has a master's of arts in Latin American and Caribbean studies and a master's of public health in epidemiology. Most recently, she was the research associate for Planned Parenthood of New York City, where she focused on the research and evaluation of sexual and reproductive health projects. She also has worked as a foster care case manager and health educator/advocate for at-risk youth in New York City.

STACEY J. COOPER is a doctoral candidate in the human development training area in the psychology doctoral program at the City University of New York Graduate Center. Her work focuses on tapping into the cultural knowledge and cultural strengths held by immigrant college students from ethnic minority backgrounds and using them to create novel and effective culturally relevant pedagogical methods.

MYRTLE DICKSON holds three master's degrees in science and nutrition, English language and literature, and educational leadership. She began her career in education as a high school teacher. She has held various administrative positions at the elementary, middle, and secondary levels and presently serves as an educational human resources administrator.

MARC FOWLER is a doctoral candidate in St. John's school psychology program. He earned an MS in education from Brooklyn College and works as a school psychologist in the Seattle, Washington, area. Marc is the coauthor of the article "Traumatic Brain Injury and Personality." His research interests include the effect of attention deficit hyperactivity disorder on academic achievement and multicultural issues in education.

ANNA MALYUKOVA was born in a small provincial town in Russia, where she planned to study hydraulics engineering. She arrived in the United States in 2001. She is currently a media specialist on a Russian language television station and a candidate in the master's program in urban education at the Graduate Center of the City University of New York. She plans to continue her studies toward her Ph.D. in the field of education.

JACQUELIN MUELLER is a group facilitator and program coordinator for Middle Earth, a nonprofit, delinquency prevention agency in New Jersey. She completed her undergraduate degree at Rutgers University and in the spring of 2013 completed an MA in child and adolescent clinical psychology at Montclair State University. She is currently studying in the advanced certificate program in play therapy at Brooklyn College and plans to continue her education toward a Psy.D in psychology. Her hobbies include photography, typography, and cooking.

ALEXANDROS ORPHANIDES is a New York City–based writer of Honduran and Cypriot descent. He holds a master's of science in education from Brooklyn College and is a candidate for the master's of arts in political science at the Graduate Center of the City University of New York. He teaches high school history and writes about political, cultural, and social issues.

ANGELICA ORTEGA is a Ph.D. candidate in urban education at the Graduate Center, City University of New York. Her research looks at the music-making practices of emergent bilinguals in formal and informal learning environments. She holds a master's degree in literacy from Teachers College, Columbia

University, and a bachelor's degree from Barnard College. She is a musician and music teacher in New York City.

ALEXANDRA PONCE DE LEÓN-LEBEC holds a BA in psychology from the University of Pennsylvania and a master's degree and advanced certificate in school psychology from Brooklyn College. She worked as a senior research analyst for a global media agency where she conducted research and published on consumer media habits and emerging trends. She is currently employed as a bilingual school psychologist and works with a large immigrant student population.

SALLY ROBLES is an assistant professor in the Department of Psychology and director of clinical training in the Brooklyn College Personal Counseling Program, where she oversees the clinical training of doctoral externs and interns and teaches in the master's program in mental health counseling. Her interests include bicultural identity development, acculturation and mental health, Latino college student retention rates, ethics, and clinical training. She is a member of the American Psychological Association Minority Fellowship Program Training Advisory Committee, the New York State Office of Alcoholism and Substance Abuse Services Talent Management Committee, and the National Latino Psychological Association.

MALYA SCHULMAN is a master's candidate in liberal studies at the Graduate Center, City University of New York, with a concentration in psychology of work and family. She is interested in child development and especially in the effects of trauma on child and adolescent development.

PARVONEH SHIRGIR is a second-generation Middle Eastern and white feminist, educator, and writer. She was born and raised in the Midwest and currently teaches High School Equivalency in New York City. She holds an MA in liberal studies, City University of New York Graduate Center. She works toward justice in adult education, feminist/queer, diaspora, and reentry communities.

JOHNNY THACH is an MA candidate in liberal studies at the Graduate Center, the City University of New York, with a concentration in human rights and international migration. He is passionate about amplifying the narratives and experiences of youth and immigrant communities. He was a museum educator at the Museum of Chinese in America (MoCA), where he coordinated exhibition-based gallery programs, tours, and discussions with grades K-12 children, families, adults, and teachers from across the world. He is a community organizer with an interest in youth empowerment, community engagement, and developing volunteerism and service.

Index

abandonment. *See* loss
abuse, 5, 48, 134, 136–137, 141, 143–144
accent, 72, 154, 157, 176,
acculturation, 1–2, 12, 16–17, 19–34, 39, 48, 51, 91, 97, 99, 100–101, 107, 108, 111–113, 115, 123
achievement, 16, 34, 68, 75, 148, 152, 171, 175–176 181, 190; academic, 27, 33, 77–79, 83, 107–110, 114–116, 147, 156, 170–171, 195, 201. *See also* Underachievement
adaptation, 4, 12, 16, 19, 22–23, 27–34, 147–148, 157–158, 193–196
African-American, 28, 46, 91, 98, 162, 169, 192, 193, 194,
after-school program, 21, 82, 122, 128
AIDS, 138, 140
alienation, 15, 23, 34, 39, 48, 112,113,192, 193, 195, 197, 206
ambition, 22, 23, 51, 101–102
ambivalence, 20, 49, 62, 64, 105, 117
anxiety, 5, 15, 34, 63, 64, 86, 94, 98–100, 106, 112, 113, 123, 137, 192, 201; social anxiety, 29, 32, 117, 156, 163
assimilation, 22, 23, 27, 29, 33, 176, 179, 194
attachment, 7, 13, 14, 23, 25, 53, 54, 56, 58–59, 65, 66, 74, 77, 79, 93, 188, 189; multiple, 57, 79; secure, 57, 59, 79, 94. *See also* Bowlby, J.
attention deficit hyperactivity disorder (ADHD), 163, 164

behavior, 33, 44, 47, 79, 112, 113, 115, 124, 128, 159, 164, 171, 172, 176, 185, 189; externalizing, 193; oppositional, 7, 77; problem, 30, 31, 47, 101, 111, 114
bicultural, 2, 13, 23, 27–29, 124, 189, 195. *See also* bicultural identity
bicultural identity integration (BII) model, 28
bilingual, 15, 41, 42, 48, 106, 108, 114, 121, 124, 125, 129, 148, 154, 185, 195; assessment, 114; education, 2–3, 110, 114
Bowlby, J., 59, 79

childcare, 79, 124, 190
college, 16, 21, 29, 33, 41, 47, 67, 73, 75, 93, 107, 124, 128, 143, 150, 160, 176, 181, 185–197; community college, 169–181
coping, 4, 5, 17, 25, 29, 64, 88, 96, 112, 164, 195, 201, 202, 204
creativity, 2, 83, 86, 126–127
cultural difference, 43, 114, 123, 156

cultural harmony, 30
cultural values, 176, 179
culturally and linguistically diverse (CID), 114–115
Cosmopolitanism, 165

deferred action for childhood arrivals (DACA), 67, 185–186, 190–191, 197
deportation, 67, 138, 143, 185, 186, 191, 192
depression, 7, 10, 14, 27, 29, 32, 50, 63, 64, 67, 91, 94, 98–102, 201; risk for, 7, 14, 23, 91, 100, 196
descendants, 19
discrimination, 4, 17, 25, 29–34, 43, 99, 100, 101, 107–108, 204
dominant culture, 39, 51,108, 185. *See also* national culture
DREAM Act, 186, 192–193, 196–197
drug abuse, 15, 141

eldercare, 190
emotionally disturbed, 114
enculturation, 97, 160, 178–180
English as a second language (ESL), 10, 92, 93, 97, 121, 124, 171
English language learner (ELL), 4, 73, 107, 127, 150

family, 6, 7, 102, 106,109,110, 124, 126, 137, 138, 140, 141, 142, 148, 149, 154, 157, 159–161, 165, 171, 173, 176, 179–180, 186, 188–189, 205; dynamics, 91, 95, 101, 105; extended, 8–10, 14, 23, 79, 99, 102, 106, 177, 186, 187, 194; honor, 15, 133, 136, 142–143, 150; separation, 5, 13, 63, 186, 190, 205–206; structure, 11, 14, 42, 91, 100, 102, 109, 153, 179
familismo, 14, 99–102
fatalism, 44
five factor model (FFM), 25

gangs, 7, 41, 48–49, 51, 134, 136, 161

gender, 2, 14, 27, 32, 45, 51, 57, 76, 95, 101–102, 140, 142, 172, 181, 203
gifts, 57, 122, 125–126, 195
grandparent, 1, 7, 9, 13, 28, 53–54, 56–60, 75–77, 79, 106, 149, 186; grandfather, 57; grandmother, 9–10, 19, 45, 56–57, 72–75, 77, 86, 92–93, 96, 205

habitus, 125
high school equivalency (HSE) program, 147, 150, 211
holding environment, 13, 57, 59, 75, 78, 85–87, 123, 126
homelessness, 16, 133–134, 136–139, 143, 161

incarceration, 50, 149, 162
idealization, 83
identity, 2, 4, 10, 12–13, 17, 25–30, 32–34, 40, 42–52, 71, 75–77, 87, 96–97, 105, 124–125, 139, 152, 161, 177, 180–181, 186–188, 191–197, 202–203, 205; bicultural, 12, 25, 27–29, 49; ethnic, 25–27, 30, 33, 42, 87; national, 26, 34
integration, 23, 28–29, 32–34, 101, 128, 176, 192, 195

Latina, 22, 39, 46–47, 91, 98, 101
Latinos, 1, 39, 43–45, 187–190, 195
learning disability, 106, 114–115, 117, 163
LGBT (lesbian, gay, bisexual, and transgender), 16, 133, 135–136, 138, 143
loneliness, 7, 64, 100, 170, 176
loss, 14, 53–59, 61–68, 71, 74, 75, 81, 85, 89, 95–96, 99, 100, 102, 123, 136, 162, 176, 186, 187, 193, 195, 205, 206

marginalization, 24, 204
marianismo, 189

mental health, 1–2, 4–5, 10, 12, 14, 16, 19, 25, 27, 30, 34, 40, 43, 47, 50–52, 65, 79, 81, 85, 91, 94–95, 98–102, 116, 143–144, 147, 165–166, 173, 175, 178–179, 181, 201–202, 204–205
migrant, 12, 15, 33, 89, 133, 135–136, 139, 143, 202
migration, 68, 71, 74, 81, 82, 83, 84–85, 86–87, 88, 89, 96, 99, 102, 122–124, 125, 135, 136, 138, 141,143, 160, 189, 201, 202; Postmigration, 8, 13, 14, 61, 62, 64, 66–68, 74, 75, 78, 79, 86–87, 99, 202; Premigration, 63, 76, 84, 99, 174; Serial, 74, 123, 125
minority group, 47, 158, 204
mourning, 13, 53, 193–195, 197

narrative, 40, 54, 58, 59, 61, 65, 68, 76, 81–83, 85, 88–89, 127, 165, 169–173, 181, 196, 201–202
national culture, 22–24, 25, 28, 31–34. *See also* Dominant culture
native culture, 51

parenting styles, 29–34, 50
peritraumatic dissociation, 137
posttraumatic stress disorder (PTSD), 5, 136, 201
prejudice, 192, 204, 205,
psychopathology, 17, 29, 201
public education, 2, 109
public school, 2, 3, 52

racism, 28, 162
reciprocity, 32, 79, 171
refugee, 1–2, 6, 10, 29, 139
relative acculturation expanded model (RAEM), 24
religion, 23–24, 26, 86–87, 142, 203
resilience , 4, 10, 13–15, 17, 44, 59, 61, 68, 73, 81, 83, 87–88, 91, 95, 97–100, 122–124, 126, 162–163, 195, 201

reunification, 13–14
risk factors, 15, 78, 83, 133–136, 139, 141, 143

school, 2–9, 13, 15–22, 24, 29, 31, 33–34, 39–50, 52, 58, 63–64, 66–67, 71–80, 82–83, 86, 89, 91–100, 102, 105–117, 121–124, 128–129, 140, 144, 147–151, 153–155, 157–165, 169–181, 185, 187, 191–192, 196–197, 203–205
selective mutism (SM), 113
self-esteem, 27, 30, 31, 112, 154, 163, 187, 192, 194, 195, 196,
separation, 4, 7–8, 13–14, 24, 31, 33, 43, 53–54, 57–58, 60–66, 68, 71, 74–79, 83, 88, 95–96, 99–100, 124, 181, 186–187, 202, 205. *See also* Loss
sex trafficking, 15, 133
sexual abuse, 6, 137
sexual orientation, 3, 16, 43, 133, 138, 143, 203
shame, 6, 16, 133–134, 136, 142–143, 158
social mirroring, 108, 110
special education, 72, 106, 114, 116, 150, 163
specific language impairments (SLIs), 112
stress, 3, 5, 10, 13, 15, 17, 25–28, 32, 34, 39, 43–45, 50, 52, 56–57, 61, 63, 65, 67, 74, 83, 88, 93–94, 97–99, 101, 107, 111–113, 115–117, 121, 123–127, 129, 136, 160, 177, 180, 186–188, 190, 195, 197, 202, 205
students with interrupted formal education (SIFE), 107
suicide, 94, 98, 101, 193

teacher, 2–4, 8, 13–14, 16, 20–21, 40–41, 50, 66, 68, 72–75, 78–79, 92, 97, 99, 105–106, 108, 110, 112–113, 115, 124–125, 128, 148–153, 159, 162, 164, 169–172, 174, 177, 179–180, 195

tests, 107, 116, 162, 163, 176, 203
tradition, 1, 20, 22, 23, 79, 88, 102, 124
Trafficking Victims Protection Act (TVPA), 134
transference, 75, 78–79
transitional object, 58
transitional space, 2, 14, 86–87
transnational family, 14, 75, 91
trauma, 4–5, 7, 10, 13, 15, 57–58, 61, 63, 68, 71, 74, 86, 88, 95–97, 99, 111, 122–125, 133–139, 141, 143–144
truancy, 6, 40, 47

unaccompanied minors, 1, 133, 135–136

unauthorized immigrant, 110, 185. *See also* undocumented immigrants
underachievement, 109, 181
undocumented adult identity development model, 17, 186, 192–193
undocumented immigrant, 62, 67, 143, 191, 194, 196, 198, 202

Vygotsky, L.V., 152, 178

well-being, 2, 4, 13, 25–26, 28, 30, 31, 34, 53, 59, 61, 66, 78, 95, 165
Winnicott, D.W., 13–14, 57–58, 60, 75, 85–87, 108, 123